Christa Paula

was born in Berchtesgaden, Germany, and educated at universities in Japan, the USA and Britain. Bilingual in German and English, she has published articles in scholarly journals in both languages. This is her first book.

CHRISTA PAULA

The Road to Miran

Travels in the Forbidden Zone
of Xinjiang

Flamingo
An Imprint of HarperCollins*Publishers*

Flamingo
An Imprint of HarperCollins*Publishers*
77–85 Fulham Palace Road,
Hammersmith, London W6 8JB

Published by Flamingo 1995
9 8 7 6 5 4 3 2 1

First published in Great Britain by
HarperCollins*Publishers* 1994

Maps drawn by John Callanan

The Author asserts the moral right to
be identified as the author of this work

Author photograph by Caroline Forbes

ISBN 0 00 638368 8

Set in Bembo

Printed in Great Britain by
HarperCollinsManufacturing Glasgow

Contents

Illustrations

Author's Note

EVEN THOUGH the People's Republic of China has in recent years opened itself to an ever-increasing flow of *waiguoren*, outsiders, it still looks with some caution at the contact of its citizens with Westerners. In order to protect the many people who have helped me along the way, who have shared their stories and concerns, and who have offered their friendship, it was necessary to change most names, some place names, and in one case a location.

Each location in Xinjiang carries a Uighur and a Chinese name. Kumul, for example, is Hami to the Chinese, Qiemo is Qarqan to the Uighurs – and depending on whom you are talking to, one or the other form is used. The use of place names in this book reflects this.

In most cases the Pinyin transliteration system has been used for Chinese names; for most Turkic geographical names the convention of the *Times Atlas* was applied, with the exception of some long-established usages, e.g. Uighur instead of Uygur, Turfan instead of Turpan. It might be helpful for the reader to know that the letter 'q' is pronounced as 'tsch' (i.e. Qarqan = 'Tschartschan'; Kuqa = 'Kutscha'). Umlauts and diacritical marks have in most cases been omitted.

There are many people to whom I am indebted, most of all 'Chang', who time and again placed himself in great danger by travelling the road with me.

Others have helped to make this book a reality: Neil Kreitman, inadvertently, by financing my field work; Nick Danziger by suggesting I should write one in the first place; Mark Lucas and Richard Johnson who believed that the story was worth telling.

I would also like to thank my friends, who have taken an interest both in my work and in my well-being, particularly David Owen for providing endless patience and physical comfort; Nico Mann for teaching me about writing; Wilhelm Kudorfer for listening to a good part of the first draft; Susan Whitfield for her help with Pinyin and other useful comments; and Maggie Gilchrist, whose comments on the final draft were invaluable.

Finally, my special thanks to Ian Prew, computer whiz at HarperCollins, who, without a murmur, printed out drafts and copies throughout the writing process.

CHRISTA PAULA
February 1994

MAPS

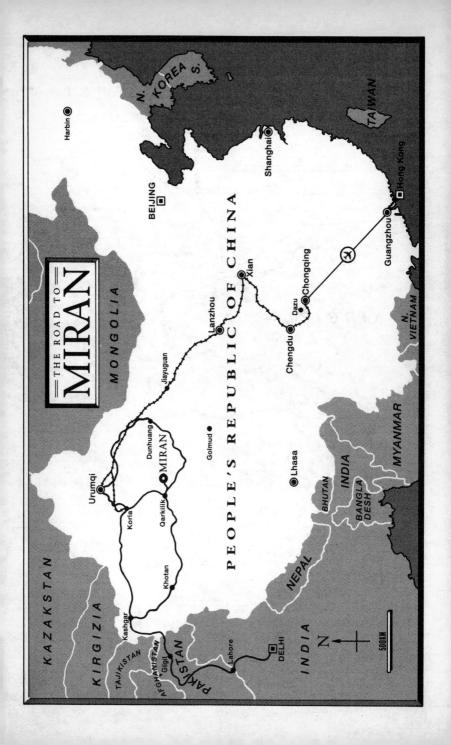

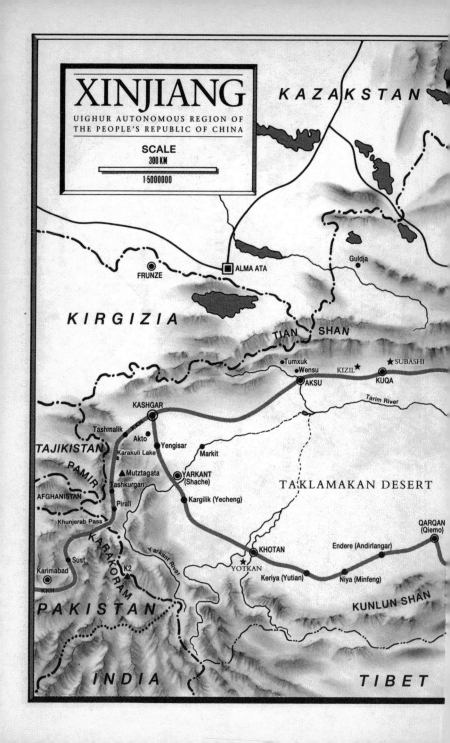

THE ROAD TO MIRAN

ONE

Prologue

I FIRST WENT TO XINJIANG in the late summer of 1989, to follow my old Professor's dream. He had always wanted to travel the eastern part of the Silk Road but couldn't; first because China had closed itself to the outside world, and later, when it might have been possible, because of his failing health. He got as close as he could, becoming one of those rare academic characters who could tell you about everything between Istanbul and Tokyo in its original language and all the time longing to go to Xinjiang.

There have been times when I suspected that he tricked me on to this path because he believed that if anyone could get there, I could. 'The tall Hun' was his not-so-secret nickname for me. In many ways my journey was his journey. I remember well the day when he set me on course for the study of Central Asian antiquities.

It was one of those afternoons when the most exciting occurrence was the specks of library-dust dancing in the broad band of afternoon sun which always fell past my desk about this time of day, the angle varying with the time of year. My thoughts were lost in the rustling oak tree in front of my window just at the edge of the Panther Hollow, a deep wooded gorge separating the student slums of Oakland from Shenley Park. Smog and heat had been pressing down on Pittsburgh all week. People moved listlessly through the day and were silly at night. I was bored with studying Japanese culture, fed up with university life and the incestuous quarrels in my department.

The monotonous hum of the air-conditioning and the drowsy

flicker of the overhead light were suddenly enlivened by the *swish-tok-swish-tok* of the Professor's approach. He moved with difficulty and the help of a walking stick. It was very unusual for him to come looking for me in my carrel, and my heart missed a beat. I had a perpetually bad conscience in those days, and was seriously considering leaving academic life. He entered my dark sanctuary without knocking. His slight frame dressed in a glorified mechanic's one-piece elegantly topped with a beige cravat, he struggled with a large canvas-bound folio. With a dramatic gesture he threw it on my desk, blurted out, 'They even had a Blue Period', and left.

The folio held large colour reproductions of paintings brought back by expeditions at the beginning of this century from oases around the Taklamakan Desert in China's westernmost province, Xinjiang. Paintings of gently smiling Buddhas, proud nobles clad in western-style overcoats, long swords dangling from their sides, and sensuous princesses stared at me, all taken from caves and mud-brick structures buried in the sands for hundreds of years. These were accompanied by place names of pure magic: Kashgar, Kizil, Turfan, Lopnur, Tarim river, Khotan, Miran, the Kingdom of Shanshan – in one, the Silk Road. But it was Miran that jumped out at me.

In 1907, and again in 1914, the celebrated archaeologist Sir Aurel Stein had excavated Buddhist wall-paintings from the shrines of Miran and placed them in the New Delhi Museum. They were considered the earliest paintings of Chinese Central Asia. Generally dated to the third or fourth century AD, but most likely belonging to the late first or early second century, the paintings had variously been described as ranging in style from classical to near eastern, Roman-Egyptian, Byzantine and Coptic – it was even claimed that they were the only surviving example of an early, but lost, tradition of Indo-Greek Gandharan art. In other words, the paintings from Miran were an art-historical challenge.

I brought the folio of illustrations to my next tutorial. The Professor smiled and leaned back in his flexible swivel chair, letting the back drop against the bookcase behind him, while I settled in the big red leather chair.

'Nice day,' he observed, gazing out over the mock-Renaissance fountain, which was crawling with undergraduates in short shorts and T-shirts.

'Miran,' I said, bringing him back. 'The kingdom of Shanshan . . . do you really believe a Roman Titus went there to paint Buddhist pictures in the middle of the desert?'

'No!'

This notion that Miran lay 'at the furthest edge of the dying classical world', as one art historian wrote, had been reinforced by an inscription naming the artist, *Tita*, which had often been interpreted as deriving from the Latin Titus. A Roman citizen, supposedly, had travelled along the Silk Road to the south-eastern border of Shanshan, to the very gateway of China, to decorate Buddhist shrines.

'A case of cultural arrogance,' I asserted with confidence.

'Surely, western elements are apparent in the paintings,' the Professor rebutted.

'True,' I conceded, then asked if he had ever been there.

'No! It's impossible,' he said.

Sometimes I think that it was this very word 'impossible' which persuaded me to continue my studies. And perhaps he knew this. I've never put much trust in the judgement of authority without testing it.

Even though a visit to the site was not necessary for the study of the paintings – they had been excavated and could be viewed in the safety of museums around the world – I decided that I was going to Miran, the easternmost terminus of the ancient kingdom of Shanshan at the edge of the desert of Lop. Checkpoint, trading post, military colony during the heyday of Silk Road traffic – and at the time when explorers such as Przhevalsky, Huntington and Stein roamed the southern parts of the Taklamakan still a formidable ruined city over several square kilometres.

'It would be necessary to see the site,' I suggested, to the Professor's amusement.

'Not possible,' he repeated, chuckling to himself.

The area had been closed to foreigners for many decades, and while the People's Republic of China had started to open its doors, much of Xinjiang still lay under a veil of obscurity. To my knowledge, the last western archaeologist who set foot on the site was Sir Aurel Stein in 1914.

But I knew, in that hot summer of 1984, that somehow, sometime, I would get there.

Five years later I was stuck in a Land Rover which was stuck in an ocean of sheep. The animals were being driven from the high pastures of the Pamirs to winter in the valleys of the Hunza, squeezing by either side of the vehicle which cowered on a ledge blasted into a sheer cliff. Icicles bled from the grey rock-face, in contrast to the hot Pakistani countryside I had just left. All of it made me shiver.

The company of local traders and western travellers, thrown together for the duration, mumbled impatiently and someone complained that the Chinese border at Pirali was open for only a few hours a day. A leather-faced man from Chitral pointed to a burnt-out skeleton of a jeep in the gorge below us and told stories about the dangers of the Karakoram Highway, the KKH, opening his ruined hole of a mouth in loud bellows of laughter. Despite our ignorance of Khowari, his native language, we could read the content of his tales easily enough from his gestures. Luca, a Swiss ex-punk who had nursed me through a bout of food poisoning in Karimabad a few days before, had folded his six-foot frame between three men from Gilgit. With every bump or sharp turn, he let go a muffled but emphatic 'damn'. I shared the seat next to the driver with the English Catherine, who followed our progress pale-faced and wide-eyed in a mixed state of fear and pleasure.

I admired her. Fed up with the yuppy atmosphere of upwardly mobile trend-setters, as she called them, she had taken voluntary redundancy from her job in advertising and had 'hit the road'. We had met at Sust, the Pakistan border post, where she had been deposited by her hired tour guide. From there, she said bravely, she planned to travel on her own. For the first time in her life.

'Just a few miles to the Kunjerab!'

The jeep laboured towards the pass, through a moonscape of slate-coloured rock and sugar-coated peaks shaped like pyramids.

The scenery was awesome, humbling, and I longed to escape from the crammed vehicle and continue on foot. A comforting sort of camaraderie had developed among the passengers, enforced, it seemed, by the drama of our surroundings. The men shared their travel rations: nuts and dried apricots, some soggy chapati and water.

The highest point reached by the KKH, the Kunjerab pass, is marked by a simple monolith, a slab of concrete edged with blood-red symbols of China and Pakistan and the date 7 (2) 1986, commemorating the inauguration of the highway. Around it brown and yellow grass struggled for life between patches of hardened dry snow. Drab-clothed Chinese officials, on their way to Islamabad, and a French tour group took turns photographing each other in front of the pillar. A sharp wind hurried us back into our vehicles.

In anticipatory excitement, I gave up my map of Pakistan to the young man on the backseat who moved uncomfortably in a suit jacket that was too small for him. I wouldn't need that map any more. It was his first trip to the Kashgar Sunday market, he said. 'Mine too,' I muttered back.

Aeroflot had brought me to New Delhi in late July, via London, Moscow and a four-hour lay-over in Tashkent. Delhi was my first stop on a six-month field trip, to research the material extracted from Miran at the beginning of this century for my doctoral thesis. I had moved from Pittsburgh to England in the autumn of 1987, to London's School of Oriental and African Studies, and was now expected to gather data in various museums from India to Japan. In my pocket I carried a letter from the Academy of Social Sciences in Urumqi, the capital of Xinjiang province; it contained a vague promise of a trip to the actual site. I disembarked full of impatient nervousness.

Nothing had prepared me for the busy, washed-out heat of India's capital. Its impact was instant: the stench of *tuk-tuks*, three-wheeled motorized rickshaws, the lame boys and beggars, the beautiful women in rainbow saris and the smiling skinny kids selling garlands wrought from fragrant jasmine flowers – it was all overpowering when combined with my expectations and jet-lag. I settled in a small, 30-rupee-a-night hotel in the busy main bazaar of the Pahar Ganj area, which smelt curiously of a mixture of piss, armpit, cheap aftershave and milky tea.

Next day the city was paralysed by an all-out strike called by the opposition party. Armoured vehicles moved through masses of people, while policemen dispersed pockets of demonstrators and holy cows with surprising lethargy. It would be futile to visit the National Museum today. Instead, I got lost trying to get to Connaught Place, the 'economic and financial centre of Northern India', as my guidebook called it, a dilapidated quarter of ever narrowing concentric roads leading to a crescent with some brown grass, a dirty fountain and an undefined concrete structure. A small man with dark skin and white pantaloons offered to clean my ears, waving a list of signatures from satisfied customers. I was not convinced. On my way back to the hotel, I bought a pair of gaudy flip-flops, two cassettes of Indian film music, coconut shampoo and some vanilla oil to disperse the smell in my room. I was exhausted and wondered if I could endure the months of travel ahead.

The following morning, I went to Janpath, New Delhi's main boulevard, before the museum was due to open. I was welcomed by a shy, lanky assistant, who led me around the building to a quaint bungalow, 'the Archaeological Survey of India, during colonial times,' he said, and left me on the threshold of the exhibition rooms which were dedicated to Stein's exploits. Illuminated by a lone, bare light bulb, it was difficult at first to see anything. Then some large wooden and glass showcases came into focus; these were filled from top to bottom with treasures from Turkestan, and looked as though they hadn't been opened for half a century.

The Miran cases were on the left. Pressing my nose against the dusty glass, I could barely recognize the paintings I had been studying from pictures for the last few years. There were the pieces from the 'Garland Dado', once located on the bottom register of the circular cella of a shrine which Stein had labelled MV. Painted in tempera, in frail reds, greens and yellows, and outlined in dark brown, busts of men and women smiled serenely from the lunettes of an undulating garland carried by small boys. Local beauties, similar in dress and hairstyles, appeared alongside men of various origins: an Indian prince, a bearded man in Parthian-style costume, another with cropped hair, representing the multitude of nationalities engaged in travel and trade along the Silk Road in antiquity. Next to it leaned a convex fragment from the 'Angel Dado' once located at the bottom register of shrine MIII. With their shaven heads and large wings, it was difficult to believe that these other-worldly beings came from the very borders of China. Others, Buddhist in iconography, showed Indian ancestry. The inhabitants of Shanshan, a mixed population related to the Indo-Germanic-speaking Tocharians, embraced the Hinayana sect of Buddhism, the earlier and perhaps simpler form of the religion (derogatorily called the 'Little Vehicle', in contrast to Mahayana, or the 'Big Vehicle'), dedicating shrines, stupas, sculptures and paintings to their new-found belief.

I asked the dozing guard in the corner if it would be possible to get any closer. 'The keys,' he said, 'have been lost a long time ago.'

I spent several days working through the Miran inventory, checking it against Stein's catalogues. On the night before my departure, I was almost mugged by a drugged-out riksha driver near the Jami Masjid, the great mosque of Delhi. Doubtful about my aptitude as a traveller, I boarded the plane to Lahore. 'Maybe it's true that money can't buy you love, but it certainly helps to dress for the occasion,' read the caption underneath an advertisement in the Indian Airlines inflight magazine, illustrating a well dressed (western) couple strolling in a mountain meadow. Overcome with nausea, I ran to the toilet and threw up. 'Delhi belly,' said a kindly English voice, as I clambered back into my seat.

For the next six weeks I wandered around the northern parts of Pakistan, discovering for myself the remnants of the great Kushan empire. Dominating the ancient lands of Gandhara, from Swat and Buner into the Kabul valley and down the Indus, it had flourished under its great king Kanishka during the second century AD. The Kushans grew rich on trade, regulating Silk Road traffic, spending lavishly on culture, most strikingly manifested in the creation of a vast body of Buddhist stone sculptures. In Lahore I found that the *Ajaib-Gher*, the 'Wonder House', as Kim, Rudyard Kipling's boy-Sahib in native clothing called the local museum, still looked as he described it: 'There were hundreds of pieces, friezes of figures in relief, fragments of stones and slabs crowded with figures that had encrusted the brick walls of the Buddhist stupas and viharas of the North Country . . .'

I went on to Taxila, the valley where Alexander the Great had rested his army, where a succession of kings of Greek ancestry had ruled, and where later the Kushans built their cities and temples. The ruined sites were overgrown with man-high plants of cannabis. Staying for a week in Sir John Marshall's bungalow near the Taxila museum, I imagined the ghost of that formidable archaeologist, who had tirelessly uncovered treasure upon treasure in the time of the Raj. For me he still roamed the valley. But noises in the night usually came from the cook, who walked round and round the small house, trying windows and doors. I was quickly learning about male sexual frustration in Pakistan, and how not to smile too much. I also learned about taking siestas, boiling water, and accepting gastric problems as par for the course. Gradually I stopped being a tourist and became a traveller. By the time I made my way up the Karakoram, I dressed like a man in *shalwar kamees* (long shirt and baggy pantaloons), had lost five kilos, and had gained an appetite for the road. I couldn't wait to get to Xinjiang.

TWO

Highway and Fort

IN THE EARLY AFTERNOON we arrived at the Chinese border.
The vehicles which had carried us from Sust, the Pakistan border
post, through no-man's land had to be abandoned. Chinese buses,
we were told, would be provided to take us to Kashgar at the
western edge of the Taklamakan. We were ushered into a low
T-shaped building surrounded by chain-link fencing, and told to
fill out immigration papers. My belongings were superficially
checked by a mask-faced Chinese woman in uniform, while her
equally arrogant cousins took apart the luggage of my companions, fastidiously exposing lengths of red nylon cloth and
machine-made frills destined for the Kashgar market. Their abuse
had an air of routine; no one seemed bothered by it. We were
ordered to wait outside, and joined a group of men squatting on
their haunches, smoking.

Luca pointed to the far end of the compound, littered with
animal bones and machine parts, to a tent-like shambles which he
called a yurt. It hardly resembled the beautifully decorated felt
constructions I had seen in books. Oil drums were arranged to
one side, a few children played around them. A tiny, unbelievably
dirty toddler stared at us from large dark eyes. He started crying
as we entered the tent. The interior was a draughty smoke-filled
cavern and I wondered about the winter months. I noticed some
cots in the back, half-shielded from view by a colourful rag, and
some plastic boxes like Tupperware in a corner. This was home
to an old Khazak and his family who came up to the border
seasonally to help with road repairs. A few people sat around a

large iron kettle simmering with mutton bones. On a wooden board next to it lay a heap of steaming noodles. The old man held up two fingers to indicate a selling price and ladled broth into a chipped tea bowl. I found the smell noxious, and despite great hunger could not finish the greasy noodles. The contrast between the brick and concrete building with its smartly uniformed officials and this hovel was striking: two different worlds within ten paces.

The ticket counter opened and everyone rushed into a low side-building to have their luggage weighed. Huge sacks were thrown arbitrarily on to metal scales and pulled off again. Eventually we all crammed into an old bus, north-east bound. We wound our way down a few serpentine curves, then joined a road which cut through the high plateau of the Pamirs and followed a small creek. After some time the creek met with the wild waters from the Mingteke valley, through which travellers used to enter the plateau before a road was blasted into the Kunjerab; together the waters create the Tashkurgan river, which flows all the way to Yarkant beyond which it drowns in the desert.

The afternoon sun splashed gold over the sterile landscape. The foothills were a muddy beige of folded earth, nestling below umber peaks dusted with white. Only the clouds torn by high winds and snow-banners drifting into a dark-blue sky reminded me that we were moving at an altitude of over 4,000 metres. Like a Sioux warrior racing a train in an old Western movie, a rider appeared in full gallop alongside our bus; his body did not seem to move at all as he floated effortlessly above his horse. He disappeared as suddenly as he had come into view.

Night had fallen when we arrived in Tashkurgan, the first real settlement after the border. Tashkurgan has often been connected with the ancient 'Stone Tower', described by the second-century geographer Ptolemy as the place where traders from all directions met, exchanging their goods and relaying them to merchants responsible for the next stage. The same caravan would never travel the entire length of the road between Rome and Changan, the Sera Metropolis or City of Silk, today's Xian.

There were a few dirt roads, and a large compound full of buses and trucks. For a moment I thought about exploring the town, but the mountain chill drove me inside our nondescript hotel. We were ravenous and searched for a proper meal. Laughter and singing came from the direction of the dining-room, a large hall with big round tables and metal chairs. Left-over tinsel and paper decorations somehow only underlined the institutional feeling. We joined the company, and for the first time in six weeks I had a beer. I was relieved to find that Xinjiang, even though it had a Muslim population, was much less strict about alcohol than Pakistan.

A tall young woman entered the room and immediately commanded our attention.

'She's probably Tajik,' Luca said, guessing at her nationality, and gaped at her.

She was beautiful. There was a defiant toughness in her movement, accentuated by a cynical smirk around her full lips and tight angular face. She was a mess of reds: tight red trousers and shirt, maroon woollen sweater and cinnabar tailored jacket with frayed seams. A wisp of a red scarf covered the crown of her head; a single black braid, escaping from it, fell down to below the small of her back. She positioned herself on the edge of the truck drivers' table and with a deliberate gesture squeezed a cigarette between her lips, then twisted slightly backward to receive the flame of the match a fat man held out to her. Not for a second did she take her eyes off us.

'Change your money!' she suddenly spat at us.

'FEC-renminbi?' Luca grinned back.

'Dollar!'

'No dollars, FEC,' answered Luca with genuine regret in his voice. Without another word she turned regally and sauntered off.

FEC, Foreign Exchange Certificates, was the currency issued to foreigners and overseas Chinese, compared to the renminbi, the people's money. Since the FEC was introduced in 1980, it had become the prime monetary vehicle of the black market economy, at that time exchanging at almost double the value allocated to it by the Bank of China. I was to find it an accurate indicator of the internal political and economic situation of the country. Luca heard that the ratio had been falling, and locals were buying up foreign currency as a safeguard.

*   *   *

My damp bedclothes had just started to give off some heat when a noise in the hall signalled our departure. It was still night when we left the Pamir inn, too early for the electricity to have been switched on. Feeling our way, we took our seats in the bus again. We passed the Takhman checkpoint to climb the Pamir plateau as the sun rose magnificently. Camels were grazing on small patches of green, and in the distance a young boy on horseback herded some yaks. There were no trees or cultivation.

Still we gained in altitude, our ears popping, when to the right the cold vastness of the Muztagata massif, the father of all ice-mountains, came into view. Glaciers and snowfields glistened in the distance, the early sun playing with shadows and light on the expansive dome. The mountain continued to overshadow us all the way to the Karakuli lake, summer home to nomads living in colourful yurts, spaced wide apart over a narrow valley of fine grass.

Held in awe as a sacred mountain, many legends and superstitions are woven around the Muztagata. A hairy creature called a Pir, perhaps related to the Yeti or the Tibetan Migou, lives on the inaccessible peak. To others it is one gigantic Mazar, a sacred place, where the souls of Islam's holy men abide. Buddhists see an enormous stupa, one of the religious monuments based on burial mounds and central to their belief. My favourite legend tells of an ancient city, a paradise hidden in the ice where dwellers live for ever in happiness. A sort of Shangri-la.

Another bus had overturned and lay like a helpless insect beside the road. The passengers, apparently unhurt, sat beside it and waved to us as we drove by. Water had gouged deep crevasses into the road, and had swept away many bridges. Here and there, teams of labourers worked large stretches of the sand and gravel highway but seemed to have little effect.

Some of the men in the back had started to beat against the side of the bus and forced a long-needed stop. The sun stood high and gave off a welcome warmth. Children from a nearby hamlet came to see the bus, sneaking closer to appraise the foreigners. Luca began to tease the youngest, playfully pulling some bean-bags from his pocket, and started to juggle. A Pakistani teenager in white *shalwar* performed acrobatics with a bicycle. Much to the delight of the crowd a competition began between him and Luca . . . we were a veritable travelling circus. As a spectacular finale the young man balanced the bicycle on his chest and, by common consensus, won the event. The children cheered us on and we continued our journey towards Kashgar.

After winding through the gorges of the Gez river for some hours we were abruptly thrown upon the oasis of Tashmalik. Mountain stillness, coolness and grandeur were replaced by sun-drenched streets lined with tall green poplars and teeming with life. Suddenly I felt I had arrived in Xinjiang.

We spent only a little over an hour in Tashmalik, but I still remember the feeling of aggression I had built up over the last months slowly seeping from my body. Wandering through the town's dusty streets, I came alive again. The main road was flanked by wood and mud-brick stalls, noodle-makers, tea houses and, it seemed, hundreds of people buying, selling or just watching. Melons, stacked high on carts drawn by small donkeys with large eyes and delicate pasterns, were cut in slices by old men with round white caps and long beards. A boy in a blue worker's jacket magically produced spaghetti-like noodles by rhythmically slapping and pulling the dough as though he were conducting a symphony. The smell of burnt mutton and acrid smoke mixed with that of dust and diesel.

Catherine and I walked up the road towards a new mosque, a shell of mud-brick with a Thousand and One Nights entrance painted in sky-blue with red, yellow and white patterns, and two pillars topped with the crescent of Islam. Young girls in short skirts and tailored red jackets laughed at us behind their hands, while the men in front of the mosque stopped in their tracks, ready to confront us should we attempt to enter. Later I understood that this was a town like any other in Xinjiang.

Ceremoniously I pulled out a crisp new map of China and folded it to show all of Xinjiang, or rather, as it is officially labelled, Xinjiang Uighur Autonomous Region, the former Eastern Turkestan.

*   *   *

Xinjiang is the largest administrative division of the People's Republic and covers one-sixth of China's land mass: larger than France and Germany combined. It is divided into two large basins by the Tian Shan range: the Junggar and the Tarim. I was interested in the Tarim basin in the south, an area occupied by the Taklamakan, the 'If-you-go-in-you-won't-come-out' desert. Oasis towns bearing names redolent of the kingdoms which flourished during the heyday of Silk Road traffic are dotted around the desert's edge. This was where the Shanshan kingdom once lay.

The boundaries of Shanshan are not clearly known, though it could be surmised that, during its heyday, from the first to the fifth centuries AD, it included the Lopnur region in the north, reached towards the Altyn mountains in the south, and bordered on the Khotan kingdom in the west. The country was traversed by the southern and central branches of the Silk Road, and had access to Turfan and Karashar. As a result, Shanshan controlled the flow of traffic between east and west in the south-eastern sector of the Tarim basin, ultimately linking China with the Pamirs, and thus with the western part of the Silk Road. Miran was its easternmost terminus. At the moment it still looked very far away.

Xinjiang, which by the early nineteenth century had been a geographical black hole in the European perception of the world for the better part of six centuries, was 'opened' for decidedly political reasons. Having effectively established themselves in India by the late 1850s, the British rulers became interested in its neighbouring regions, primarily as a reaction to the Russian advance towards the subcontinent. There ensued a competition between the powers, popularized by Kipling as 'The Great Game', in the wake of which spies, explorers and, later, scientists uncovered some of the greatest treasures known to archaeology.

Reports of ancient ruins in the Taklamakan Desert first reached western ears in 1855 from the papers of a certain Mohamed-i-Hameed, an agent hired by Her Majesty's Government in India to conduct a secret exploration of the Taklamakan oases. He spent six months in Yarkant, where he heard rumours of an 'ancient capital of Khotan'. His mission was followed up in 1866–7 by William Johnson, an intrepid young Englishman in the employ of the Survey of India. Though primarily interested in the burgeoning Russian activities in the region, he pursued Mohamed's report and visited a ruin near Khotan. He was, in fact, the first of many Europeans to explore the eastern Silk Road and hunt its treasures.

The following year Russia took Samarkand and slowly encroached upon Xinjiang. In 1870, Tsarist troops occupied Guldja in the north-west of the province. The same year, and again in 1873, the British agent Douglas Forsyth led a mission to Yarkant to establish diplomatic relations with Yakub Beg, the feudal warlord of Kashgaria, who was consolidating his rule over the area. Forsyth's expedition brought back small artefacts and coins which he discussed at the Royal Geographical Society in London, in a lecture entitled 'On the Buried Cities in the Shifting Sand of the Great Desert of Gobi'. With the continuing Russian expansion, similar reports began to trickle back to the academic community in St Petersburg. Albert Regel, a Russian physician and botanist stationed at Guldja, in 1878 described his visit to Turfan and its ruined ancient capital Gaochang. One year earlier, Nikolai Przhevalsky, who was to become Russia's most formidable Central Asian explorer, had returned from his first expedition. Nevertheless, real academic interest was not kindled until the 1890s when a series of ancient manuscripts came to light.

A fifth-century Sanskrit text in Brahmi script written on birch bark was purchased by Hamilton Bower, a young Scottish lieutenant, in Kuqa. This was older than any known Indian manuscripts. Other fragments, written in the old North Indian script Kharosthi and dating from even earlier, were bought by the French cartographer Dutreuil de Rhins in 1892 at Khotan. A Russian expedition to Turfan in 1897 brought back more manuscripts, as well as the first wall paintings cut from Buddhist shrines. The same year the Swedish explorer Sven Hedin returned from his first two-year mapping expedition in the southern Taklamakan Desert with additional fragments. These new finds were presented to the Indian Section of the 1899 International Congress of Orientalists in Rome, causing a considerable stir in the academic community and resulting in financial support for a number of subsequent expeditions.

Those first reports were followed by almost three decades of concentrated archaeological exploration. In a series of expeditions, often carried out under trying climatic conditions and in a none too stable political environment, Russian, Swedish, German, British, French, Japanese and towards the close of the period even American expeditions excavated and bought artefacts of a hitherto unknown nature. Up to this point, the material had been cheaply purchased and easily carried. During the first decade of the twentieth century a new type of archaeological expedition emerged with the aim of retrieving bigger and better treasures from the caves and temples of the Taklamakan. Its leaders were trained in the study of antiquity, cartography and languages. For a brief period, international teams competed against each other and increasingly against the deterioration of the political situation in a frantic 'Race for the Treasures of Chinese Turkestan'.

Perhaps the greatest of all Central Asian explorers was the Hungarian-born British cartographer and archaeologist Sir Marc Aurel Stein (1862–1943). Having studied Oriental languages and archaeology in Vienna, Leipzig, Tübingen and Oxford, at the age of 26 he moved to India and joined the Educational Service in Lahore, and later the Archaeological Survey of India. Stein conducted three successful Central Asian expeditions during his long and varied career: in 1900–01, 1906–08, and 1913–16. He attempted a fourth in 1930, but had to abort it for political reasons. The Chinese intellectual community had finally woken up to the bleeding dry of their cultural heritage and Stein was boycotted.

Stein's first expedition followed in the footsteps of Sven Hedin along the southern edge of the Tarim basin and inaugurated a fifteen-year period of excavations. Upon his return to Europe in 1902 he spoke at the 13th Orientalist Congress in Hamburg. Count Kazui Otani, patron of the subsequent Japanese missions to Xinjiang, probably met Stein during the same year in England. Prompted by this information and Stein's preliminary reports, he set out immediately upon his first journey. But he was not alone. He had a rival, Albert Grünwedel, who led the first German expedition and was on his way to Turfan at the same time. The Germans, with Grünwedel and later Albert von LeCoq, consequently embarked on four highly sucessful missions (1902–03;

1904–05; 1905–07; 1913–14) mainly in the vicinity of Turfan and Kuqa. With the outbreak of World War I their exploits came to an abrupt end.

The French entered the race with the outstanding young scholar Paul Pelliot, and excavated between 1906 and 1908 at 'Tumquc' and in the Kuqa area, concluding with a fruitful visit to the Thousand Caves at Dunhuang. Considering their geographical proximity, formal Russian exploration was surprisingly low key. The Klements expedition was followed by a short journey by the Bersovskys in 1905, by the Koslov expedition of 1908–09, which concentrated on Karakhoto (Etzina) on the Mongolian–Chinese border, and by the more elaborate Oldenburg expedition of 1909–10. Finally, in 1923, in the afterglow of an exciting exploration period, the American art historian Langdon Warner, with Horace Jayne from the Museum of Pennsylvania, attempted one final expedition. Troubled by many misfortunes and the general hostility of the local population, they managed to visit Karakhoto and Dunhuang. With them the first period of archaeological activity in Xinjiang came to an end.

Considering its geographical and art historical importance, Miran commanded comparatively little attention from the early explorers. Only Stein and Tachibana of the second Otani mission retrieved objects from the site, and Stein alone carried out scientific surveys and systematic excavations there.

The first to mention the ancient site was Colonel Nikolai Mikhailovich Przhevalsky. Nominally in search of a route to Lhasa, he was more concerned with geography and general information-gathering than with archaeology. He conducted a series of four expeditions from Russia into the depths of Chinese Central Asia, dying in 1888 at the age of 51 shortly before his planned departure for a fifth. His second expedition, funded by the Russian Ministry of War, left Guldja in 1876, crossed the Tian Shan and continued via Korla down the Tarim river to the small village of Qarkilik (Ruoqiang). He reached the Lopnur lake in December, thereby proving its long-doubted existence. Przhevalsky settled to winter at 'Chargalyk', as he called it. Among his detailed observations of plant and animal life there was a note mentioning three ruined sites in the vicinity of the village. One lay at the edge of Qarkilik and consisted of a mud wall, of about two miles in circumference, and an ancient watch tower. Locally it was called *Ottogush-shari*, a name referring to a former Khan of the area. Another, *Kunia-shari*, or Old Town, he simply described as a very large city near the Lopnur. From the entry on his map it is certain that Przhevalsky's large city was the ruined Miran. It is also certain that the Colonel never actually set foot in it.

Almost thirty years after Przhevalsky's excursion, a group of American geologists embarked on the study of the physical environment between the Caspian Sea and Turkestan. Among them was Ellsworth Huntington, whose interest in the effect of drastic climatic changes upon human, plant and animal life brought him to the region around the Lopnur. More sensitive than his predecessor to archaeological remains (Huntington had discovered and described a number of ruins near Korla), he followed Przhevalsky's mere footnote, and found himself on Christmas Day 1905 among the ruins of a large town. He left a fairly detailed description, observing that Miran covered an area of at least five square miles 'all of which, judging from the canals and pottery, and still more from the number and location of public and religious structures, must have been thickly populated.' He briefly examined the structures which were excavated by Stein only two years later. In total, he recorded thirteen free-standing ruins, spread over a large area. Unfortunately, Huntington did not construct a plan of the site. His primary interest was the way the water supply affected the region; indeed, he identified an intricate network of canals and dams at Miran. This system, he asserted, was much the same as the one still used by locals. His observations were verified independently by the Beijing archaeologist Chen Ge in 1973. Huntington also argued that drastic climatic changes had reduced the water supply and caused the abandonment of the site. This theory later influenced Stein, who contended that the population of Miran left the oasis in the late third or early fourth century because the Tarim river had changed course.

Stein first visited Miran during his second expedition into the deserts of Xinjiang. He left for the Tarim basin in 1906, revisiting Khotan and the sites along the southern route – Niya, Endere, and Qarqan (Qiemo). From Qarqan he travelled to a small town on the Tarim river called Abdal, and from there, guided by a local *Loplik*, he came to Miran. He stayed for two days, identifying a Tibetan fort from the eighth century. Only when he returned in January did he realize the importance of the site. He came upon a series of Buddhist shrines, the earliest in Chinese Central Asia, decorated with wall paintings and filled with sculptures. Under extreme weather conditions – the temperature never rose above freezing – he extracted a large quantity of materials and in early February, from his base in Abdal, dispatched a convoy of six camels loaded with antiquities to Kashgar.

In 1914, during his third expedition, Stein briefly returned to Miran intending to remove some wall paintings left behind previously. At that time he found that the Japanese had become interested in 'his site'.

Between 1902 and 1910 the Japanese carried out three missions in Western China. All of them were apparently funded by Count Kazui Otani, the spiritual leader of the *Jodo Shinzu*, or Pure Land sect of Japanese Buddhism. From the rather brief notices in the *Geographical Journal*, it can be ascertained that Zuicho Tachibana, leader of the second and third missions, reached Miran some time in the winter of 1908–09. Rumour had it that his presence in Xinjiang was motivated by more than the recovery of archaeological treasures. Indeed, George Macartney, the British representative in Kashgar, suspected Tachibana of espionage and speculated that he was actually an officer in the Imperial Japanese Navy. He retrieved little from Miran, and did so, it seems, in a highly unprofessional manner. Five years later, Stein lamented the destruction of the painted interior of shrine MV, a ruin he had left buried for protection under layers of sand.

Stein was the last western archaeologist to work at Miran.

THREE

Kashgar

'KASHGAR IS THE MOST romantic place in the world,' a frail Japanese girl sighed dreamily, clinging to the arm of her strong Scottish boyfriend.

The sweet aroma of hashish wafted over to our table, which was cluttered with yoghurt bottles and empty plates. A group of Italian boys, well-groomed and fashionably dressed in Kathmandu colours, Pathan hats and Kashmir jewellery, argued loudly with a money-changer; three Afghan students in crisp white shirts and tight grey trousers lounged in wicker chairs slowly sipping Xinjiang beer from large bottles; a few northern Europeans in lycra shorts, singlets and blond crewcuts, complained that they had cycled the long haul up the Karakoram Highway, only to be told at the border that they had to take a bus to Kashgar. The makeshift outdoor café, constructed for the tourist season, was patronized exclusively by foreign travellers who were catered to by a group of Chinese women. Li Shiang, a pretty waitress with a welcoming smile and rudimentary English, served some more drinking yoghurt and apple fritters, and asked if we had any foreign stamps to add to her collection. It was Friday morning with a Sunday feel to it, and the scene could have been taken from any Club Med advertising pamphlet.

The bus from Tashkurgan had arrived late the previous evening, discharging us in front of the metal gate of the Qinibagh, the once-upon-a-time British Consulate. In the cold fluorescent light of the street lamps, the two-storey main building with its crenellated roof mouldings, recognizable from countless photographs, loomed familiarly, but the once-famous gardens were gone. The grounds had been ripped open and a trench cut from the water mains to the stables, which now served as dormitories. A few men from across the border shouted wearyingly familiar greetings: 'Hallo Miss, hallo Miss!'

Most of the Pakistani traders visiting Kashgar took lodgings at the Qinibagh, which is probably why the bus driver didn't even bother to take us to the depot on the other side of town. I had to admit that the previous month and a half of travel in Pakistan had disinclined me, probably unfairly, towards any unshaven male in *shalwar* and *kamees*. Too tired to make a decision, I stared forlornly at the gaggle of eager young boys and their donkeys and carts crowding around the entrance.

'I heard the Seman had better baths,' said Luca, and climbed on to the carpeted platform of a donkey-taxi. Catherine and I followed without much protest.

The Seman Hotel, the former Russian consulate, had survived the last half-century visibly better than the Qinibagh. (The Russians played the Xinjiang-game with a bit more endurance than the British.) Low buildings, some new, sprawled across a large walled compound. Next to the gate nestled a vine-covered café run by an enterprising Han Chinese, who advertised himself and his services with carefully crafted lettering painted on the back wall. Mister John catered to tours, provided guides, bicycles and overseas phone calls. His restaurant served pseudo-English breakfasts and gin and tonics without the tonic. Apart from a collegiate-looking young woman in pastels, the place was empty. We were assigned a room in the building just behind the café.

The dark, cool space was spartan, with three sturdy beds and a high ceiling which hadn't been painted since it was built. Green mould crept up the wall and chewed into the faded carpet, clashing with the orange and pink design of oil-lamps and debased Chinese characters. A creaky wooden wardrobe looked bulky and out of place. I threw myself on to the bed between Luca and Catherine, sinking almost to the floor; the springs had lost their elasticity many decades ago. The lack of luxury was compensated for by the adjoining bathroom. It was large and tiled, and taken up almost entirely by a tub fit to grace any turn-of-the-century hotel in

St Petersburg. Boiling water steamed out of brass taps, transform-ing the room into a plausible facsimile of a Turkish bathhouse. Feeling clean for the first time in weeks, I fell into a satisfied, dreamless coma.

The outdoor café was opposite the entrance to the Seman, and we had settled there for a long, languid breakfast before exploring the town. Li Shiang had just brought the third bottle of yoghurt, having convinced me that it was the only antidote to gastric upset. Luca took turns arguing with the money-changer, a short, thin Uighur wearing a pin-striped suit, cloth cap and a long frozen smile. Speakers piped Hong Kong pop music on to the street. Suddenly, a group of uniformed officials accompanied by a squat Chinese woman clad in medical whites swarmed between the tables, marching purposefully towards the kitchen. Without intro-duction, completely ignoring the dozen or so foreigners, they proceeded to close the shutters, padlock the door and tape a thin piece of paper on the wall declaring the establishment closed. 'Closed by the Department of Hygiene', the flimsy strip read in large red characters. Then they turned and left. All this had taken no longer than a couple of minutes, and we suddenly felt rather dumb sitting with full plates in the garden of a closed café. Li Shiang shrugged her shoulders and smiled, then fetched her bag and bicycle and went home.

'Don't forget to send me stamps,' she reminded us as she took off.

'Happens all the time,' Ian the Scotsman commented, break-ing a long nervous silence. He regarded the incident with an air of complacency and a superior 'insider' expression. He had been in Kashgar for three weeks, and was considered an old hand. 'She probably didn't pay off the right people,' he added knowingly. 'Or she was too much competition for Mister John.' Then, after a moment he sounded truly worried: 'There won't be a single good café in Kashgar, until the Oasis opens again.'

Kashgar, the most romantic place in the world!

We disbanded slowly. The Italians were debating whether or not to return to Gilgit immediately or to stick around for the Sunday market. Someone suggested hiring a jeep to visit the tourist sites near the town, and Luca was excited about rumours that Tibet was opening to individual travellers again. I asked Ian if he would show me around town. He said he'd be glad to, if I didn't mind stopping at the Qinibagh first.

Stein had always stayed at the Qinibagh during his expeditions, as the guest of the legendary representative of the British Empire, George Macartney and his wife Catherine. Of unusual background for the period – his Scottish father had married a Chinese woman – Macartney was ideal for the job and served for 28 years in Kashgar. He and his wife were renowned for their hospitality and, over the years, entertained scores of travellers and explorers. Stein seems to have enjoyed the safe haven provided by the consulate gardens so much that he hardly ever left the compound. Of his first visit during the summer of 1900 he wrote: 'Most of my time was spent in busy work at Chini-Bagh; and to the little oasis of Anglo-Indian civilisation which my kind hosts had created around themselves cling my main recollections of Kashgar. There was little contact with the outer world to vary the pleasant round of our daily life.'

My feelings for Stein have always been ambivalent. I admired him as an explorer and scholar, but had never been able to grasp Stein the human being. Very little personal information can be gleaned from his vast literary corpus, his scientific papers, personal narratives and endless articles. He was a short man, barely five foot four, strong, and physically very active. He enjoyed the rough life, and enjoyed advertising it. Reading his biography, qualities such as systematic, organized, methodical, frugal, keep coming up. His life belonged to his work; he never married, nor is there any indication that he ever had an intimate relationship with anyone, man or woman. Instead, Stein had three heroes: Alexander the Great, the Chinese travelling monk Xuanzhang, who became the patron saint of his expeditions, and Marco Polo.

I wondered if he had ever been in love.

Near the Seman was a small liquor store, and in front of it, beneath an awning constructed of three red blankets, roosted a row of squat billiard tables. A couple of drunk Uighur youths attempted shots: one of them was quite good. To our right appeared a few ugly concrete structures in the best socialist style.

To our left, and in contrast, small shops and eateries lined a dusty sidewalk, shaded by a row of slender poplars.

'Ugly,' I commented, looking at the concrete buildings.

'Part of the Chinese assimilation process,' Ian said, somewhat sarcastically. 'They've been cutting more and more into the old city; trying to turn it into Chinatown.'

We arrived at the Qinibagh, which looked even worse in daylight. Ian hurried through the gate and into the main building. Through a side entrance we climbed a wooden staircase and entered a series of large, dark rooms, filled with beds, rucksacks and hashish smoke.

'How ya doin', man,' a figure crouched in the corner of a bed greeted Ian. Glazed eyes and tousled shoulder-length blond hair were illuminated by a candle.

'Stoned again, Steve?'

'Yeah man . . .'

Ian picked though a pack at the foot of a bed in the adjacent room and let something slide into the pocket of his jeans, then motioned me to follow him.

'All roads lead to the Idga Mosque,' he said as he led me into a small alley crowded with life. Stalls, piled high with fruit and vegetables, gave way to those selling household goods, boots and books, presided over by bearded men with thick round black-rimmed glasses, *chapans* – the Uighurs' traditional padded coats distinguished by their sashes – and fur-edged hats. Women in colourful dresses, with long braids and pill-box hats, argued loudly with naked children or toddlers with slit trousers, a convenient way to avoid the nappie problem, I thought. Some of the children had the large protruding bellies of the underfed, and I saw an infant with ugly sores on his face and arm, being pulled along in a cart by his older sister. Dust mixed with the smell of fresh bread, baked in conical tandoori ovens, and kebabs. There were noodle-makers and tailors, cobblers and knife-makers.

We emerged on to a large square, presided over by a mosque: the Idga, religious and social centre of old Kashgar. A rectangular façade was squeezed between two slender minarets, faced with tile-work of light yellow, pale blue and faded purple, arranged in geometric patterns. Niches decorated the structure surrounding the main gate, reminiscent of the Buddhist practice of incorporating sculptures in the architecture, only here the niches were empty. In front of the mosque a crowd of men and boys had gathered, encircling a troupe of jugglers and acrobats. A young performer in electric-blue trousers offset by a magenta cummerbund, and a tanned naked upper body exhibiting his tight muscles, walked on his hands, his legs swaying to Uighur music screaming from a ghetto blaster. An older man with a billowing white shirt and a Zorba the Greek face balanced two small boys wearing lavender and pink outfits and yellow turbans on his outstretched arms, while dancing around a teapot strongly reminiscent of Aladdin's lamp. The onlookers must have recently emerged from Friday prayers, and now sat on their haunches cheering the actors; most of them wore dark suits and cloth caps, creating a sombre background to the frenzy of sound and colour.

'I've got to take off . . . you mind?' said Ian, pointing to his watch as he disappeared into the crowd. I didn't mind.

I turned into another dim alley, which led into an old covered market smelling of must. Swathes of cloth and clothes hung thickly from small stalls, encroaching upon the narrow path. There was much nylon and fake lace, some familiar fabrics imported from Pakistan. I asked for the traditional ikat cloth, silk woven into a pattern from a single multicoloured thread, and was directed to an old man's shop. The owner dug deep beneath a pile of synthetics and proudly brought forth a few metres of the rare material. It was too expensive for my tight budget. Instead I bought some strands of freshwater pearls. I had noticed them around the necks of most Uighur women, the number of strands corresponding to their status or income. I paid eight renminbi for the white ones and twelve for the more precious pink ones.

Then I moved on and got lost in a cul-de-sac of mud-and-wattle walls. An older woman threw a brown veil over her wrinkled face as I came near her, and I remembered hearing someone say that only the old and the ugly wear veils in Kashgar. Indeed, most women did not hide their faces, and only covered their braids with the flimsiest of nylon scarves. Many wore rouge, and accentuated their eyes and brows with kohl. Though most dressed in a neo-traditional manner, high heels were definitely fashionable and a few women sported leather jackets over short skirts. I couldn't help but make a comparison with Pakistan where, under the strict Islamic rule, women were kept behind walls and veils. But even historically Kashgar and its women were known for their independence and freedom. When Yakub Beg, the boy-dancer turned Turkic leader from Khokhand, seized Kashgar in 1865 and proclaimed it an independent state, he was appalled at how easily women consorted with travellers and introduced the law of temporary marriage, making it obligatory for male visitors to 'marry' within three days of arriving. A similar law of temporary marriage, termed *sighe*, is now current in Iran, where, with the sanction of a mullah, the duration and price is fixed prior to the union. It is frequently a form of legalized prostitution.

The more I drifted around Kashgar, the more apparent became the contrasts, the tensions, the incongruities, boiling beneath its medieval charm. Large posters were plastered on wooden bill-boards urging harmony among the minorities; crude paintings showed Uighur and Han children hand in hand. Others propagated birth control, for the sake of the survival of the motherland. Broad avenues divided the old town; large concrete buildings clashed with the traditional Uighur architecture, grey next to painted carved woodwork, geometry next to playful verandas and balconies. Here and there a television blasted from the depths of a *chai kanah* – a traditional tea stall; billiard tables looked out of place next to donkey carts and skinned carcasses of sheep. My favourite was a large painted sign suspended above the entrance of a department store, advertising traditional Uighur riding boots, a painting-set, an array of ladies' shoes and a standard issue Chinese military gas-mask. The motherland was squashing its adopted child.

Kashgar has a violent history, mirrored in the faces of its population: there were Caucasian faces, narrow and oval, with green or grey eyes; round, flat Mongol faces; brown curly hair; black straight Chinese mops. Most of its people call themselves Uighurs, a Turkic nomadic tribe which exercised considerable

political power throughout the oases from the ninth to the thirteenth centuries.

Squeezed between the western edge of the Taklamakan Desert
and the Pamirs, Kashgar has been a trading town ever since its
founding over 2,000 years ago. Toba, White Huns, Turks,
Tibetans, Mongols and Chinese have repeatedly struggled for
domination over the roads and the oases which grew rich from
the exchange of goods between east and west. In Chinese annals,
the kingdom of Kashgar appears as Shule. Indeed, the contemporary city grew out of a union of the previously independent cities
of Shule and Shufu. Shule used to be known under the name of
Hancheng, China town, and Shufu as Huicheng, Muslim town.
The old city, the heart of Kashgar with its mud-brick buildings
and markets, is identical with Huicheng. The new city is still
primarily inhabited by the Chinese, often closed to non-Han, but
is no longer separate.

The Chinese managed to include Kashgar in its 'protectorate'
during the Han dynasty (206 BC – AD9 and AD25–221) until they
were expelled only to be replaced by the White Huns who sacked
the town in the third century. The Chinese were back during the
Tang dynasty (618–907), but were pushed out by the Tibetans
who had slowly been conquering the oases along the southern
road. Subsequently, Kashgar was ruled by a confederation of
Turkish tribes who, in alliance with the Arabs, took it in 725.
The primarily Buddhist-dominated community adopted Islam,
although other religions including Manichaeism and Nestorian
Christianity continued alongside the new faith, to succumb gradually to the word of Muhammed. Kashgar became the capital of
the Kharakhanit Khanate, which ruled between Bokhara and Khotan for almost 200 years. World history took a swipe again in the
thirteenth century, when the city fell into the hands of Gengis
Khan, flourishing during the *pax mongolia*, only to be destroyed
by Tamerlane who swept through the region at the end of the
fourteenth century. China returned in the form of the Manchu
dynasty of the Qing in the seventeenth and eighteenth centuries,
a period during which the Turkic people managed to stage 44
separate uprisings against their oppressors. Finally in 1865, Yakub
Beg declared the independent state of Kashgaria, wooing both the

British and the Russians who had increasingly become interested in this far-away place. Yakub's state was short-lived, and by 1877 he disappeared, defeated, leaving the whole region to be incorporated as a province into China: Xinjiang, it was named, the New Dominion. A year after the fall of the Manchus and the declaration of the Chinese Republic by Sun Yatsen in 1911, a bloody revolution once again swept through the oases. Kashgar found itself eventually ruled by the bloodthirsty warlord Ma, a Chinese Muslim, fond of torture and pretty women.

Xinjiang finally had enough, a pan-Turkic movement developed, and pockets of rebellion broke out throughout the province, culminating in the founding of the short-lived Independent Muslim East Turkestan Republic on 12 November 1944.

All that came to an end when Mao and the Chinese Communist Party assumed power in 1949, and the People's Liberation Army moved into Xinjiang to subdue the 'minorities', followed by a steady stream of Chinese immigrants. Mao used a strategy which had proved effective throughout Chinese history: destruction, assimilation and diffusion. First, Arabic letters were eliminated and replaced with Latin script; books were destroyed. Land reform removed private ownership; so-called *waqif* lands owned by mosques were confiscated, depriving religious institutions of income. Minority groups were defined as such, and Turkic people categorized as 'Uighur', thus weakening the traditional allegiances to oasis, tribe and family. Traditional bonds were further destroyed by forcing people into communes and camps, run on military lines and ruled by the red book. Some 29,000 mosques were closed, imams arrested, and religious services replaced by political indoctrination. It is almost impossible to obtain concrete information – the Chinese government is not in the habit of advertising its atrocities – though Uighur groups outside China estimated that during the hard years of 1950 to 1972 some 360,000 Turkic people were executed, while half a million were pressed into labour camps. Another 200,000 fled to neighbouring countries; many of them are still exiled in Turkey, led by the head of the separatist movement Isa Yusuf Alptekin, now over 90 years old.

Not until the late 1970s, after the end of the Cultural Revolution and the dawn of a new 'liberalism' in Chinese political thought, was the plight of Xinjiang's native population eased. During the early 1980s mosques were once again opened, and many of them restored. The Latin script reverted to Arabic. Life assumed an air of normality as people returned to their villages, and now, with increased prosperity, the standard of living was steadily rising, though the average income is still 20 per cent below the national average.

When the government relaxed its iron grip, voices of the resistance began to be heard once again. In 1985, Uighurs demonstrated in cities throughout China, bringing forth a long list of grievances and demands. Among the slogans displayed on banners were: democratic election of officials to replace the Chinese autocrats appointed by Beijing, economic self-determination, an end to the practice of sending Chinese convicts to Eastern Turkestan, and an end to nuclear testing. As a result, 60 so-called ringleaders were arrested at Urumqi University in May 1986 – never to be heard of since. June 1988 saw renewed demonstrations, this time against the new policy of birth control among Turkic people, proclaimed by the central government on the first day of that month, with births of more than two children per family being heavily fined. The publication of a book called *Sex Habits*, a derogatory exegesis on supposed amoral tendencies among the minorities, caused another outcry. Protest marches in Urumqi in May the following year culminated in violent demonstrations in June, at the same time as the pro-democracy movement in Beijing which ended in the massacre of Tiananmen Square on 4 June 1989. In Urumqi, government buildings were stormed and windows smashed. Arrests certainly followed, though it is not known how many people fell into the hands of the Public Security Bureau.

Getting news from Xinjiang in the West is like squeezing water from a stone. Getting news about Xinjiang in Xinjiang is almost as bad. People don't like to talk about their current affairs to foreigners; people don't like to talk to foreigners, period. But the local and national press started to acknowledge the existence of a separatist movement – difficult to ignore after the 1985 demonstrations – and Tumur Dawamet, the puppet governor in Urumqi, has gone as far as blaming the exiled Alptekin for fuelling unrest.

It is certain, however, that Beijing has no plans for letting the province go. Not only is it of the utmost strategic importance militarily, but Xinjiang is rich in mineral resources, namely oil and gas. Han Chinese now make up more than half of the population of almost sixteen million and the immigration process is far from finished.

I returned to the Seman, to find the three Afghans seated nonchalantly around a table at Mister John's. All three were students in Peshawar, having lived there in exile since the outbreak of the war in their country. They came to Kashgar for a holiday and to have riding boots made for themselves and three of their cousins. The oldest had already the appearance of a fierce Pathan, with thick hair and a proud black beard, symbolizing his recent pilgrimage to Mecca. An animated conversation was in progress between them. I slumped into a chair at the next table and ordered a gin and tonic which, predictably, came without the tonic. I was listening to their discussion without understanding a word, when the name 'Salman Rushdie' jumped out at me.

'Have you read the book?' I asked, turning round to face them.

'Of course,' the bearded one answered haughtily in good English.

'Only some excerpts,' admitted the younger cousin, a pretty boy with large bedroom eyes and well-styled wavy hair.

'Actually, the mullahs read some parts to show us the blasphemous nature of the book,' said the third.

'Have you read any of his other books . . . *Midnight's Children*, for example?' I asked. (I had read *Midnight's Children* during a journey through Morocco the previous year, and loved it.)

They shook their heads.

'Anyone who defiles the teachings of Muhammed in the way Rushdie has done deserves to die!' the bearded one stated fiercely. His cousins looked at him uncomfortably.

'Bullshit.'

He looked at me with pity, and I realized that there was a gap too vast to be bridged. I excused myself and went to my room to rest, recalling that the Afghans had told me yesterday that they had applied for admission to Oxford, Cambridge and London's School of Oriental and African Studies.

I didn't wake until late the next morning, almost lunchtime.

'Finally,' said Luca as I opened my eyes. He and Catherine had organized a jeep to take us to the Abakh Khoja tomb on the north-eastern perimeter of the oasis and a Buddhist monument called the 'Caves of the Three Immortals', not exactly a Buddhist name. Together with a thin Japanese girl named Mayumi, who had been travelling in Africa and India for two years and looked as though she needed a vacation, and Gary, a footsore Brit, who had embarked upon a hike with too tight shoes, we piled into the vehicle. Our driver raced through narrow shady lanes accompanied by the vocal complaints of scattering chickens and people, never once taking his hand off the horn. He came to a halt in front of a beautiful blue and white tiled gate and pointed to it, indicating that he would wait for us by the car.

The Abakh Khoja is known as one of Islam's holiest places in Xinjiang, named after a popular Muslim leader and religious figure who had organized an uprising against Qing power in the seventeenth century. Under the Qianlong emperor, the rebels of Kashgar were all executed, including Khoja. The only one spared was his daughter Iparhan, who, renowned for her beauty and her 'exceptional good smell', was brought to the forbidden city to enter the imperial harem as *Xiangfei*, the Fragrant Concubine. She was later strangled, it is said, for her never-ceasing drive to avenge her family; her remains were brought back to her homeland, and interred in the family tomb.

Built in a style reminiscent of the great mosque in Samarkand, the broad domed structure, framed by two short, fat minarets and faced with bottle-green tiles with multi-coloured facets, showed signs of serious deterioration. Tiles had come off the roof and sides and lay shattered on the ground. Still, it was beautiful, surrounded by an aura of ancient calm. The keeper, a short man in black clothing and a white turban opened the door and we peeped into the semi-dark interior crowded with sarcophagi. The cool space smelled of dust and death, and I followed the urge to escape back into the sun for want of oxygen. Mayumi stayed inside for a long time, re-emerging with an elated expression on her face.

We continued our ride, due north-west, for some ten kilometres, then turned sharply into a broad, dry river-bed, shaded by a tall cliff. Engulfed in a dust cloud, we sped down the river and halted by a collection of water-starved trees, facing the cliff. There, high above the river-bed, were three tiny openings hewn into the wall. Remnants of wall paintings and a blue halo were visible in one cave, having at one time surrounded a Buddha statue. We lounged in the shade, looking at the remnants of early Buddhism in Xinjiang; I was trying to hide my disappointment. Lulled by the heat and arid serenity of the place we fell into siesta mood.

Buddhism, the religion of compassion, had come to the oases of the Taklamakan around the turn of the millennium, six centuries after it was founded by Siddartha Gautama, a prince of the Shakyas, a hill tribe in the Himalayan foothills of present-day Nepal. Based on the doctrine of the 'Four Noble Truths' and the principles embodied in the 'Noble Eightfold Path', a series of moral and behavioural guidelines, it aspired to the 'Middle Way', a life devoid of extremes. The goal was nirvana, enlightenment, and ultimately escape from the endless cycle of birth, death and rebirth.

The driver, who had not spoken during the whole trip, urged us to leave. We ignored him, and Luca threw him a few words about getting your money's worth. He sat at a distance from us, and seemed agitated. After some time he returned to his car, and sounded the horn, until we reluctantly climbed back into the vehicle. On our return to the main road, we saw a number of black, human silhouettes leaning against the cliff-side. Then an army jeep came speeding towards us, and a soldier reprimanded the driver in harsh, fast language. The river-bed was used for shooting practice by the army.

We returned from our outing late in the afternoon, tired and sunburned. I left Catherine in the room waiting for hot water. She was mystified that the promise of a bath had been reduced to a tepid rust-coloured trickle and went out into the hall to ask the *furen*, the keeper of keys in any Chinese hotel, if there was a defect.

'Hot water at six o'clock', the woman told us. We had forgotten to ask whether she referred to Xinjiang or Beijing time, a confusing system of official and unofficial time-keeping. Xinjiang time runs two hours behind the official, or Beijing, time; in summer months this gap extends to three hours, when daylight saving time rules most of the People's Republic.

I went over to registration to complain about the laundry, which had reduced all my clothing to a washed-out, yellow glob with little speckles of grey fuzz, and to pay our room bill, which had to be taken care of daily. The girl behind the counter smiled, and, successfully diverting my attention from my ruined clothing, told me about a big party at a disco in the centre of Kashgar that night.

'There will be dancing,' she nodded enthusiastically.

The water came on at eight, and I decided to go to the dance.

The disco was held in one of the massive concrete buildings on Renmin West Road, the six-tank-wide grey ribbon which divides old and new Kashgar. Uniforms and colourful dresses, a few leather jackets and lots of red ribbons in glossy black hair, crowded round the entrance and stairs. Cigarette smoke mixed with the loud brassy noise of a military march. The party appeared to be on the first floor. From the street I could see rainbow-coloured disco lights flashing through the windows, and little fireflies from those rotating glass balls danced against the ceilings. The building vibrated with the stomping of hundreds of feet, echoing the martial rhythms. A big bouncer eyed me with suspicion.

'This is not for foreigners,' came out of the side of his mouth while he checked the ticket of a young girl with too much rouge. 'This is the celebration of the fortieth anniversary of the People's Republic of China,' he added.

'Well, I want to celebrate too,' I challenged him in my imperfect Mandarin.

'No,' he growled as he shoved me aside.

'How much are the tickets?' I said as if I hadn't heard him, edging my way up the steps.

'Han Chinese only,' he barked, now openly antagonistic. 'Get out!'

Reluctantly I gave up, and forced my way back against the stream of the crowd. People turned and stared. A few young girls giggled stupidly. '*Waiguoren, waiguoren* . . . foreigner!' There were no Uighurs. As the man had said, this celebration was for Han only.

On the way back to the Seman I passed a cinema. Rows of benches were arranged in a rectangular open space facing a white-washed wall. Another wall shielded the enclosure from the street. Sultry, erotic sighs and gunshots blasted into the night; a few men had placed chairs near the doorway to catch a glimpse for free. Kashgar loved the movies almost as much as its mosques: in the last days I had seen six cinemas in the city centre alone.

Next morning I got up early. The sky hung low; a heavy lead sheet filled with sand from the desert crushed down upon the city. The atmosphere was murky and hot. It was Sunday, the first of October. After a quick breakfast at Mister John's, I went off in the direction of the Qinibagh, but took an early left into Shengli Street to pay a visit to the Public Security Bureau. The Kashgar PSB was housed in a large, walled compound. Granters of visas, givers of permits, keepers of information, it had the reputation of not being exactly the friendliest police station in the province. I entered a small side building next to the main gate. The interior was dark, and my eyes focused slowly on the human shapes inhabiting it.

Was it possible to visit these archaeological sites on my way to the capital, I inquired, listing Tumxuk, Kizil and Karashar?

'Kizil is closed,' insisted a rotund Uighur in uniform.

'But I heard it's open,' I countered.

'Closed,' he maintained.

'Can I get a permit?' I smiled at him.

'Try in Kuqa,' he replied, oblivious to my charm.

'What about Tumxuk?' I tried again. His expression unequivo-cally told me that I was a bother.

'Tumxuk?' I repeated, pulling out my map and pointing to a small dot north of the town of Aksu.

'Aksu is open,' he snarled, and gestured with his head to a

large poster on the wall which cited the so-called 'open' towns in Xinjiang. Aksu was indeed open. Another officer, no older than eighteen, balancing his boots at the edge of a bare wooden desk while cleaning his dirty fingernails with a knife, snickered, and mumbled just audibly enough '*lao wai*', a colloquial abbreviation for *waiguoren*, foreigner. I felt anger rising from the pit of my stomach, but managed to delay a strong, uncontrolled curse until I stood once more outside the gate.

From the PSB compound, I followed the tiny alleyways which all led to the centre of the old town. I passed the silver market, then the box-makers whose workshops spilled out into the street, and entered the market of the hatters and cap-makers. Business was thinner than usual and a few of the stalls were shut. Sunday was the day of the great market in the eastern part of Kashgar, I recalled. I emerged from the maze on to the open plaza in front of the Idga, bought some ripe figs, then crossed over to Jiefang North Road and headed south.

Two blocks before I reached the intersection with the main avenue, I became aware of the rhythmic drumming and whining sounds of Uighur music. As I came closer I saw three men in brown suits and green, embroidered *dopa*, standard Central Asian headgear, perched on the awning above the entrance to Kashgar's largest department store. They twisted to the music on a space no larger than a horse blanket, beating the drums and blowing the *sunai* (an instrument related to the clarinet) with the intensity of a heavy metal band. A crowd had formed below them. Improbably, the volume increased at the same moment that I heard a marching band. A sea of red banners rolled towards us, propelled by the sound of snare drums and horns. Party officials in uniform marched by, wearing faces of marble. They were followed by local representatives of the government, wearing traditional embroidered shirts and caps; then came rows and rows of school-children of all ages.

The Uighur beat filled the air, drums and *sunai* working into a frenzy; defiantly at first, then triumphantly, the volume increased again. Beat and counter-beat competed with military noise. The snare drums lost their rhythm, the children's feet – more familiar with their native instruments – stumbled. Bodies bumped into one another, interrupting the marching order. The whole parade fell apart. On the corner, a group of teenage boys unfurled a white bed sheet, displaying a crudely painted green crescent moon and a star, the banner of the East Turkestan Republic. Suddenly, uniformed PSB officials swarmed among us, hurrying the confused children along. The banner vanished. Quickly the parade disappeared up Jiefang Street.

'Musical anarchism,' I laughed to myself, and continued on my way. Families that had lined the street were dispersing. I noticed that the onlookers had consisted almost exclusively of Han Chinese, and realized how little they figured in the street picture of daily Kashgar life. Prim women in trousers, a uniformed child hand in hand with a uniformed father, promenaded on the sidewalk, returning to 'their' part of town. They struck me as uneasy, their clothing more adapted to a Beijing shopping mall than the dust and heat of the desert.

On my left loomed the eighteen-metre-tall concrete statue of Mao, grey except for the painted red star on the famous cap. I passed the sports field, covered in brown dusty weeds, and turned towards the bus depot, a sandy compound accessible through a surprisingly narrow gate. Mud-brick huts were sunk halfway into the ground. These were the ticket offices. Destinations were written in Chinese characters and Arabic letters. People were crowding in front of the small holes in the wall, screaming names of towns, pushing money between iron bars. There was a separate office for foreigners. I asked for Aksu.

'Thirty-eight FEC.'

' I'm a student.'

'White card?' the voice asked.

'International Student Card,' I answered.

For some reason the shadow in the wall accepted my credentials and let me pay for the journey in renminbi. I pushed the amount between the metal bars, a brown hand took it and handed me a little bundle of thin papers stapled to a cardboard ticket.

'A good omen,' I thought, and instead of going to the Sunday market I went back to the hotel to pack.

FOUR

The Tumxuk that Wasn't

I LEFT THE SEMAN before the call to morning prayers. By daybreak I had travelled beyond the last of Kashgar's cotton fields, and had entered a monotonous grey and yellow landscape. All day I watched bald, wrinkled foothills pass by the window on my left and became mesmerized by the gravel desert on my right. We stopped at a few caravanserais that all looked alike. Time ceased to exist, and did not start again until we approached the first green of the Aksu oasis. Suddenly, there was an overwhelming impression of fecundity.

The bus driver was surprised that I alighted there. Foreigners don't often visit Aksu, he said.

But I hadn't come to stay: my goal was two ancient Buddhist sites built into cliffs near a town called Tumxuk. I had not read much about them, and had neither source material nor maps regarding the location with me, but recalled that Paul Pelliot had worked the site for several months in 1906. He had found an extensive monastic complex and a large amount of sculptures and paintings. Stein snubbed the place (probably out of a sense of competition), exploring it only superficially, but mentioned some fourteenth-century coins, though it is generally assumed that the town had declined by the eighth century. I like to think that it was sacked when Tamerlane swept towards Kashgar, trampling everything in his path. At least that would explain the coins.

It seemed easy enough to get there; there was only one town named Tumxuk on the map, located north of Aksu.

Our bus had stopped in front of the Aksu bus station, a massive building faced with bile-green tiles. A group of men hung around a *kavabchi* beside a shack selling scores of different brands of cigarettes, none of which I had heard of. I asked for directions. Unanimously, they pointed to a waiting bus at the far end of the depot, then turned their attention back to pulling bits of mutton from metal skewers. I shoved my luggage into the vehicle and relaxed in a seat.

'Aksu-Tumxuk, this is Tumxuk,' the driver announced impatiently about twenty minutes later.

I must have dozed off, for I noticed with a start that I was the only remaining passenger on the bus. Unsure where I was, I found myself facing a construction site and a section of paved road at the transition to gravel. There were a few buildings on the opposite side of the street, next to a field planted with vegetables. I sensed that I hadn't left Aksu at all, but had ended up in its suburbs. My feeling of being lost increased when I discovered that I had left my roll of maps on the bus. And, to make matters worse, it was getting dark.

The speed at which sunset turned to night in this part of the world struck me once again. It was violent in its abruptness. Like a door being slammed in your face. I shouldered my bag and walked towards a small window garlanded with round light bulbs and a miniature red lantern.

A crude wooden entrance disappeared below street level, leading to a sparsely furnished room. There were two tables and a bar draped with silver tinsel. Strips of white and pink paper were pasted on the wall, advertising a variety of Chinese dishes. The place was empty. Loud pop music drowned laughter emanating from a second room, lower still than the first. I dropped my luggage, took a seat in the corner and waited.

A short, fat Chinese woman with uneven hair entered with pert little steps. Head turned over one shoulder, she carried on a conversation with customers in the back room, expelling piercing staccato laughs. She hurried to the bar, opened a massive white refrigerator and slammed three bottles of *Aksu Pijiu*, the local brand of beer, on to the counter. Then she noticed me. Her verbal explosion came to a dramatic halt, her eyes widened and her jaw dropped. I managed a polite '*Nin hao.*'

The woman spun on her heels and fled back to the other room. I sat for a moment, contemplating whether it would not be better to leave, when a young man, tailed by a handful of people, crept up to my table.

'Do you speak English?' he asked diffidently.

'Yes!?' I answered, drawing the syllables into one long question mark.

The young man laughed proudly, as did the others around him. They slapped his back, exclaiming a few 'hao, hao's, poured clear liquor into cups and toasted in unison with an emphatic 'ganbei'.

'I study English at university,' he explained. 'I'm returning to Urumqi tomorrow, this is my goodbye party. Won't you join, please?' he added politely. Then he introduced his mother, Mrs Yang, uncle, younger brother, cousin and his friends.

They hung on Yang junior's every word. Uncle offered cigarettes all around. It was my first exposure to a Chinese family, and their first meeting with a foreigner. Their hospitality was direct and unexpected. In Kashgar I had instinctively sympathized with the Uighur view of the Chinese as the oppressors, the colonialists; now I was served a generous helping of mixed vegetables and noodles, some dumplings and clear soup with greens in it, while Yang interrogated me about my vital statistics. He seemed a nice young man with his mother's round face, and a few hairs on the upper lip.

For the first time he was able to practise his English with a non-Chinese, he told me. His dream was to go to Beijing, maybe even work for a foreign company; he'd do anything to leave Xinjiang and was hoping to get out soon. The problem seemed to be one of registration. There were country and city registrations, and the government had made it almost impossible for people with country registrations to move to the city.

'It can't be all that bad here?' I asked.

'It's a . . .' he stalled, searching for words, '. . . it's a prison,' he said finally. His voice trembled with emotion, but then he became blank again. His family was from Shanghai, but had been living in Aksu since 1968. He had come here with his mother at the age of three. They had repeatedly petitioned the government to be allowed to return to Shanghai, but had always been refused.

'Many others have gone back . . . so maybe we'll be lucky some day,' he shrugged. Then he laughed, poured me another beer and changed the subject: we talked about brothers, sisters and how much video recorders cost in the West. Xinjiang was a complex land.

Using Yang as a translator, the uncle asked about my business in Aksu. I explained that I had come to their neighbourhood by mistake and that I was on the way to a small town in the north. Tumxuk. Did he know about it?

'Why do you want to go to Tumxuk?' uncle wanted to know. I explained all about the archaeology, glad to be on familiar ground again, but he shook his head, and said that he had never heard of an ancient site near Tumxuk.

'Do you have permission?' he asked, adding, 'Even Chinese need permission to go there.'

'Well, yes of course,' I lied, and even more boldly added, 'they are expecting me.' A white lie, but his last comment worried me.

He nodded and promised to put me on the right bus in the morning. After long goodbyes and a group photo, I followed the uncle to a compound where I was shown to a small room next to the stables. It was filled with a penetrating odour, redolent of childhood summers spent on my grandfather's farm in Bavaria. But I couldn't quite place it . . .

Shortly after dawn I was woken by loud grunting noises and the clanking of metal buckets. This racket was produced by three fat pigs fighting over a foul-smelling brew of vegetable matter and starchy, steaming glue. Then I remembered the pigs kept by my grandfather's neighbour, to whom I would deliver potato peelings and bread crusts in the evenings during my holidays.

Uncle joined me at the restaurant. He was in a hurry. I had barely finished my noodles when he grabbed my red bag and tied it on to his bicycle. In silence, we walked towards the centre of the city. Daylight hadn't improved it much. Clean broad streets were lined with grey socialist architecture, unrelenting in its monotony, but occasionally interspersed with ornate European-looking buildings – reminders of Russian–Chinese friendship before the 1960s. A few faded shop signs incorporated Cyrillic letters, which, I guessed, were an attempt at a more readable alphabet than Arabic for the Uighur language. Uncle couldn't answer my questions about it.

The streets were already busy. People crowded at corners, and clogged the sidewalks. Scores of bicycles circled roundabouts with green metal fencing and grimy red geraniums. There was a marked absence of Uighurs, donkey taxis, horses and melons. Aksu belonged to the Han Chinese.

We stopped in front of a jewel-like mosque: aquamarine and turquoise tiles with colours reminiscent of the Abakh Khoja tomb in Kashgar decorated the delicate façade squeezed between two monstrous brick buildings. Slender columns topped with graceful half-moons framed the deep-set, arched entrance, but the wooden gate had been boarded up and pasted over with slogans.

A bus was waiting in front of it. Uncle exchanged a few words with the woman behind the wheel whom he apparently knew, threw my bag into the bus and waved. I turned to thank him for his kindness but he had already mounted his bike and disappeared in the crowd.

'*Meiguoren?* American?' the driver asked. She had an extremely warm, almost motherly face, with nests of laugh lines at the sides of her eyes. Her strong body was stuffed into tight blue trousers and a white, short-sleeved man's shirt.

'No, I'm German, *Deguoren*,' I answered, to which she responded with raucous laughter. I didn't know what was so funny about that. She assigned me the seat on top of the motor, usually reserved for the ticket girl. We headed north, keeping a small creek with overgrown green banks on our left. To the right were vertical sandstone cliffs in bizarre formations. Every once in a while we passed a brick factory with huge hive-shaped kilns. The bricks and the houses had the same ochre colour as the cliffs, and it was at times difficult to tell man-made dwellings from natural geology.

After an hour or so the driver insisted I get off. I was at an empty crossroads on the outskirts of a small village. To one side stood a forlorn-looking donkey hitched to a cart loaded with water melons. Its driver dozed in the cart's shade. I asked him for the bus to Tumxuk.

'*Sanji* . . . at three,' he said in a broad Uighur accent. Only

43

then did he look up at me, and baring a full set of yellow teeth grinned at me: '*Waiguoren,*' chuckled heartily, and fell back asleep. It wasn't even eleven yet.

This was Uighur territory. Tree-shaded lanes meandered between walls and fields planted with tomatoes, aubergines and beans. Irrigation canals fed each individual poplar. A handsome woman with a naked baby riding on her expansive hip smiled at me, children stared with blackberry eyes. On the bank of a creek a boy of about five and an old man wearing a thick fur cap despite the midday heat, his grandfather perhaps, were spinning wool into yarn. They stood almost thirty metres apart linked by two thin strings, twisting and turning them. The boy tried not to lose his rhythm as I walked by, while the old man didn't even notice me. There was a mosque under construction of the type that I had already seen in Tashmalik. Open space was surrounded by simple walls and a colourful painted entrance. Here also, they seemed to prefer garish primary colours.

Coming to a building which resembled a garage with a dilapidated pick-up truck in front, I enquired about renting a vehicle.

'*Meiyou* . . . there is no car,' answered the attendant. He gave me the same smile that I had been receiving a lot in the last few days, the smile one benevolently bestows upon a child or the village idiot.

'How about a bicycle . . . or a donkey?'

He laughed again, and shook his head. I had no choice but to wait for the bus.

On my way back to the intersection I passed a farrier's shop. A horse had been put into a leather body-harness and suspended from a cross-beam held up by two posts. Its tail was bound to one post and the smith was busy changing its shoes. It hung there completely docile.

The only inn in town was a cool dark place with concrete floors and an institutional smell. Huge round tables stood like islands among metal chairs. Chopsticks lodged in marmalade jars in the centre of each table. A drunk in the corner offered to buy me a beer.

'*Gonggongqiche, gonggongqiche* . . . *Autobus,*' a child screamed brightly. The double doors flew open and a panting six-year-old announced that the bus for Tumxuk had arrived. I paid up and hurried back to the crossroads.

Someone had already tied my bag on to the roof of an antique bus, along with a sheep too petrified to protest, a bicycle and numerous bundles packed tightly in white, roughly woven rice sacks. The air was thick with cigarette smoke, the bus almost full. The passengers appeared to be exclusively Uighur. Women in colourful dresses and tailored jackets of burgundy or dark blue, all wearing headscarves, held dirty infants with slit trousers, laughed and shared out food; men in brown or grey suits, sweaters and the inevitable cloth caps chatted excitedly. I found an empty seat beside an old man. All I could see was his scraggly grey beard, for he stared intently out of the window-hole, ignoring me. (Apart from the windscreen there was no glass in the bus.) A woman in front of me turned round and tried to get my attention with a high-pitched 'Oiy . . . Oiy.' We had no common language, but she gently grabbed my arm, pulled me to her side and offered me some sunflower seeds. The old man looked relieved.

We left the green oasis behind and travelled towards the mountains. Fine sand blew into the gaping windows, slowly building up a glistening layer upon our clothing and skin. After crossing a washed-out river-bed, we entered pure, ochre desert. The supreme emptiness cloaked us with almost heartbreaking silence. Soon there was only the grinding noise of the engine and most of the passengers went to sleep.

Four hours later we reached our destination. The bus halted beneath the arch of a huge metal gate, its wrought Chinese characters and red star almost completely obscured by thick vines. The gate opened on to a single, unpaved road which made up the village of Tumxuk. Tall poplars threw the street into a twilight streaked with wild geometric patterns of sunbeams. A few naked boys threw stones at a donkey. They were filthy, but well fed. Dust stirred up by the arrival of the bus gave the scene an air of unreality.

I felt at a loss for a moment, when the Uighur lady from the bus took my hand and marched me off to the only walled building in town, leaving me at the entrance of a courtyard. The double-storey structure, with its wooden veranda and balcony, was overgrown with vines. Thick clusters of grapes hung suspended from rafters, walls and wires. A Chinese grandmother with the face of a mummy sat knitting in a rocking-chair. Almost as though she had been expecting me, she rose and, without so much as a word, fetched an unwieldy iron key. Then she pointed to a door and went back to her knitting.

I turned the key in its rusty lock. The room was dark and I wondered why it had no windows. I felt for the light switch and turned the old-fashioned knob. Neon lights flickered, illuminating the chamber – inadvertently I let out a muffled scream. There were thousands upon thousands of fat black flies in the room, completely covering the window in a crawling mass and swarming on the ceiling and walls. No one had used this room for some time. One of the window panes was broken. I stuffed a scarf into the hole and lit an incense coil. To regain my composure I slammed the door behind me and asked the old lady for water. She smiled enigmatically, pointing to a creek behind the house.

Through an opening in the back wall I entered a story-book meadow. Horses were grazing idyllically on the opposite shore of a babbling white creek; there were a few willows. Behind me the ranges of the Tian Shan hovered above the desert. I knelt down to wash the dirt out of my hair, when suddenly a pebble landed beside me, splashing me with water. I turned, but there was nothing. I proceeded with my toilet when, splash, another stone nearly hit me. This one was accompanied by some giggles. I turned again, and saw a gaggle of children disappearing behind a mound.

Sunset was staining the snow-capped summits pink and purple. As the temperature dropped, the lower part of the range became obscured with mist echoing the colour of the blue-grey sky, leaving the peaks floating in a void like air-castles. Indeed, I thought, Tian Shan, the Heavenly Mountains.

The evening stillness was abruptly violated by blasts of military music. There were speakers everywhere, mounted on trees and the sides of buildings. I hurried back to my room. Someone had pointedly left a broom in front of my door.

I shovelled out the dead flies, changed and went to find some dinner. The street was clogged with people, slowly promenading up and down in the amber light thrown from the houses. Whenever I passed, they stopped and stared. Though the women wore the traditional skirts, scarves and jackets, I noticed that the men were exclusively dressed in workmen's Mao suits and caps. No one was veiled. The noise from the speakers was maddening; aggressive speeches interrupted sometimes by marching band recitals. Gangs of children would run close to me, then recoil with screeching voices. I ducked into the town's only eatery where a Chinese woman, outlandish in tight trousers and woollen jumper, entered from the kitchen area and eyed me with a mixture of superiority and outright antagonism. I ordered noodles and beer. A few minutes later she slammed a plate in front of me on the table. I ate quickly, paid up and went back to my room. Near the gate a stone hit me on the ankle. It hurt.

Disturbed about the change of atmosphere, I plugged my Walkman into my ears and put on the *Jungle Book*. Why the antagonism? The light flickered on and off several times, as though someone was playing with a switch, then went off altogether. I got scared, and angry with myself for being scared, for being here, and for being such a fool . . . I lit a candle, pushed the bed across the room to barricade the door and went to sleep.

Next morning I was woken by military music blasted at full volume outside my window. My body was covered with perspiration and my tongue stuck in my mouth like a dry sponge. It was six o'clock. Wondering why no one ever thought of sabotaging the speakers, I threw on a T-shirt and some shorts and went back down to the river to wash the night away. White morning fog still hung over the oasis, and the mountains sparkled in the distance. It was going to be a hot day.

I guessed that Tumxuk was some sort of agricultural commune. There was no mosque and no evidence of a school, nor were the houses laid out in the traditional Uighur manner. I also noticed the absence of small fields and gardens, such as I had seen in other villages. The only store-cum-restaurant was run by a Han Chinese, and the house where I was staying evidently represented the centre of power. None of the Uighurs spoke Chinese, not even the children, which made communication almost impossible.

I had no choice but to return to the store in order to find out about those archaeological sites. Before I could say anything, the woman who had served my dinner the previous night asked me for a permit. Taken aback, and feeling uneasy, I pulled out various papers and letters. She grabbed my passport, leafed through it and again demanded a permit. Laughing at her, I took my papers back, turned and left her dark store. This wasn't going to be easy.

Outside the door a group of onlookers had formed.

'*Mingoi*', I asked them, using the Uighur word denoting ancient remains. 'Is there an archaeological site near here?' The men continued to stare. Then the crowd parted and a tall man came forward self-importantly. He spoke a little Chinese and I repeated my questions.

'*You liang ge* . . .' he exclaimed, 'there are two places, Mazar and Tulumush Mazar.' I was ecstatic. Those had to be my two sites. The man took my pen and diary and drew a simple map, according to which Tulumush Mazar lay about seven kilometres north-west from Tumxuk, the other about thirty kilometres further to the west. I decided to walk to Tulumush, shouldered my pack and hurried out of town.

I passed a stream of people, donkeys packed high with goods, and a horse-drawn cart. In Tumxuk market was held on Wednesdays. From behind me came the noise of an engine. It was a truck, laden with sacks of flour. I flagged down the driver, a Han Chinese in grey clothing, and asked him for Tulumush. He gestured to the back of the truck. Three kilometres down the road he stopped and pointed north into the desert. I thanked the driver and started walking towards the mountains. Soon I left behind the strip of green along the river and entered a desolately beautiful landscape. The track was washed away as if by a torrent of water, though it was impossible to imagine that it ever rained here. The temperature rose quickly.

After two and a half hours' march due north-west, I reached a tiny oasis, inhabited, it seemed, by just one family. In the heart of a dense poplar forest hid a mud-brick hovel. An old man in a long padded black coat with cornflower blue sash was shovelling dirt in front, gawking toothlessly as I approached. I greeted him and asked for Tulumush. He pointed to the ground. This was Tulumush. 'No *Mazar* . . . I'm looking for Tulumush Mazar,' I tried to make myself understood. The old man smiled, turned and pointed to a stone cliff, rising from the desert about a kilometre from the house. Then he mumbled something about a bazaar, from which I gathered that the family had gone off to the market in Tumxuk, and invited me into his home. It was a poor dwelling, a one-room affair, taken up by a sleeping platform and a kitchen area. He brought a piece of nan from a cupboard and poured hot water from a thermos into a bowl. Politely, I sprayed a few drops of it on to the clay floor and drank. '*Yakshi* . . . good,' I mumbled as I chewed on the stale bread. As I was leaving the old man pointed at my camera; I obliged him with a picture, waved and headed towards the mountain.

Tulumush Mazar was a steep sandstone cliff, topped by a pinnacle of heavily eroded stone and rubble. I climbed to the peak. Someone had erected a cairn and decorated it with long sticks from which flew colourful bits of cloth indicating a holy site. There was a breeze, and I sat down to have some lunch and take in the view. Around me spread a vast grey desert, defined by the foothills and peaks of the Tian Shan, its uniformity interrupted only by the green smudge of the small oasis I had just visited. At the edge of the poplar jungle grazed about twenty camels. But there was no evidence of an archaeological site. I stayed for a while, bathing in the wild stillness of the place, then descended along a ridge. About halfway down, nestling in a deep ravine, I came upon a shrine of whitewashed mud-brick, square in plan and surmounted by a shallow cupola. I looked inside and saw a man with a turban and a long beard, kneeling on the straw-covered floor, chanting and clicking some beads. A book lay open in front of him. I apologized and moved on.

Walking quickly, I headed back south-east, skirting the small oasis of Tulumush, and once again entered open desert. The sun had passed its zenith and the heat was subsiding a bit. I mulled over my failure to find a Buddhist site, meditating to the steady rhythm of my steps, and realized that I was content, not disappointed at all. I might not have found what I was looking for, but the sense of peace and wellbeing which flowed from the place I had just visited fully compensated me.

I recalled an experience I had in Japan, almost five years before, when at the close of a year-long stay I accepted the invitation of a distant friend to visit the Zen monastery where he had been studying as a novice. His directions had been vague: first I went by train to Nara, then by bus to the countryside, and by nightfall found myself trudging through terraced rice paddies up a hill. I still recall the humid night air and the deafening love song of crickets. I was almost ready to give myself up for lost, when the shadow of a large gate loomed above me. I knocked. Suddenly, a tiny door opened at the side of the gate, framing the stately figure of a bald monk in long robes. He looked at me and smiled. 'Howdy, we've been expectin' ya,' he drawled in an unexpected Texan accent. I must have gawked at him speechlessly, but he assured me I had come to the right place. The man was John Toller, Tora-san as the Japanese call him, the only *gaijin* in Japan who had ever been granted his own temple. In the end I spent several days at Shogen-in, never quite reconciling the blatant 'Americanness' of my host with the setting, but finding a serenity and calmness similar to that communicated by Tulumush Mazar.

A cloud of dust rolled down from the hill, turning into a big blue truck loaded with tar. I waved and asked for a ride, then jumped on to the side-board and, hanging on to the door, raced through the desert back towards Tumxuk. The driver dropped me off just before we reached the oasis.

In town the weekly bazaar was coming to an end. There were a dozen or so stalls, no animal market; various bits of produce, second-hand clothing, old boots and beat-up ironware were laid out on tables. I tasted some strips of milky gelatine made from cucumber, which, dipped in hot sauce, was delicious. The villagers followed my every move, and now stared expectantly. '*Yakshi* . . . good,' I said, and everyone laughed. The tension from last night had disappeared. On the way back to the guest house I stopped for some noodles and a beer, and bought a second bottle for later. I planned in the evening to visit the local cinema, which only showed films on market days. It was of the outdoor variety, like the ones in Kashgar. Military music blasted again from speakers, interrupted only for a few announcements I couldn't follow. Then came the news, and I realized it must be eight o'clock in Beijing.

When I entered the overgrown veranda I found the grandmother waiting for me. She looked worried. Anxiously she laid a frail hand on my arm and whispered: '*Jing cha* . . . police.' The door to my room stood open. A middle-aged Chinese man wearing a tightly-belted beige trench coat sat in the chair smoking a cigarette. Another was going through my bag, but prompted by a gesture from his boss, he ceased and left. The man in the chair stared at me from little eyes, his face frozen. His cigarette had left a trail of ashes on his coat. He said nothing. I was feeling exceedingly uncomfortable. Then a young woman dressed in slacks, white shirt and red cardigan came into the room, first greeting the seated man in Chinese, then addressing me in English.

'Can I see your passport, please?' she asked politely. Usually I carry my documents and money in a thin cotton purse lodged comfortably in the small of my back, and reaching it is awkward. The girl turned away as I unzipped my trousers, while the boss continued to stare at me with the same expression, sucking on his cigarette.

He took my passport, studied it for a second then pocketed it.

'This is a closed area . . . you must leave at once,' the girl informed me. I packed my bags in defeat, wondering how I would get my passport back.

Escorted by the three officials I left the government rest house, sending a smile and a '*Zaijian* . . . goodbye' in the grandmother's direction, while she stood rooted to the spot kneading her apron in distress. To her this must have been a picture reminiscent of much harder times.

The bus which had brought me to Tumxuk two days ago was waiting beneath the metal gate at the end of the main street. Villagers, who had surrounded me in the bazaar only an hour ago, crowded silently at a distance. The bus was full. Rudely, the boss appropriated the seat of a Uighur man by the door. Sensing that I had been arrested, the Uighur passengers drew a cloak of friendliness around me, found me a seat and started offering food. My Chinese escorts were isolated; as in Kashgar I felt a suppressed but distinct animosity between the two nationalities.

We arrived in the dark. 'Wensu Town,' the girl replied to my question of where we were. I was marched off to a hotel and put up in a comfortable room. There was a bathhouse which I used at leisure.

Next morning martial music blasted me out of bed. It seemed that Wensu was under the same regime as the little oasis of Tumxuk. I dressed and went downstairs in search of food. Through the glass windows of the front door I saw that the street was crowded with people exercising in unison, following instructions from the loudspeakers: '*Yi er san si . . . yi er san si . . .* one two three four . . .' They looked like robots in their blue and grey Mao suits.

The girl from yesterday escorted me to the Public Security Bureau. I looked around; Wensu did not appear very old. Grey-looking buildings delineated broad streets, planned in that unmistakable socialist style. Then I noticed the remains of a citadel high on a cliff, overlooking the town. I tried to ask about it, but the straight-faced girl only urged me ahead. I was taken to a small rectangular building at the edge of the police compound and deposited in a stark room. There was an oak desk and three wooden chairs. The boss was seated in one of them, smoking. His trench coat was still tightly belted, and I wondered if he'd slept in it.

'You broke the law of the People's Republic of China,' the girl started a solemn litany. I tried not to smile.

'How?' I asked.

'You went to a closed area,' she stated.

'I didn't know it was closed.'

She conferred for a moment with the boss, then handed me a small booklet delineating in several languages the proper conduct for foreign visitors. Heading out into the sticks was definitely against Chinese law.

'What were you doing in Tumxuk?' the interrogation continued.

'Looking for archaeological sites.'

She translated, glancing at the boss, who shook his head. She repeated the question, I repeated my answer.

'Write that you broke the law . . .' she said, pulling out a piece of paper. She meant a 'self-criticism'. I wanted this farce to end, and wrote as she demanded, and promised that I wouldn't do it again. She looked at the illegible scrawl, and put it away in the desk drawer.

'Who incited you to break the law?' she continued.

'I wasn't aware that I broke the law.'

'But you just confessed that you did,' she said, sharply holding up my self-criticism for evidence. I wasn't smiling any more.

A few more officials crowded into the room, keen on watching the spectacle.

'Who was the bus driver, what did he look like?'

I was getting cautious.

'Oh, I don't know, medium height, black hair, black eyes . . . could have been his brother,' I pointed to the boss, who looked as though he was about to lose control.

'You were seen making photographs in Wensu,' the girl said finally, looking triumphant. I was about to reply that I had never been to Wensu before, when I realized that the small village where I was dropped off by the bus driver from Aksu must have been a suburb of the city where I was now. I silently thanked the friendly driver, and denied the accusation. The boss asked for my camera. An assistant grabbed hold of it and opened the back to remove the film. Pulling it out of the cassette, the assistant held the film up to the window, and exclaimed disappointedly that he could see nothing. My jaw dropped. The man grabbed hold of my bag. Panicking for my thirty or so exposed rolls of film I went into a frantic explanation of the developing process. Reluctantly, he left off.

Five hours later the interrogation finally drew to a close.

'You must be punished for the crime,' the girl said. My heart sank.

'Please pay fifty yuan.'

I couldn't restrain a relieved laugh. That amounted to barely five English pounds – hardly a punishment. The boss, who had monitored my response, said a few angry words to the girl.

'One hundred and fifty yuan,' she said.

I must learn to keep my emotions off my face.

In the afternoon I was finally let go. A bus took me back to Aksu. Much later I learned that Wensu harboured a Labour Reform Camp with some 23,000 inmates.

FIVE

In the Capital of Xinjiang

URUMQI WAS WET, COLD AND GREY. Broad avenues separated concrete buildings; a traffic light looked incongruous with the Xinjiang I had seen so far. It had started to snow and my body took the abrupt climatic change with discomfort. Stiff-fingered, I groped in my pocket and pulled out the crumpled letter from the academy. The address read Beijing North Road.

A plausible facsimile of a Fiat 500 pulled up at my side. 'Taxi?' a Chinese face wrapped in woollens called to me. I nodded, pushed my bag on to the back seat, squeezed next to it and held the envelope under the driver's nose. Three minutes later we stopped in front of an austere four-storey building. Two uniformed boys ran up and down an ugly forecourt just inside the gate, trailing rolls of wire. They were practising laying cables for dynamite charges.

'Two hundred renminbi,' the driver demanded, while pointing to the door. I made a mental note to negotiate the price next time, before climbing into a taxi.

The place looked deserted. I left my bags in the semi-dark foyer, and climbed a flight of creaking stairs. They led to a dimly-lit hallway, terminating in front of a half-open door. I stuck my head through the gap, and startled a pudgy young Chinese hunched over a desk, pruning a small potted plant.

'Ah, *Paula Xiaojie* . . . Miss Paula,' he smiled after a moment of fiddling with the business card I handed him, 'we have been expecting you.' Perfect English. He introduced himself with the unlikely name of 'Goethe', pushing back his black-rimmed glasses on to the flat bridge of his nose with quick, nervous jerks of his middle finger. A name he chose in English class. The specs were held together by a dirty Bandaid, and I was unable to keep from staring at it. Goethe escorted me to another office and left me there. He said he would go and find Madame Wu.

The room was crammed from floor to ceiling with books, files, objets d'art and photographs. A wooden desk hidden beneath papers took up most of the space. I moved a box filled with assorted clay sherds and sat down. It smelled of archaeology, that unmistakable musty odour of dust mixed with chemicals.

When I was searching for possible contacts in preparation for my journey, Madame Wu's name had cropped up several times. I had written to her and, in return, received an encouraging, albeit noncommittal letter. It was one of my former professors who told me, with a tone of nostalgia and admiration, that in her youth she was a Beijing University student leader and had stood next to Mao in 1959 in front of an eager young crowd on Tiananmen Square. She had volunteered to come to Xinjiang with the first waves of students sent out to develop the frontiers – and had stayed. A pillar of Xinjiang archaeological society for many decades, she had now retired from most leading posts, but remained active and influential. The letter I had received in London six months earlier was written in her name.

Madame Wu was a short, sturdy woman with wavy hair and an oversized, dark blue hand-knitted cardigan with patches on the elbows. She edged through the door behind a young woman in a yellow tartan skirt, and clasped my hand with both of hers, smiling from a smooth, ageless face. She also said she had been expecting me, then referred me to the severe girl at her side, who addressed me briskly in English. Pan Xiaojie came straight to the point.

'We have received your letter, and hope to include you in an expedition going to Miran in one week,' she said, much to my delight. 'But we first have to get permission from the Ministry of Foreign Affairs.'

'In Beijing?' I asked.

'No, here in Urumqi. We will know in a few days.' Her

pronunciation was as precise and clipped as her hair, which had not a strand out of place.

'Do you think there'll be a problem?'

'No problem!' she stated confidently.

Madame Wu witnessed the conversation with a smile reminiscent of the octogenarians plastered over the *People's Daily* front pages. Quietly, she instructed Goethe and Pan Xiaojie to take me to the Academy compound and find me lodgings. The audience was over.

Pan Xiaojie said that the Toyota truck had been paid for by the Japanese Silk Road expedition a few years ago.

'They have a lot of money,' she added.

We drove north and entered a concrete village, laid out in strict institutional geometry. This was where Urumqi's scientific community lived. Women with brush brooms were sweeping yellowed leaves into mounds and burning them. The trees seemed to have lost their plumage overnight. We stopped in front of a guest house for visiting scholars and students, a grey and lime-green building indistinguishable from the rest. Pan explained my presence efficiently to an arrogant young receptionist, who registered me. The pink bow in her hair was incompatible with the expression on her face.

'Second floor,' said Pan Xiaojie, handing me piece of paper. 'You'll need to buy food tickets and sign up for a shower.' Then she smiled. 'Call me Youyou . . . if you like.' There was a heart after all, underneath that stiff façade.

'*Mingtian ah . . .*' she said and waved, 'see you tomorrow.'

On the second floor I was turned over to the *furen*, who took the paper, fetched a key and opened a door.

'It's not supposed to be winter yet – the heating won't come on for another week,' she apologized, rubbing her gloved hands together, and pulled the door behind her with a sharp bang. 'Are rules in China stronger than nature?' I wondered, standing in the ice-cold room. I stowed my gear in the closet, tried out both beds and settled for the one to the left of the door. There was a pump thermos filled with hot water and tea, and a few plastic bags with sweets, labelled CAAC; 'China Airline Always Cancelled,' its ironic acronym among long-suffering China travellers.

The washroom was a dank cube with two rows of large concrete basins, five doors down from my room. The row along the left wall was dedicated to cold water, while the other spewed boiling water only. (It wasn't only the British who had problems providing comfort from single taps.) A cleaning woman was washing out her mop. Next to me, an embarrassed young man with an exposed torso, shorts and flip-flops was laundering his clothing. Probably his only set. He avoided eye contact, but glanced over every time he assumed that I was not watching. After he'd left, the cleaning woman, pushing her metal bucket on wheels and dragging the large hairy mop behind her, came close and stared at me. Her face below the white cap was worn and creased. One of her incisors was broken and brown from not having been treated.

'*Sie sind aus Deutschland?*' she asked in impeccable German, leaning heavily on the mop handle. I nodded, and asked where she had learned to speak so well. She had studied German for five years at university, she said.

The *furen* must have been standing there all along, just outside the washroom door, hidden in the gloom of the hall. She shouted something at us, her sharp voice reverberating in the bare space. The cleaning lady shuffled off trailing an odour of sweat and disinfectant. I noticed that her ankles were painfully swollen, and thought that she was old enough to have been the *furen*'s mother.

The receptionist had sold me a stack of paper tickets: white for dinner, pink for breakfast and green for lunch. I presented the whole bundle to a student guarding the door of the dining-hall, which lay opposite the guest house. He extracted one of the white tickets and led me through the hall. Most of the area was taken up by students eating noisily; some stopped and stared. To the right of the door, barely visible through hospital-like white cloth screens, sat the senior staff. I was guided to a third enclosed zone, holding a few large round tables, neatly decorated with flowers and napkins. Save for a single place-setting, it was empty. The young man left and pulled the screens closed behind him. I was isolated, shielded completely from view. Quarantined like some-one carrying a bad virus. A Uighur servant brought a feast of pork, vegetables, rice and Xinjiang beer. I asked her for chop-sticks, but she didn't reply. I ate quickly and returned to the guest house. I don't like eating on my own.

Later, I grabbed a towel and fresh clothing and asked directions to the showers which, I was told, were located in the basement. On the way I passed an open door, and threw a glance at three Chinese women who lay, college-girl fashion, on their beds, smoking. One of them got up and closed the door. I felt that I wasn't doing too well in China, and wished I were back in Xinjiang.

The shower-room was a steamed-up, tiled cavern, with eight doorless cubicles containing efficient industrial showers. Chattering women vigorously scrubbed each other's backs with what looked like pan scourers. I stripped and padded to the only unoccupied cubicle, feeling all legs and big tits. The chatter sud-denly ceased as they stared at my tanned face, neck and arms, dark against my white torso, and sun-bleached hair.

The Professor had once told me a story of a Portuguese sailor who had been captured, brought to the Tang capital, and paraded through the streets as a curiosity. His upper body was tanned almost black, while his lower half, protected from the sun by trousers, had remained white. There was a debate whether or not to cut him in two, to see if the differences were more than skin deep. I can't remember if he escaped or fell victim to science.

Back in my room, I settled down to work on my notes. There was a timid knock on my door. One of the girls from the shower-room, her face still glowing, bashfully asked if she could speak with me. She had the thick glasses and neglected hair of a scholar. I asked her in and offered tea. Balancing herself on the edge of a chair, she folded her hands in her lap and asked nervously if she could practise her English with me.

'Sure.'

'What would you like to talk about?' she asked in fairly good English. I felt put on the spot.

'Tell me about yourself,' I said.

She told me she was a biologist, specializing in desert vegetation; she was from Beijing University, on a two-month research trip to Xinjiang. I asked her if she'd been in Beijing during the pro-democracy demonstrations four months ago. She nodded uncomfortably. This was one subject she did not want to talk about.

'What did you do?' I persisted.

'I stayed in my room and studied,' she said. 'Politics don't interest me . . . only my work.' With that statement the conversation faltered. She got up abruptly and left. I never saw her again.

Next morning after breakfast, again in isolation, I set out for the institute. The freezing air and the fog, mixed with acrid smoke, burnt in my throat. Youyou, Madame Wu's assistant, had written instructions in careful letters. I followed them and caught an overcrowded number 2 bus across the street from the main gate. The fare was half a yuan. A loud-voiced ticket girl extracted a note from me and handed me back the change.

Youyou was already waiting for me. She led me to the storeroom where the material from Miran excavated by Chinese archaeologists over the last few decades was housed and gave me a brief introduction to the collection.

Between 1957 and 1958, the late Professor Huang Wenbi of the Institute of Archaeology, Academy of Social Sciences, toured Xinjiang and conducted his preliminary survey of the major sites. He spent less than a week in Ruoqiang county and only a few days at Miran, focusing on the Tibetan fort, from which he recovered a small number of objects. The year after Huang's visit, an archaeological team from the Xinjiang Museum in Urumqi conducted a ten-day survey of the site. Again, they concentrated on the Tibetan fort from which they excavated a large number of Tang period objects. The structures from the earlier Shanshan period were, however, left untouched. In 1965, Mr Rao Reifu, an agricultural reclamation engineer, visited Miran and included a brief description of the ancient water system in his report, 'A Preliminary Study on the Reclamation and Irrigation during the period from the Han to Tang Dynasties'. His visit was followed in 1973 by another archaeological team from the Xinjiang Museum which included the Beijing archaeologist Mr Chen Ge. Chen Ge mapped the intricate canal system at Miran, dating from the first century BC onward, while the survey undertaken by the team seems to have provided the basis for all subsequent Chinese studies of the site. During the period 1978–80 Messrs Huang Xiaojiang and Zhang Ping of the Xinjiang Museum visited Miran several times and conducted yet another survey to supplement that of 1973, but once more concentrated on the Tibetan fort. They did, however, 'measure' (survey) eight stupas, three temples, and two beacon towers.

I was surprised to find that Chinese archaeologists had been so busy. News of their activity seldom hit the western academic press, and local publications were difficult to obtain.

In two weeks there would be another expedition . . . and the letter in my pocket contained a vague promise that it might include me.

I surveyed the material which was mainly from the Tibetan fort of the eighth century, rather than from the earlier, Buddhist structures which were of interest to me. Numerous wooden strips with Tibetan writing and some military equipment were displayed in glass showcases. But there was the head of a colossal Buddha, familiar to me from a photograph taken by Stein in 1907. He had discovered it between two decapitated sculptures, seated in a row near the *vihara*, the monastic complex he had labelled MII. He had left it in situ for fear of damaging it in removal. Now it sat on a shelf in a dark store-room, and for a moment I wished Stein had taken it to the British Museum, where it would be exhibited to the public along with the others.

There wasn't much for me to do. Youyou was hovering close for fear I would photograph the precious spoils. 'Photography is not allowed,' she had instructed me. A hushed, uncomfortable silence lay over this building, causing one to talk in whispers and as little as possible. I asked her if there was any news about the Miran expedition. She shook her head and said to come back on Monday.

'By the way, I would like to join the ranks of students,' I mentioned before leaving. She looked perplexed, and I explained that

I felt rather uneasy isolated behind closed screens. She said she would make a phone call.

On my way out, Goethe hurried out of his office, pulled me in and secretively shut the door behind us. He unlocked the pencil drawer of his desk, and carefully drew out a leather-bound Bible. He handed it to me reverently, then without speaking took it again and restored it to its place. He had obviously shared an important secret, but didn't want to talk about it.

At the post office I found a stack of letters waiting for me, most of them from my boyfriend in Italy. I thanked the smiling young man, and surprised myself by thinking that he was handsome.

I walked across the road, past the Hongshan department store towards the centre of town, and turned into a small eatery which advertised a menu in English. Over a large bowl of soup I read through my mail, thinking how far away Europe was.

It had started to snow again.

In the Urumqi Museum I was followed by the shadow of a guard, who switched on the lights in each successive gallery individually as I wandered among the exhibitions. In the centre of the last room stood a solitary showcase containing recent discoveries from Lop Shanpula, a burial site east of Khotan. Among household goods, combs and axes lay, slightly raised on an incline, a pair of trousers fashioned from a patchwork of multicoloured pile and 'shag' carpet-cloth. Into each leg was sewn a patch of tapestry, depicting the head of a youth on one and the playful image of a classical centaur on the other. I guessed it to be from the first or second century.

The 'Portrait of an Arian', as the left patch had been named by the museum staff, showed the face of a clean-shaven youth turned in three-quarter position, surrounded by a chaotic background of floral and geometric patterns, dominated by a red lozenge filled with blue four-petalled flowers. He had striking azure blue eyes, and his equally blue hair was held back with a broad golden band: a warrior prince. I had seen faces like his before in pictures from the ancient Kushan palace of Khalchayan, near Termez in Uzbekistan, where the aristocracy had been modelled in clay reliefs and mounted on walls. The centaur, on the other fragment, was squeezed tightly into a lozenge frame made up of white and buff coloured flowers, over a dark-blue background. In full gallop, his cape swinging behind him, playing his double flute, he came straight out of Greek mythology.

'Bactria,' the guard stated, having come up nosily, wondering what took my attention for so long.

'I don't think so,' I said thoughtfully.

'Rome?' he questioned again.

'No, Xinjiang,' I said finally. The guard snickered condescendingly: '*Bu shi* . . . no it isn't,' and turned the lights off.

'Yes, Xinjiang,' I mouthed stubbornly.

During his third Central Asian expedition Stein went back to Loulan, deep in the Lopnur Desert. In one of the grave pits, among numerous textiles, he had found part of a decorative hanging woven in similar colours and the same tapestry technique as the Lop Shanpula examples. I remembered it well. There was part of a young man's head, with curly brown hair, large eyes with the iris and pupil outlined. Hues of brown, beige, pink, red, grey, green and gold were set delicately next to one another while crisp outlines sharpened the features. Next to the head appeared a caduceus, the winged staff entwined by snakes, symbol of Hermes. This tapestry had struck me for two reasons: one, stylistically it showed great affinity to the Miran paintings, and two, I had the suspicion that it was produced in the kingdom of Shanshan, though this theory was not a popular one. Perhaps it was more convenient to assume that civilization was imported wholesale into the barbarian backwater, brought along the Silk Road from the classical West.

Yet hundreds of woollen fabrics have been found in digs around the Taklamakan, most of them just ordinary pile carpets used for keeping the cold out of mud-brick buildings. Many were woven in the same tapestry technique, using the colours the Shanshan industry was famous for in its time, as the fabrics with figures. The third-century Kharosthi documents mention them – *tavastaga* they were called – and they were used as payment for goods, in one case as the price of a girl.

I left the museum. In the foyer I noticed for the first time the

RIGHT: It sometimes seemed as if we were a travelling circus. Rest stop on the way to Kashgar in the shadow of the Muztagata, father of all ice mountains.

BELOW: Strings of spaghetti miraculously emerge from globs of dough – a noodle maker in Tashmalik conducts his pasta symphony.

ABOVE: The religious and social centre of Kashgar, where performances take place in front of the Idga mosque on a Friday afternoon, the Muslim Sabbath.

RIGHT: There is a popular saying that only the old and the ugly wear the veil in Kashgar.

ABOVE: The old man of Tulumush, keeper of an Islamic hermitage which I came upon during my search for the Buddhist sites of Tumxuk.

BELOW: This hand-painted advertisement above a department store on Jiefang Street, Kashgar, includes a reference to a standard-issue People's Liberation Army gas mask.

LEFT: Ming Oi, the thousand caves of Kizil north-west of Kuqa, one of the most important Buddhist centres along the Silk Road.

BELOW: Barber at work in Kuqa.

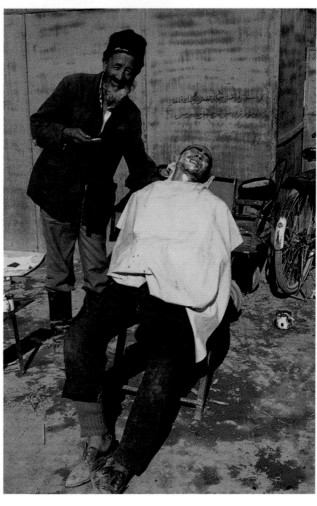

ABOVE: The 'forbidden' half of Subashi – a stupa and monastic complex from the seventh century, twenty kilometres north of Kuqa bazaar.

RIGHT: Sometimes the ruins resembled sculptures by Henry Moore.

Women have caught on to the new market economy with a vengeance; this entrepreneur uses her stocking as a purse.

BELOW: A beacon tower from the third century, still guarding the approach to the Buddhist caves of Kizil Kara near Kuqa.

ABOVE: Woman and child in the old city of Kuqa.

BELOW: A mender of metal pots and vessels in Kuqa.

ABOVE: The local version of a mini-cab service – my camel guide in Qiemo. After my return from searching for ancient ruins, I was stopped and arrested.

ABOVE: A one-man Uighur bank, *bureau de change* and building society.

LEFT: Old man in Khotan. Each region has its own head-wear and facial characteristics.

row of life-size busts, idealized images of the Xinjiang 'minority nationalities' cast in bronze, lined up under the flag of the People's Republic.

Back at the academy I found my room the temperature of a hothouse. Nature had won, after all. The window was steamed up and the condensation quickly froze into organic patterns.

The receptionist had reluctantly exchanged my white tickets for blue ones, and when the bell rang for the evening meal, I joined an aggressive crowd of students in front of a window, elbowing my way to a bowl of gruel, some pickled vegetables and a steamed bun. I steered to an empty table, and started eating the tasteless mush. Suddenly I understood Youyou's wonderment. To her it must have seemed crazy to want to give up the privilege of better food.

A tall, chubby Chinese with sideburns and stiff hair bristling over his woollen turtleneck sweater asked to sit at my table.

'Not very good,' he commented on the food in English, while sliding into a chair.

'Better than eating alone behind the screen,' I said.

'We saw you there yesterday, and thought that you were someone important.'

'No one important,' I insisted and introduced myself.

'Yang Shu.' He extended a hand. 'I'm a geologist.'

'From Xinjiang?'

'No, Xian. I've come here to do a survey . . . like most of us.' He made a sweeping gesture around the room.

We quickly finished our meagre rations.

'Feel like some more food?' he asked.

'Yes, why not?' I said, not wanting to offend. But I was famished.

We left the compound and crossed the street to a small covered market. He led me through alleys selling clothes smelling of mothballs, stalls with toys, shoes and tools, to a *kevabchi*. We settled on a narrow bench and ordered some skewers dripping with mutton rolled in crushed chilli from a Uighur man who obviously knew Yang.

'I thought Chinese didn't eat mutton,' I commented.

'They don't . . . but I like it; anyway, one couldn't survive on the food in the canteen.'

'You speak good English . . . a lot of people here seem to.'

'I listen to the BBC every night,' he said, hesitated, then continued in a quiet voice, '. . . and I study very hard. I want to go to America.'

'Why?' I asked, expecting a answer about the tough life and political situation.

'Study about the environment,' he said to my surprise. 'There isn't a river, stream or lake in China that is not polluted,' he went on heatedly.

'Isn't that a bit exaggerated?' I asked.

'Not really, or maybe only a little, it's just that we don't talk much about ecology here. Fact is, industrial waste, sewage, agricultural chemicals, all goes into the water, untreated. Off-shore, fish are poisoned by the oil industry. And what water there is, is being used up too fast. In cities, we have to dig deeper and deeper to get to the groundwater, and here in Xinjiang, well, you can see for yourself, salination due to faulty irrigation, erosion, desertification,' he exclaimed with passion.

'That is a pretty bleak picture; is it all that bad?' His outburst astonished me.

'Probably even worse,' he continued, stabbing the air with the skewer to underline his points. 'We are an agricultural nation, moving towards industrialization. Only a sixth of our land is agricultural land, and only a sixth of that again is good agricultural land. From that we feed over a billion mouths. But the land is exhausted. We've lost maybe a third of it in the last thirty years.'

'How?' I asked naïvely, dodging his sabre.

'Are you going to go to Xian?' he asked.

'Yes, probably.'

'Just take a look out of the train window on the way there. You'll see flat lands covered in fine earth going off into the distance. Then look at the telegraph poles. Each of them sits on a mound two to three metres high. That is how far the ground has lowered since the poles were put there.'

'What happend to the soil?' I asked. He shifted along the bench and laughed sarcastically.

'When it's harvest time in Shaanxi province, we have beautiful sunsets. We lose five billion tons of soil a year,' he exhaled noisily, '. . . into the air, into the river. The Yellow River is yellow from the soil washed away.'

He fell silent for a moment, his brow furrowed.

'Most of us at the academy have been sent to Xinjiang because of oil, minerals, and to find more water, make more land. But no one thinks about the future . . .' he trailed off. 'That's what I want to study. The future. If China is to have a future, we have to care for the land.' He spoke with convincing determination.

It had grown dark and cold. Slowly we walked back to the academy.

'Can you change some money for me?' he asked hesitantly before we entered our building.

'You mean dollars?'

'Yes, I need fifty dollars to take exams to go to America.'

The number 2 bus was filled to bursting capacity, but Yang the geologist forced his way in anyway. No one seemed to mind. Squeezed tightly together, almost to the point of suffocation, the whole mass moved with the motions of the bus. Yang handed some money to his neighbour who passed it on to the next until it reached the ticket girl, a young woman with a tough frown, who screamed out the individual stops at the top of her range. She passed back two slivers of ripped green paper.

Sunday was the day off for the working classes. Yang had offered to show me around town and to take me to the telephone exchange, to send a sign of life to my parents. The bus moved sluggishly through a sea of cyclists and pedestrians.

Urumqi – 'The Beautiful Grassland' – was created by the Chinese following the demise of Yakub Beg and Kashgaria and the official annexation of Xinjiang to the 'motherland'. Dihua, as Han officials referred to it, 'Return to Civilization', became the capital of China's newest province in 1882. It looked it.

Tree-lined, wide and very planned roads, crowded with cyclists, buses, jeeps and the occasional car, converged around the Hong Shan, the Red Hill, which, for better or worse, had become the symbol of the city. Utilitarian architectural styles dominated, with an occasional relic from the time when the Russians still flirted with their Communist neighbour. Most of them are from the 1950s. With their blue and yellow painted stucco façades, corrugated iron roofs and columned porticoes, they suited the city better than the new, so-called modern Uighur architecture, a hodge-podge of styles and tiles, Islamic arches and arabesque designs set off by the red star of China. But there weren't very many of them left.

Urumqi was not a friendly city. Once it spread over three separate quarters, Muslim, Chinese and White Russian, surrounded by tall mud walls. The walls were gone and the quarters have merged into one big urban sprawl. It is probably most famous for its short but colourful history, and most of all for the deeds of Governor Yang, who for seventeen years from 1911 ruled the province with an iron fist from his seat in the capital. Yang had a reputation for dealing with his enemies in a decidedly resolute manner. During a banquet in 1916, he had a band of Yunnanese rebels beheaded, one by one, while he looked on, calmly finishing his meal.

I asked my guide if he was related to the old governor.

'I don't think so,' he laughed, 'but Yang is a very common name.'

We alighted near the post office and walked up to the telephone bureau, a large hall with a mezzanine floor, resembling a stock exchange. The office for overseas calls was on the right, a glass cubicle presided over by an elderly official and a young assistant. There are few private phones in Xinjiang, and fewer yet with direct access to the international communications network. I filled out a form, then searched in my bag for the deposit. 'Shit! My wallet's gone.' I looked again.

'My wallet is gone,' I shouted to Yang, and stormed out of the office. There was a credit card in it, my brother's credit card.

'We'll have to go to the police,' I shouted and started walking.

'Was there a lot of money?' he asked, following me.

'Only about a hundred yuan. But it's the credit card I'm worried about.' I was beginning to panic.

'What is a credit card?' he asked. I tried to explain it to him, but all I could think of was reporting the loss as soon as possible.

'Can you use it here?' he asked calmly.

'I don't think so.' I couldn't imagine Urumqi joining the age of plastic money for a while yet.

'Then why do you want to go to the police?' he asked.

I stopped and looked at him, puzzled.

'Do you think it's useless?'

'Theft is common in Urumqi,' he explained. 'They'll catch the thief. They'd look hard because you're a foreigner.'

'Good!' I said angrily.

'Miss Paula, punishment here is very severe . . . and sometimes much more severe than the crime.'

As I absorbed the implications of what he was saying, I began to feel silly.

'Come on, let's go have some food instead. I know a nice restaurant,' Yang said, consoling me. I followed him, wrapping my scarf over my nose and mouth. It was still snowing.

On Monday I visited the Institute again.

'No news yet,' said Youyou barely looking up from her desk. I bought some postcards and returned to the Academy compound.

'Einmal ist keinmal'. If we have only one life to live, we might as well not have lived at all, is how Milan Kundera makes his protagonist Tomas contemplate the popular German proverb. I disagreed with his sombre fatalism, preferring my own interpretation: once doesn't count – you are therefore at liberty to try anything at least once, with a stress on the 'at least'.

Catherine had presented me with Kundera's novel *The Unbearable Lightness of Being* and I dived into it gratefully, escaping from China and the mood of foreboding. I was starved for a book, and this was the first piece of literature I had held in my hands for two months. A friend had slipped a book into my bag at Gatwick: *Ulysses*, one of the fattest books ever written. I had left it with the houseboy at Hotel Anand in New Delhi before I'd even read the introduction and was already regretting my hastiness by the time I reached Lahore.

67

In the evening, grabbing my toiletries, I headed for the basement. The receptionist stopped me. 'You can't have a shower every day,' she said briskly and sent me back to my room. I was starting to get depressed.

Tuesday's visit to the Institute was a near replay of Monday's. I finished Kundera that afternoon and shed a tear for Sabrina.

On Wednesday morning the receptionist's shrill voice got me out of bed. '*Dianhua* . . . *Dianhua* . . . telephone,' she cried, between loud knocks on the door.

Barefoot, I traipsed after her down two flights of stairs. She held open the door to her cubicle, and handed me the receiver, all the time keeping a suspicious eye on me.

'*Wei?* . . . Hello?' It was Madame Wu, requesting me to come to the Institute at once. As usual, her voice was friendly and noncommittal. I threw on some clothing, snatched a pear from the fruit tray and hurried out into the cold. My watch read six thirty-five. I hadn't changed it from Xinjiang time.

Madame Wu, Youyou and Goethe were waiting in the office. Goethe rose from his chair and politely offered it to me, while Youyou poured me tea. Madame Wu started talking, smiling all the while. Youyou translated.

'We regret . . .' her voice faded into the background after these opening words, but I didn't want to hear any more. Free fall with a scream.

Having said her bit, Madame Wu pulled a book from the shelf, her own *Xinjiang Archaeology*, and ceremoniously signed the title page.

'Hundred and fifty renminbi,' she asked, handing it to me. I paid, thinking that I had seen it for less money in the museum bookshop. I didn't want to stay around, or listen to explanations. Perhaps I simply had not been 'approved'.

Youyou escorted me down the steps.

'I'm sorry . . . what will you do next?'

'Don't know,' I shrugged. I was not a master of face, and my disappointment must have been very obvious.

'There is much to see in Xinjiang, Turfan, Kizil . . .' she tried to console me.

'Yes, I'll probably do that . . . or maybe I'll try on my own.'

She paused for a moment. 'Miran is closed to foreigners . . . but then, why not?' With that she turned and went back indoors.

I needed to think. I walked into town, not looking at anything, then climbed the Red Mountain, which sat like a manicured mole-hill behind a department store. I watched a Chinese family having a picnic in an open concrete pavilion, its red-painted roof mocking that of a Buddhist pagoda. The air smelled of smoke and snow.

Yang was waiting in the foyer the next morning. He would come to the station to see me off, he said.

On the way a black limousine passed us slowly. We stopped and stared along with everyone else.

'Rabbia,' said Yang, 'she is the richest woman in Urumqi. She owns a department store. They say she takes her holidays abroad.'

'Uighur?'

'Yes.'

I boarded the bus and squeezed in next to a very bulky man in a white leather coat. With his white hair, pointed beard and moustache, pale skin and blue eyes he looked like Colonel Sanders from the Kentucky Fried Chicken advertisements. On my other side, across the aisle, sat a Chinese girl of about eighteen. A large teddy bear was embroidered on the left breast of her coat. She worked in the yoghurt factory in Kuqa, she told me, and she was going back home after a two-week seminar on hygiene. In Korla, where we stopped overnight, we shared a room at the bus station, and I promised to meet her and her friends some evening after work.

'There is only one place for foreigners, I'll come and see you there,' she said as we pulled into the Kuqa bus station.

SIX

Kuqa

I HAD BEEN TOLD there was only one place for foreigners to stay in Kuqa, the Waibinguan, advertised as the Kuqa Number One Guest House on the small pamphlet the girl handed me with my first night's receipt. The picture on the cover had a green tinge to it. It was an overgrown inn in the north-western corner of the new town, with a rusty metal gate, a fountain filled with sand and thistles with magenta flowers, and a squat building with a few rooms. The kitchen lay opposite the sleeping quarters, and at right angles to that was a dining-hall. Behind it a new hotel, oddly colonial with porticoes and wooden columns, was still under construction, quietly anticipating the tourist trade. Kuqa had only 'opened' this year, and could be visited without permit for the first time. But few travellers seemed to know that.

The 'Kuqa Wai', as the donkey driver who had deposited me on its threshold, called it, was run by a collection of women, with no one in particular in charge, and a fierce cook from Hunan province. The cook had grey-streaked greasy hair tied into a rat-tail, and a horse's face, and I never saw her without the same padded jacket with yellow and orange floral patterns. She claimed to have been born in Shaoshan near Changsha, Mao Zedong's home village, and she told everyone. How she came to work in Kuqa remained a mystery. The quality of her cooking was determined by her mood, which was usually pretty foul. She announced meals by bashing a frying pan, and if the response was not immediate, one of the girls was sent to escort the culprit to the table. I liked the hotel.

'*Chi fan* . . . food,' a girl yelled, knocking on my door. I had ignored the racket from the kitchen, and was still settling in to my room, a basic arrangement of two beds, a table, chair and a metal brazier.

The other diner, and the only other guest in the hotel, was hunched over a bowl of noodles, slurping noisily, in the middle of the large, empty dining-hall. His back was turned to me. Cook slammed a second bowl opposite him, muttering under her breath that I was late. I apologized.

The man looked up and introduced himself with a brisk bow as Kitagawa.

Kitagawa was forty-something with a slight build and a permanent five-o'clock shadow. Until last year he had worked for a Tokyo bank, he told me. After his father's death he gave up the job he never liked to pursue his only passion: calligraphy. Three days after the funeral he booked a flight to Shanghai, found a teacher, and had been living there ever since. This was his holiday, and he was tracing the '*Siruku Rodo*', the Silk Road, hunting for early examples of script. He had never married. Talking rapidly in a mix of Japanese and Chinese, with the odd English word thrown in, he was starved for conversation. His high voice had a whiny sub-tone, and rose even higher when he asked me to come along to see the caves of Kizil the next day. I said that would be nice.

Cook's signal for breakfast worked like an alarm clock. I rushed to the dining-hall, and imagined a satisfied expression on her tanned, ugly face as she served a plate of tomatoes fried up with eggs.

Kitagawa said that he had arranged a vehicle for the morning with the Foreign Affairs Bureau and asked me to contribute 130 FEC.

Moments later Cook returned, a pretty Uighur girl with a round face and dimpled cheeks in tow. A thick chestnut-brown braid lay over her shoulder, covered by a flimsy scarf woven with silver thread, which had slid into the nape of her neck. With her red tailored jacket and tight grey skirt she belonged on a 1950s movie screen. Like most Uighurs she looked older than her twenty-four years. Fine webs of wrinkles surrounded her eyes, a result of the relentless summer sun and a permanent lack of good cosmetics. She introduced herself as Aertosen, the head translator for the Foreign Affairs Bureau.

'Where are you from?' she asked me with a smile. I noticed her elegant movements and long slender fingers. Kitagawa gave a glance, got up and left.

'Strange man,' she said following him with her eyes. 'He's been here for a few days and he won't talk to anyone.'

'He's Japanese,' I said, as though that were an excuse.

'Are you a student?' she returned her attention to me. Her English was good, with a broad Uighur accent.

'Yes, in London,' I answered between bites.

'Oh, my old English teacher has gone to London . . . do you know her?'

'Not Hakime?' I asked, making a wild guess.

'Yes, you know her?' She sounded very pleased.

There aren't many Uighurs in London, and most of them sooner or later come to SOAS. I had met Hakime briefly, and gathered she was working on her PhD at the Institute of Education next door to SOAS.

The horn of a jeep sounded outside the window.

'Your car,' Aertosen mentioned superfluously, as I got up to leave. 'The princess's tears, watch for the princess's tears, she's still crying for her lover,' she yelled after me and waved.

'Xinjiang must have made a deal with Toyota.' I tried a joke on Kitagawa as I climbed into the four-wheel drive. It was lost on him. Our driver, a heavy Uighur who smelled of a sleepless night, tapped his fingers to the beat of arabesque music blasting from his cassette deck. We drove speedily. After ten kilometres, leaving the oasis behind in a dust cloud, we turned into a brush and gravel desert studded with mounds and clay sarcophagi. Pink, red and white cloths fluttered from wooden sticks. The desert was a cemetery. In the distance lay the silhouette of a factory.

We halted in front of a mud-brick monolith, a beacon tower left over from the third century, when communication posts followed the roads and the river. It overlooked a bluff of white rock set with yellow doors: the caves of Kizil-Kara, poorer cousin to the Kizil caves. No one answered to our shouts and knocks on the caretaker's bungalow, and without seeing the promised paintings we left again, with Kitagawa complaining about the expense of the tour.

Kuqa was settled by a branch of the Tocharians, an Indo-Germanic tribe which had migrated from the vast steppes west of the Chinese heartland, and grew into the largest of the 'western kingdoms' by the second century BC. It adopted Buddhism along with an enthusiasm for trade in the first century AD, and remained an important economic nexus along the northern Silk Road until the Mongol invasion. It was famous for its dancers, its music and its wine. The kingdom was rich, charging high taxes to passing caravans, and wealth facilitated culture. Monasteries were built all around the oasis, lavishly endowed by the pious aristocracy. By the eighth century it was reputed to support some 5,000 monks.

We continued north-west on a freshly tarred road – a rare sight in Xinjiang – into a strange landscape. Sedimentary beds of sandstone and shale jutted into the sky at 45-degree angles. A bridge had the same colour as the jagged rocks. The driver pointed into a gully and to a cliff which had the quality of an abstract painting. Wind had scoured shallow holes into the wall, making it look like Swiss cheese. I imagined moving through this environment two millennia ago, no road, no bridge, only dead, dry silence and dragon bones. I dug into my bag, found a cassette and stuck it into the machine. 'A Whole Lotta Love', played at full volume, shut up Kitagawa and the driver who were arguing over two kilos of grapes. To our left lay an ancient alluvial plain with winnowed dunes, each small hill glistening with a crown of salt. Led Zeppelin was strangely appropriate.

At the apex of a sandy hill, the driver stopped for a moment. 'Kizil,' he said with reverence, and even Kitagawa gaped in silent astonishment.

Below us lay the sparkling Muzart river snaking through a gorge, a smudge of green willows, and a long sandstone cliff. We slowly descended into the narrow valley. Then we saw the bright yellow doors, concrete balconies and metal railings, which clashed with the almost white cliff-face. Archaeology had been busy here.

We parked by a building with a shady garden, and were greeted by a red-cheeked Chinese girl in a track suit who called out for a guide, an old man who shuffled towards us in felt slippers.

Despite his awkward footwear, he nimbly climbed the steep concrete steps and opened the first cave. It was empty, save for a sign condemning imperialist art thieves for the destruction of Chinese Cultural Heritage (in capital letters), and a short essay on the caves. There are 236 of them, I read, the earliest remains are from the third century, and most of them date from between the fifth and the seventh; as a community it flourished until the Mongol invasion.

They had all been here: the Otani expeditions, Grünwedel and LeCoq, the Bersovsky brothers, and Stein's closest rival, Paul Pelliot. Stein, who had organized his trans-Taklamakan expedition of 1908 in Kuqa, had written about Kizil with an unde-niable note of jealousy. 'The caves proved disappointing with their frescoes terribly mutilated by pious vandals and collectors . . . The ruined monasteries and temples had all suffered so badly through moisture that Japanese, Germans and Russians contented them-selves with mere scrapings . . .' Mere scrapings they weren't, as anyone who has had the pleasure of visiting the Indian Museum in Berlin can verify, but the description of the state of the caves wasn't that far off.

Our guide opened another dark and empty chamber, then another. Finally we entered a rectangular hall with a central pillar, symbolic of the cosmic centre, the world mountain Meru. The pillar functioned as a stupa and a pathway led around it, like a circumambulatory. In the back of the narrow tunnel lay the reclin-ing figure of the dying Buddha.

Slowly the guide traced the walls with a weak beam from his inadequate flashlight. Above the entrance levitated Maitreya, the Buddha to come, surrounded by devis and apsaras, graceful heavenly dancers with musical instruments. On the side walls, badly rubbed by time and use, were images to aid in teaching Buddhist scriptures, and just below the lantern ceiling appeared abstracted landscapes in the form of large lozenge shapes, each containing tales from the previous life of the Buddha, reduced to single scenes. All were painted in the cool blues and greens the masters of Kizil were so famous for. Donor figures faced the central pillar, and I pointed out to Kitagawa their red hair and blue eyes; Tocharian princes, who, with their tight smart jackets and long swords, could have graced King Arthur's Round Table.

On the dado of one cave was painted a familiar narrative: the Vessantara Jataka, the best-known epic in the Buddhist world. It recounts the pious deeds and trials of the Buddha's penultimate reincarnation as Prince Vessantara, son of King Sanjaya and Queen Phusati of the Sivis. Together with his wife Maddi and their two children, he lived as heir apparent in Jetuttara, the capital of the kingdom.

From birth, Vessantara practised complete and unconditional generosity: 'If I met anyone who asked for it, I would give my right arm and not hesitate. My mind delights in giving,' he exclaims in the first verses of his story in the Pali canon, the scriptures of Theravada Buddhism.

Vessantara owned a magical white elephant, regarded by all as the key to the country's prosperity. One hot summer a drought threatened a neighbouring kingdom and, having heard of the luck-bringing beast as well as of Vessantara's vow, Brahmins were sent to ask for the elephant. It was presented without hesitation. There followed an angry outcry as the citizens of Jetuttara rose in protest, forcing Sanjaya to expel his son from the kingdom. Maddi and the children chose to share his banishment, and after making the 'great gift of the seven hundred' (seven hundred elephants hung with gold, seven hundred chariots, and so on), they left the city for exile on Crooked Mountain. On his way Vessantara was challenged again, and duly presented the horses drawing the family's carriage to begging Brahmins, and eventually the chariot itself. The family continued the journey on foot, settling in a remote hermitage. Again, Vessantara was asked to give what was precious to him, first his children and lastly his wife. He passed the test. Finally, convinced of his purity, the gods restored family and kingdom to him. The story ends with a moving scene of reunion and the jubilant return to Jetuttara.

The painting showed only a few scenes of the story. Vessantara confronted by the Brahmin Jajuka gives away his children in the centre left, while on the right, Maddi, who is away in the forest picking berries, is prevented by wild animals from returning to the hermitage. On the far left we see 'Maddi's lament', in which she weeps over the fate of her children and on the far right, Jajuka is depicted driving the children into the woods.

At Kizil, Vessantara's tale appears nine times, each one of them concentrating on the children and Maddi's lament. At Miran the Vessantara Jataka was painted in no fewer than fourteen scenes around the interior of a circular shrine. It was rendered at eye-level to the viewer and developed clockwise, following the custom of *pradaksina*, or ritual circumambulation round the central stupa. The concave wall, the continuous narrative and the movements of the devotee created a strong aesthetic relationship between architecture, art and ritual. The effect must have been almost cinematographic with the unfolding of the story-line determined by the speed of the viewer's progress.

The Vessantara Jataka at Miran was destroyed by Tachibana, a Japanese naval officer who visited the site some time in the winter of 1908–09.

The guide locked the door and said the tour was over.

'What does he mean, over?' I asked Kitagawa, whose Chinese was better than mine.

'Over. He says he is tired.' Kitagawa didn't seem to mind.

'Tired?' I repeated disbelievingly: there were so many more caves to see.

'*Tsukarete* . . . tired,' Kitagawa nodded. The guard shuffled back to the main building and Kitagawa followed him.

But my tour was not over yet. I headed into the poplar and willow forest and came to the opening of a gorge, from which trickled a muddy creek. Walls rose to the left and right, closing in until only a narrow strip of sky was visible. It was cool and moist. Caves sat high up in the walls, accessible by ladders; here there were no concrete steps. I felt myself magically drawn in and followed the creek which seemed to emerge directly from the mountain; ferns and small willows hung from crags and rocks. The narrow footpath terminated in a natural bowl, confining a small clear pool. Water dripped from the walls and the sky above seemed very blue and very far away. 'The princess's tears,' I said to myself, smiling at Aertosen's message. There was only the sound of water, the smell of moist earth and green grass, and it was easy to imagine the monks of long ago meditating in the cool sanctuary. The desert did not exist here. Inscriptions in both Chinese and Arabic were scratched into the wet wall above the pool; most of the dates were recent.

I stared into the mirror of the water for a long time, thinking of Kuqa's most famous son, the fourth-century Buddhist teacher and translator Kumarajiva. Had he ever sat here?

Later I heard the local legend Aertosen had referred to. One day, Zaoerhan, the beautiful daughter of the king of Kuqa, went hunting and heard someone singing in the woods. She dismounted and searched for the source of the song. It came from a young, handsome mason. Enchanted she listened, and fell in love with him. Angry, and unwilling to give his daughter to a lowly mason, the king called the youth and set him a task. If he would carve a thousand caves, he would be granted his daughter's hand. The young man went to the banks of the Muzart river and began the impossible work. Three years later he had completed 999 caves, but beginning the very last one he collapsed and died. When the princess found his body she grieved until she too died, and to this day, her tears fall endlessly into the clear pool near the caves.

There were shouts, and the driver materialized from behind a boulder. He waved frantically, pointing at his watch. Time to go. I had been here for two hours. Kitagawa said that he had bought a drink at the shop and that his glass exploded when he poured beer into it. Probably from the heat, he said. It was hot, and I had almost forgotten the snow in Urumqi.

We were quiet on the way back to Kuqa. There was one more stop, the driver said, and instead of returning to the guest house we drove north again towards the purple mountains, turning grey in the evening mist. In the last heavy rays, we saw Subashi, an imposing free-standing site, cut in half by a broad river-bed. Its pyramid-like ruins, stupas and mud-brick walls looked alien in the late afternoon light, reminiscent of sculptures by Henry

Moore. I asked the driver about the site on the other bank of the river, which looked far more interesting.

'Forbidden,' he said in English.

Next morning Aertosen was waiting by the fountain, leaning against her bicycle.

'Why didn't you knock?' I asked her, rubbing the night from my eyes.

'I didn't want to wake you,' she said politely.

She watched me eat breakfast without touching any food herself and I saw Cook smile for the first time.

Kuqa was a Uighur town, Aertosen told me proudly. She was wearing her tour guide expression. Less then twenty per cent of its inhabitants were Han Chinese. I wondered how soon that number would change, and said so out loud. She didn't reply.

Kuqa was divided into a new and an old town by the Urumqi–Kashgar road. The new town, a few parallel streets and a concrete monolith, had once been aptly described as 'utilitarian'. Aertosen pointed out each building, 'Bank, telephone exchange, department store . . .' There was also a hospital, a military complex with guards and a derelict Russian cinema with a crumbling stucco façade. Near the main road was a 'donkey taxi station', and a bustling daily market with both permanent and temporary stalls. Dentists went about their business with foot-powered drills, like treadle sewing machines, below large painted signs of heads in profile, partially stripped of flesh; barbers scraped away at beards and scalps, next to women selling coloured eggs and produce. There was the odd skilled worker, menders of vessels, shoemakers, knife-grinders, and some food vendors frying fish in batter. Desert fish!

'Kuqa is one of three towns in Xinjiang which still have donkey taxis,' Aertosen informed me, still in tour guide mode, and pushed her bicycle towards one of the shops lining Market Street. She said she wanted me to meet her friend. Arsalan had wavy black hair on a head that seemed incongruously small in proportion to his muscular body, but that was redeemed by sparkling coal-black eyes and high cheekbones. He ran a handkerchief-sized stall selling headscarves and trinkets. Aertosen practised English with him almost daily, preparing him to leave for Pakistan in the spring to study at university in Islamabad.

'Why Pakistan?' I asked him.

'It's the only way . . . for a Uighur,' he said. 'The mullahs are sending me on a scholarship. Do you think the Chinese would send me to the United States?' He spat sarcastically.

'Arsalan . . .' Aertosen tried to shut him up, but he was an angry young man.

'It's true, and you know it. If it were up to them, we'd not study at all. Look what they are doing to us. Bad schools, no jobs, cheap liquor. They give us freedom, but only so much.' He measured 'so much' between his forefinger and thumb.

'Arsalan,' Aertosen said again, looking uncomfortable. She turned and invited me to lunch at her home.

'Please excuse him,' she apologized.

'Is it so bad?' I asked. I would have liked to talk to him some more.

'No it is not,' she stated strongly. 'We are very well, we are wealthy peasants in Kuqa . . .'

Aertosen lived in the old town, a network of passageways with a few mosques. It was separated from the new town by a broad bridge spanning the Kuqa river. Her family occupied several houses next to an irrigation ditch leading into a field. 'Wealthy peasants,' she underlined her earlier statement, pointing to the fields.

She unlocked a blue gate and led me into a tiny courtyard with a tandoori oven in one corner, then through another door into her room. I was surprised to find that she lived alone. I looked round her sanctuary. She liked framing objects with objects: a round mirror over a dresser between two plastic miniature palms; two ornately painted trays displayed on a ledge in the clay wall, on either side of another mirror which was made up of fragments and shaped like an Islamic arch. She picked up a graceful water vessel with a long spout and ceremoniously sprayed a few drops on to the shiny clay floor.

'Excuse the mess, please, if I knew you were coming, I would have cleaned,' she said with downcast eyes, in a well-rehearsed hospitable formula. Her room could not have been tidier. Half of the space was taken up by a *kang*, a sleeping platform which in the cold winter months could be heated from underneath. It was thickly carpeted with colourful rugs, and strewn with pillows. The wall was spread with cloth. It was the kind of place I would never have wanted to leave as a child.

Aertosen was an orphan and she had inherited her parents' house. She had let most of it to a cousin's family, and her sisters and brothers, all much older than she was, lived next door. The following November she would be getting married to a local teacher, she told me in a girlish way, and showed me a white shirt she had been embroidering for her fiancé in the traditional blue and green cross-stitch. Every oasis, she told me, had a different pattern.

As we talked her aunt, a tall, handsome woman, brought in a nan as large as a cartwheel and two steaming plates with noodles decorated with mutton and peppers. We ate sitting cross-legged on the *kang*, and she showed me a few postcards written by the members of an American tour group.

Dreamily, she said: 'I wish I could come with you.'

'Why don't you?'

'I can't, my place is here,' she said after a pause, and asked me to photograph her small cousins.

I returned to the 'Wai' late in the afternoon.

'Where have you been?' Kitagawa asked me in an accusing voice.

'Out,' I said.

From my recollection Subashi lay in a straight line north from Kuqa bazaar. No more than twenty kilometres, I guessed. The girl at the reception had told me the previous evening that in the early morning a lot of traffic would be heading in the direction of the mountains. She was right. A steady procession of trucks, tractors and donkey carts moved in single file along the road; the poplars were white from the dust. I flagged down a vehicle and climbed in with a dozen Uighur teenagers carrying pickaxes and shovels.

'Subashi?' I asked. They nodded.

When the main stupa and the telegraph wires crossing the half of Subashi I had visited the previous day came into view, I was asked to get off. The boys pointed straight ahead, and the truck turned right on to a gravel plain. But it wasn't the western side I wanted, it was the eastern half, the one the driver had called 'forbidden'.

A horse and cart, driven by a white-bearded Uighur, stopped next to me with a loud hissing noise.

'*Mingoi?*' he guessed. I nodded, indicating the eastern side. He giggled like an old witch, and waved me to get on. Grandfather didn't speak Chinese.

'*At,*' he said suddenly, and pointed at his horse.

'*At?*' I questioned.

'*At,*' he repeated, touching the flanks of the old mare with a switch. *At* was the horse.

'*Kün,*' he pointed to the sun.

'*Kün,*' I repeated, realizing that the old man was teaching me Uighur.

'*Usüm,*' he grabbed a handful of grapes and pushed them into his toothless mouth.

'*At, Kün, Usüm,*' I recited.

He giggled again and pulled a pencil from my breast pocket, turned it between his fingers for a moment and stuck it behind his ear.

Near the river was a camp with grey and olive tents, and hundreds of young men shovelling gravel and sand.

'*Hasher,*' the old man said. *Hasher,* I found out, was a system of unpaid labour, which forces the donation of at least 45 days' work a year to the government. It had been thought to have been rendered obsolete with the ending of the Cultural Revolution.

Near canals and locks, used for harvesting the water from the river, the old man let out a sharp whistle. Moments later, a young shepherd dashed out from behind a wall, and the old man told him to show me the way across. The boy jumped ahead on bare feet, leading me to a set of stairs, then vanished as abruptly as he had appeared. The dry river-bed was almost 700 metres wide at this point and I crossed rapidly, hoping not to draw too much attention.

I scrambled up the steep incline and hid behind the ruined walls of the main monastery, catching my breath. Its large stupa drum, rising from a massive square base, echoed the one on the other shore. Probably from the fifth century. A gash in its side may have come from a treasure hunter's hand, and deep trenches near it indicated extensive archaeological activity. I wondered if they had been left by Pelliot, who had spent almost eight months in Kuqa in 1908.

Unconsolidated gravel swept down from the mountain had created sharp ridges. On one pinnacle sat a Muslim hermitage, similar in structure to the one in Tulumush. Erosion had made the approach to it inaccessible, completely isolating the tiny domed building. I climbed as high as it was possible, found a ledge sheltered from the wind and sat, eating the grapes the grandfather had handed me with a final pat on the hand.

I walked back to Kuqa in the early afternoon, hitching an occasional lift with a donkey cart.

In the evening Aertosen and Arsalan came to take me to the new cinema, a western installation of great pride to the community. We saw a 1970s Russian air disaster movie translated into Uighur with Chinese subtitles. Everyone talked and spat pumpkin seeds. But when I laughed at the 'Stingray'-type special effects, Aertosen elbowed me in the ribs and told me to hush.

Outside I ran into the Chinese girl from the bus. She asked me, reproachfully, why I spent time with Uighurs. I asked her, why didn't she. Without answering, she turned and walked away in the company of two friends.

Next morning I went to the Foreign Affairs Bureau to see Aertosen. I had promised to go over an English lesson she had been putting together for the officials.

'Can I see your passport, please,' read the beginning of the dialogue. 'This is a forbidden area,' it went on and, 'You must pay a fine.'

'Very practical,' I commented, trying to be suitably serious.

'Yes, I will have all winter to teach them,' Aertosen said, and sighed, 'but first they have to learn the ABC.'

'Could be helpful,' I commented.

A Uighur with a stern face stuck his head round the door, and asked to speak with Aertosen.

'My boss,' she said, excusing herself.

Ten minutes later she came back, distraught.

'I was told not to invite foreigners to my home again,' she explained.

'Why?' I asked, wondering how they had found out.

'Oh, they probably thought I was getting presents,' she laughed.

'I'm leaving tomorrow,' I told her.

'Miran?' she asked.

'Maybe!'

SEVEN

Back to Kashgar

'I AM A MUSLIM,' the scrawny kid in tattered clothing finally said. He had been watching us intently from the far end of the waiting-room, all the while expertly rolling up tobacco in squares cut from newspaper. He looked about twelve. Edging closer, he pulled his impish brown face into a broad smile, and offered a cigarette to Kitagawa, who turned away. He was not discouraged.

'What are you?' the kid demanded to know in a husky, pubescent voice.

'German,' I said.

'What religion is that?'

This was a Muslim state. Most of the so-called minority nation-alities in Xinjiang, of which the Uighurs form the largest group, were followers of the Sunni sect of the orthodox Hanafi *machhab*, though Shia fundamentalists were gaining influence, especially in the poorer south. The boy's innocent question bespoke the grow-ing religious awareness, noticeable everywhere. After decades of repression, the Chinese government had eased its overt policy of denying free religious expression; new mosques were mush-rooming, filled every Friday with an enthusiastic crowd of worshippers.

Kitagawa and I had missed the bus. Or maybe there hadn't been a bus today. Kitagawa was nervous and looked close to tears.

'I want to leave Kuqa,' he pouted. I told him to take it easy.

He had latched on to me this morning, waiting with his luggage ready by the gate when I was leaving the hotel. He was a strange man, and I did not take to him. It seemed he liked neither China

84

nor travelling, yet he was obviously in awe of the country's traditions and determined to visit every historical or culturally important site, a goal he pursued with almost heroic stubbornness. I wondered why he insisted on coming with me. Feelings of liking or dislike between people tend to be mutual.

The kid was bilingual in Chinese and Uighur and he said he wanted to learn English. I asked him if there was no school today. He laughed and lay back on the bench, puffing smoke into the air. I noticed he was barefoot.

Finally there was some space on the Urumqi–Aksu bus and by nightfall we were again at the bile-green bus terminal and the shack selling cigarettes.

'Uighur three renminbi, Han five renminbi, *Waiguoren* eight renminbi,' read the sign next to the counter. An old man sat below it. He balanced on a three-legged stool, gesturing wildly as we approached: 'English? *Deutsch? Russki?*' he bellowed, excited. He said he had fought against the Russians, and then with them he had fought the Germans in the Great War. He had been to Europe a long time ago. He even spoke English. Saliva dribbled from the corner of his toothless mouth, but his eyes were bright and friendly.

A boy reproachfully pulled him up and away before I could ask him any questions. '*Auf wiedersehen*, goodbye,' he waved, turning back.

'Drunk,' Kitagawa grumbled.

Next day at dusk we pulled into Kashgar's long-distance bus terminal, greeted by the dark shadow of Chairman Mao's concrete arm pointing east. A donkey taxi took us to the Qinibagh. Though less comfortable than the Seman, it would be a better place to gather information about going on to the southern Silk Road.

The destruction of the consulate compound had made some headway since I'd been here last. The plan for the future hotel was outlined crudely in white chalk on the dug-up ground in front of the main house. Its foundations were indicated to rise just metres from the old porch – a tribute to the inelegance of Chinese planning. A few more trenches had been dug, and the tall old trees lay in pieces on a bed of sawdust by the water pump.

We were put into the former stables, a row of dormitories at right angles to the main building ('the main building is full up,' said the Chinese at the reception), in a large hall lined with two rows of a dozen beds each. Kitagawa threw his pack on to the cot next to mine, and I tried hard not to feel annoyed by his company.

We ate some dinner at the *kavabchi* opposite the gate of the Qinibagh; the proprietor's children were fighting over the remote control for a television suspended in a corner, switching back and forth between a football game and a martial arts drama set in the Manchu era. The father finally extracted the black box from his seven-year-old's clutches and turned the set off.

I had piled several damp mattresses and blankets on the wooden planks of my bed, and after a shower in the swampy bathhouse took an early night. The large, dank hall had an air of cheerless dinginess. As a precaution, I padlocked the door from the inside.

I woke to Kitagawa's soft moans and unmistakable rhythmic movements. He was masturbating. Instinctively, I reached for my knife, which out of habit I had put under my pillow along with my money belt. At daybreak I found that I was still clutching it, and swore I would stay in Kashgar as short a time as possible.

In the morning things looked less dreary; the night's incident seemed almost funny. After all, as Woody Allen put it, 'it's sex with someone you love.'

Kitagawa had disappeared before I got out of bed, to see the ruins of Hanoi, a Tang dynasty town about 30 kilometres to the east of Kashgar. I hadn't seen them and wasn't planning to.

After a bowl of delicious home-made yoghurt and some still warm *girda*, the bagel-shaped bread rolls, sold door to door at the Qinibagh by a woman whose face was almost completely covered with a thick brown scarf, I headed upstairs to the top floor of the main building where Ian had brought me a few weeks earlier. In the half-dark I could just make out a few sleeping bodies, empty unmade beds, and the disarray of luggage. Graffiti, some in Urdu, covered the walls. 'Save the Qinibagh,' seemed to be a recurring message.

A young man, pretty, with a mop of black curls, was checking a T-shirt suspended like a sack from the ceiling. It was filled with a dry, white mass.

'Yoghurt,' he said, squeezing the shirt and laughed, 'it's for cheesecake.' He introduced himself as Kim, wiping his hand on old, faded jeans. He was from Portugal, and he had been in Kashgar almost a month now.

'Ever been south?' I came to the point after some chatter.

'You mean Khotan?'

'Hm, and further east.'

'Closed road,' he said and raised an eyebrow, looking at me with interest for the first time.

'So they say . . .'

'I haven't . . . but I've heard of some Japanese . . .' he said thoughtfully. I liked his accent.

'Think it's possible?'

'Everything is possible,' he laughed, 'but you best speak to the map-maker, John, he knows his way around better than anyone else. You can probably find him at the Oasis.'

'Oh, it's open again?'

'Didn't know it had closed,' he commented and fingered a silver concert flute.

Life in Kashgar must have a hypnotic quality annihilating all sense of time. The weeks are measured only by the Sunday market, and the daily routine is simple: yoghurt and nan mornings, kebab lunches and magic evenings. Sooner or later, everyone finds their way to the Oasis café, the Qinibagh of modern days, home away from home, Kim had called it.

A handful of global bums represented the core of the Kashgar élite, orbited by a steady stream of young passers-through. Some of them had dropped out a long time ago; others were here for business. There was Hannu, nicknamed the 'granddad of all hash-ish smoking hippies', who was an old Kashgar hand. He was loved for organizing bonfires on the flat roof of the Qinibagh and picnics in the desert. And Saddhu Babba, a New Zealander turned holy man, who had left his adopted India to travel the ancient routes of the scriptures, propelled by a dream to pray at Mount Kailash in deep Tibet. But Tibet was closed to individual travellers. 'The PLA is still busy bashing monks,' he said in a quiet voice.

In a corner sat the American, Sol, with a towel around his waist and a dishcloth on his head, one of the more bizarre figures. He refused to speak to other foreigners and ostentatiously displayed the *Renmin Ribao*, the Chinese-language *People's Daily*, which he read intently and conspicuously upside down. There was a well-known drug smuggling couple in their mid-forties, who used to do the Afghan route but had relocated their business when the war broke out. Patrick, an androgynous, well-dressed boy from Surrey, was into Korans and carpets, buying cheap and selling dear back in Europe.

The Oasis was run by a young entrepreneur, struggling to succeed in China's new brand of free market economy. Short, with a not particularly handsome face rescued by beautiful silver-grey eyes, Tahir spoke English coloured by a multitude of accents picked up from travellers. He was determined to make a go of business, though he admitted it wasn't always easy.

'I've been trying to play it straight and honest,' he said, but implied that in China, a country motivated by the principles of *guanxi*, connections, and the 'back door', that was a near impossibility.

He had opened his first café in 1986, further down the road near the Seman on the ground floor of the Oasis Hotel.

'I had just come back from Guanzhou with a degree in electronic engineering,' he said and chuckled. 'But there isn't much work in electronics in Kashgar.'

He borrowed money from his father's work unit, the bank, and from a new unit that had been established in Kashgar to foster private business ('real communists, from the Shanghai area').

'Everyone thought I was crazy,' he remembered with a crooked smile.

Within a month the café was a success. From travellers, who had started to pour into Kashgar after the opening of the KKH in 1986, he learned English and how to cook the Uighur equivalent of western food, and soon pizzas, Kashiburgers, chocolate gâteaux, were added to the standard menu. But with success came trouble.

'The police started to poke around; they said I was open too late, then they accused me of dealing on the black market.'

'Did you?' I asked.

'No, of course not, I had a business to run. I was playing it completely straight – too straight, probably,' and he shook his head.

In early 1987, Tahir was closed down. Shortly after, the café was reopened by local party officials. Their business folded within three months.

Tahir travelled to Urumqi, where he obtained a government decree permitting him to run a restaurant. In 1988, back in Kashgar, he opened the New Oasis, in the Friendship Hotel.

'I designed and built this,' he said, and I commented on the beautiful arched windows which looked almost Gothic.

'I had trouble, especially with the tax man. There seem to be no laws on taxes, and the amount you pay depends on personal relations. As long as you entertain them and their family and their friends, you're fine. But you can't run a business on free-bees. When I became strict, saying that I'd rather pay a fair and agreed sum, they tried to find ways to close me down again. I think they are jealous. Everyone thinks I'm making too much money.'

'Are you?' I asked.

'I try,' he laughed.

Tahir's story was not uncommon in China. For decades people had got by through alternative means, and bureaucrats had always increased their standard of living by receiving 'favours'. Capitalism or no capitalism, old habits are hard to shake.

John, the map-maker, wasn't at the Oasis.

I joined a group of travellers listening to the male half of a pair of honeymooners, both thirty-something, Tom and Linda. Tom was fat, imposing, and very verbal; his wife skinny, with a bored expression. They had met through a lonely hearts advertisement, got married and started travelling three weeks later. They wanted to cycle through China, but so far hadn't had much luck.

I asked if anyone here knew details about the southern route.

'Impossible, for most,' said Tom. 'Of course, we have thought of doing it, but there isn't time.'

'Get real,' laughed a friendly Australian named Alex, shaking his head. As he left the table his eyes met mine and we both fell into a fit of suppressed giggles.

I spent the afternoon wandering through the bazaar around the Idga, rummaging through dusty boxes in the antique market with the faint hope of finding some Sino-Kharosthi coins, an obscure currency that circulated in the first centuries of our era. The coins, all dedicated to the kings of Khotan, displayed legends in both Chinese and Kharosthi, the north Indian script used for a few hundred years in Shanshan and some of the neighbouring kingdoms. Some of the coins adhered to Roman weight standards, which meant that, theoretically, they could be used for payment anywhere between Changan and Rome – a sort of American Express card of antiquity. I didn't find one. At the government-run Kashgar Crafts Centre I found two signs posted on the second and third floors, beside the doors leading to the exhibition rooms: 'Unity is Strength, Unity is Victory', said the first; 'Time is Money, Efficiency is Life', the second. Slogans for a modern China.

In the late afternoon I returned to the Qinibagh and climbed back to the top floor of the main building. Candles were lit all around. A Japanese girl and three boys sat on the floor, eyes glazed over, kneading hashish. A fat man with a beard sat in a chair watching them.

'Why are they doing that?' I asked him.

'Why not, got to earn your reward,' he said with a German accent. Kim was cutting up cheesecake. He greeted me with a smile and pointed to the next room. An American girl showed off her newly bought padded Uighur coat, and handed round a joint.

On a bed, surrounded by maps, drawing equipment and papers, crouched a young man with tousled brown hair and three-day stubble. He was the map-maker.

'Kim said you know your way around the south,' I introduced myself.

'Not really, I've been to Khotan,' he said abstractedly, glancing at his notes. A folding bicycle leaned in the corner.

'What about the rest of the route?'

'They say that Keriya is practically open – you should talk to Ahmet at the CITS at the Number One hotel, he'll know. If he's in a good mood he might even help you.'

I wrote the name in my diary.

'When are you going?' he asked, wrinkling his brow.

'Day after tomorrow.'

'Staying for the market, then,' he said. I noticed a slight Irish accent.

'Yes, I am,' I said. The American girl came over and offered the joint to John. He shook his head, and she turned and went back to the others.

'Well, you'll need a map,' he said finally, and reached for my diary. Swiftly he drew a neat diagram of the centre of Khotan in my notebook. From memory he included landmarks, old city walls, the market, main hotels, the police station.

'Try the Number One, at least the showers are good there,' he informed me.

'Where are you from?' I asked.

'Harrow, outside London.'

'Might see you there then.'

'You never know.'

The cold had caught up with me again. Next morning a sharp wind blew in from the desert, throwing fine dust in the air. A parade of donkeys, carts and people was already moving in the direction of the Sunday market. Thousands seemed to pour into the town from all directions.

I went to the bus station and purchased a ticket to Khotan, than dived into the colourful chaos of the market.

Uighur doctors, their medical paraphernalia spread on blankets in front of them, lined the way to the entrance. Noodle-makers, nan sellers and sweetmeat stalls competed with temporary *chai khanas* and *kavabchi*. Women sold eggs coloured pink and orange, indicating that they had been boiled. The market proper was row after row of low tables displaying secondhand goods, old clothing, and odds and ends. The crowd moved sluggishly, body to body, and I thought of Leicester Square tube station in the rush hour – after a bomb scare. The noise, the smell, the colour, mixed with that inevitable Kashgar dust. At one end were the building supplies: large wattle mats, in stacks, ready to make a new house.

Khazak horsemen were showing off their skill and beasts, racing back and forth on a provisional course next to the Tohman river. There were a few camels for sale, each surrounded by three or four prospective buyers. Sheep, donkeys and various birds, in cages or lying on the ground with bound feet, took up another corner. I found a *chai khana* and collapsed on the carpet, following the cheerful chaos from behind the safety of a tea bowl.

A Swedish film crew busily filmed a barber and his victim. Two tall, cool blondes wearing broad-brimmed silver fox hats (the kind that had been appearing on the Kashgar market since it was noticed that foreigners, unlike Uighurs, preferred precious furs over ordinary sheep) stood in the background chatting in soft Swedish. They had been in Kashgar already for a couple of weeks attempting to film a documentary about Sven Hedin, the maverick explorer and first westerner who seriously followed up the tales of buried cities in the desert. Rumour had it that the Swedes had already spent over $3,000 in bribes, and were still waiting for official permission to follow the route of Hedin's first Taklamakan Desert crossing. That famous journey almost ended in his death.

Hedin chose his thirtieth birthday, 17 February 1895, to depart from Kashgar and travel to Markit with the aim of mapping the south-western sector of the Taklamakan. He had planned to cross the perilous empty quarter, a dangerous zone made up of shifting sand dunes, located between the Yarkant and Khotan rivers.

He left Markit (these days, well known for its cluster of labour camps) with a caravan leader, three other men, eight camels, guard dogs and some livestock, and provisions for one month.

After fifteen days, Hedin noticed that their water supply was running low. The men, he discovered, had neglected to fill the water carriers at the last well. He made a fatal decision: instead of turning back, he ordered the caravan to press ahead. Disaster struck almost immediately. Two camels had to be abandoned. Soon after, they were caught in a sandstorm, exhausting them even further, and another camel had to be left behind. Then the men discovered that the guide had been stealing precious water rations. There was none left. In anger and out of desperation the men attempted to kill the guide; he was saved only by Hedin's intervention. 'God help us,' he wrote in his diary that day.

The next five days became a nightmare. To survive, they attempted to drink cockerel's blood and camel's urine – only to become violently ill. One of the men collapsed unconscious, another was close to exhaustion. Leaving those two behind, Hedin moved on with Islam Bei, the caravan leader, and another man, Karim. Then Islam Bei also dropped out, unable to go further. Along with Karim, Hedin pushed on. On the sixth day they reached the edge of the Khotan oasis and found the river-bed. It was dry. Mustering almost inhuman strength, Hedin crawled on hands and knees until he finally reached a pool of fresh water. He drank. Then he filled his boot and hurried back to the dying Karim. Islam Bei was also found and survived the ordeal. The others had succumbed to the desert.

Hedin was Stein's closest rival and very much like him. Short in stature, the bespectacled Swedish geographer wrote profusely, bringing tales of adventure and stories of buried treasures along the Silk Road to an appreciative European public. Like Stein, he was knighted, and awarded honours from numerous universities. Unlike Stein, he died in relative obscurity. During both world wars, Hedin sided with the German cause, a political move that eventually disgraced and discredited him. Stripped of his honours he died at the age of 87 in his native Stockholm.

I came back from the market exhausted, my head full of textures, smells and colours. I hadn't bought anything. I was nursing a cold beer at the Oasis when Alex, the Australian I had met the previous day, came in laden with fur hats.

'Those are protected animals.' I pointed at a snow leopard trim.

'Part of Uighur culture,' he replied.

'More likely part of tourist culture,' I said, and ordered a Kashi-burger.

I returned to the Qinibagh to pack. Kitagawa's luggage stood, looking suspiciously ready to go, on his bed. He isn't . . . he can't!

He did. When I got ready in the morning to trek to the long-distance bus terminal, he was there. In the bus he took the seat next to me, balancing on an air pillow. We didn't talk much.

At one point we saw about a hundred women beside the road, pulling weeds from the shoulder of the gravel highway.

'They are prisoners,' I pointed them out to him.

'I don't believe you,' he answered. I was sure they were.

We stopped for lunch in Yarkant, then drove through endless desert, passing the occasional village or truck stop. I was hoping to see the Pigeon Sanctuary, the 'My Lord of the Sand Stations', a holy place in the middle of the belt of drift sand near Khotan described in detail by Stein in *Ancient Khotan*, the report of his first Central Asian exploration published in 1907. The popular name of the shrine is Kaptar Mazar. I asked the man behind me if it still existed. He said it did, then rubbed his thumb and forefinger together in a gesture I know to mean 'much money'. The pigeons are said to be the offspring of a pair that metamorphosed from the heart of Imam Shakir Padshah, who was killed during a battle with Buddhists from Khotan.

But it was already too dark to see anything when we passed the spot.

EIGHT

Khotan, the Jade Kingdom

MONDAY NIGHT. There were no stars, just velvet darkness, as we pulled into the compound of Khotan's bus station. Stiff-limbed and tired, we clambered from the bus, untangled our luggage from beneath the rope netting on the roof, and stepped on to a broad, poplar-lined street ankle deep in fine sand. With a thankful thought to John-the-map-maker's foresight, I pulled my diary from my knapsack and led a placid Kitagawa towards the Number One Guest House. He demanded implicitly that I take responsibility for him. Passive aggression. I fell for it.

'Are you sure this is the right way?' he whined after we had walked along the empty street for fifteen minutes. Wordlessly, I handed him my diary and flashlight.

'We've just passed that turn-off, the guest house should be on the left . . . any moment now,' I said after a while.

A small sign reading CITS, China International Travel Service, pointed to a paved driveway almost hidden by lush vegetation. A gate led to a compound, a few one-storey buildings with a touch of pre-revolutionary flavour and a spot of shrubbery, thick with winter weeds, confined by a circle of poplars. Inside, the hotel was like any other. Glass double doors covered with delicate wire mesh led to an empty foyer illuminated by surgically cold neon lights. It smelled of fresh paint and detergent. A desk sat in an alcove. On the wall next to it was a bell and a sign in several languages: 'Ring for service'. I rang.

A gangly Chinese girl, white sweater, skin-tight black stretch trousers, shoulder-length hair and friendly eyes, emerged from a room round the corner, accompanied by the noise of television and the clinking of beer bottles. She signed us in, took our passports and a first night's deposit and handed us two keys. Moments later I fell on to a bed noticing almost in passing that the second one in the room was not occupied.

Waking at three o'clock in the afternoon the next day, I drank a cup of tepid jasmine tea, ate some leftover biscuits, raisins and some brown grapes, while watching '*Wo ai Victor* . . . I love Victor' on television, a summertime soap opera made for twelve-year-olds, with blond and blue-eyed boy and girl actors frolicking in an Austrian country village, dubbed into Chinese. My muscles and joints were feeling sore, and I had developed a cough. I fell asleep again, remembering that it was Hallowe'en.

I was woken once more on Wednesday morning, shaky and confused with lingering dream images, by a large Chinese girl unceremoniously dropping my clothing from the other bed on to the floor. Company. I took it as a cue to get up. After a long, hot shower, I changed into some fresh clothes, and ate breakfast in the noisy hotel canteen. Fed and in better spirits, I went to find Ahmet at the CITS office, a building set at right angles to the main hotel.

I knocked on the office door and entered. A youngish Uighur in dark suit and cloth cap sat behind a desk, busy with paperwork. His mouth smiled broadly, waiting for an introduction, although his dark eyes, I noticed, did not. Eyes are important. I don't like eyes that fail to smile along with the rest of the face. They make me uneasy. His followed me around the room, unblinking, like a hawk's; his mouth all the while grinning widely.

'Ahmet?' I asked.

'Yes?' he answered in English.

'I would like to know if it's possible to go east from Khotan,' I stated without prologue.

'The road is closed, it's a bad road,' he said cautiously.

'Well, but is it possible?' I insisted.

'There is a bus, there is a bus station, and they sell tickets . . . just buy one,' he smiled. His English was good, with a soft Uighur accent.

'Just like that?' I wondered about the contradiction.

'Just like that!'

He changed the subject. 'How long are you going to be in Khotan? There are many interesting tourist sites.'

'Like Rawak, Dandan Uiliq and Domoko.' I listed some of the more famous Buddhist ruins around Khotan, rediscovered and excavated by Stein over 80 years ago. Some of them, Rawak for example, 60 kilometres to the north of the oasis, ought still to have impressive remains, even some sculptures.

Ahmet looked up, surprised, and laughed. 'They are all closed to foreigners.' Then he added slyly, 'I could arrange a car . . .'

'How much?' I asked. It was always a question of money.

'Rawak? I can get you there for 3,000.'

'Renminbi?'

'No, FEC.'

'Too expensive.' I shook my head.

'Ah, but foreigners have money. I took some Germans there recently . . .'

A Chinese woman came into the office and replaced a folder in a filing cabinet. Ahmet stopped talking and winked at me con-spiratorially.

Though I hadn't planned on it, it was tempting just to pay the money and visit some of the outlying sites. In antiquity, the kingdom of Khotan had been the most important Buddhist centre on the southern Silk Road. Faxian, the Chinese travelling monk, who had left the capital Changan in AD 399 for India, spent three months in the Gomati monastery, one of the fourteen larger insti-tutions in Khotan at the time. He wrote that there were 10,000 monks in the kingdom, lavishly endowed by local rulers. Later, in 644, when Xuanzhang, the most famous of all Chinese itinerant monks, returned from his search for scriptures in the homeland of the Buddha, there were a hundred monasteries in Khotan, its inhabitants following both the Hinayana and Mahayana schools.

The woman left again. Ahmet rummaged for a moment in his desk drawer, brought out a dark green cylinder and handed it to me. I fondled the smooth surface of the heavy stone. One end was cut at an oblique angle, rough, and I thought it might be a drill sample.

'Jade,' he said, 'my father collects jade . . . Khotan is the oasis of jade.'

I handed it back to him, but he raised his hand and told me to keep it. 'Souvenir,' he said.

Jade was as precious as water to the oasis, and as intimately joined to its survival. In the Chinese histories, Khotan is known as Yutian, the Kingdom of Jade. Trade may have begun as early as the third millennium BC and certainly flourished during the second, contributing significantly to the wealth of the oasis. When Fu Hao, the consort of the Yin-Shang emperor of China, was buried at the close of the thirteenth century BC in Anyang, then the capital of the Shang dynasty (1765–1123 BC), in northern Honan province, 750 Khotan jade carvings were entombed with her. Not only Khotan, but all the oases located on the commercial routes must have benefited from this activity. Every year when the water subsided after the summer melt, the king of Khotan would ritually wade into the river to find the first crude jade rock, swept by the floods into the valleys. Now all the finds belong to the government.

Khotan jade is graded according to its colour, Ahmet explained to me, with white being the best and the most expensive. There is also yellow, green, dark green, red, purple and blue jade. But the supply had almost gone. There were some mines in the mountains, but the rivers rarely yielded finds any more.

'It's illegal to trade privately,' Ahmet said. It seemed to be an emotional subject with him. 'But sometimes the old men sell it in the market.'

Before I left I asked Ahmet about Yotkan, the site of the ancient capital. He said he could drive me for 500 renminbi. I said I'd rather walk. John had indicated it on the map as about eight kilometres west of the oasis.

I retraced my steps to the bus station. To my left were remnants of the old city wall, probably destroyed along with much of the old city centre after the Communists took over the province and started to plough broad, straight avenues through villages.

The ticket window at the station was closed, but an attendant told me that there would be a bus to Qiemo on Friday. Qiemo was halfway between Khotan and Ruoqiang, and Miran lay less than 80 kilometres north-east of Ruoqiang. I would come back the next morning.

There was one more piece of business I had to take care of. My visa was about to run out. The embassy in London had given me only one month in China, with the possibility of two extensions. I headed for the local Public Security Bureau, indicated by John on the map just around the corner from my hotel.

Khotan was a sandy, quiet sprawl of a town, its main roads broad and geometrically aligned: a few grey buildings, on a corner the entrance to a bar with a large, hand-painted sign showing the face of a blond woman with sunglasses and the word 'Bar' written in English across it. An old man selling large water melons had parked his donkey below the sign. There was a small market selling odds and ends and Chinese army parkas with fake fur linings. There were some pool tables. I noticed that the green felt cover on one of them had been replaced with arabesque-patterned cotton cloth.

The officer at the PSB couldn't help me. They were not authorized to deal with visas. I should try the army compound. A friendly uniformed man gave me elaborate directions, but I was already lost at the first crossroads. A man in a thick black coat and black-framed glasses came up to me, wanting to help. I could not understand him. A boy of maybe sixteen, pushing a bicycle, joined us. He spoke some English and Chinese and using a mixture of both languages I explained my problem.

Khotan people are friendly, as has often been pointed out by travellers. Faxian noticed a disposition for music, and Xuanzhang described the Khotanese as soft by nature, with a love for literature. Stein's entry over a millennium later appears to be almost a copy of Xuanzhang's: he ascribed 'a peculiar softness of temperament, good-natured ease in language and manners, and a disposition even more pronounced than in other parts of eastern Turkestan to make the most of what pleasures the humblest life can offer . . .' The people had not changed.

The young man's name was Rishat. He pointed to the luggage rack of his bike, and I got on, legs swinging to one side, as I had often seen local girls do. Rishat pedalled hard, and after a few minutes we entered the army compound. Without much fuss my visa was extended. Did I want to see the market? Rishat asked. I did.

The market, a few lanes of stalls, was not very busy. The main market day was on Sunday, as in Kashgar, when people came from the surrounding villages to trade. There were a few silk shops, displaying lengths of ikat cloth. As well as jade, Khotan was traditionally a centre for silk production, ever since a Chinese princess, so the legend goes, had smuggled silk worms and mulberry tree seeds into the oasis, carrying them hidden beneath her headdress. China had jealously protected its monopoly for millennia. Not until the time of Justinian, in the middle of the sixth century, was the secret of silk production first introduced to the Byzantine Empire, and from there to Europe.

Rishat and I wandered between the stalls, most of them boarded up. There was a busy produce section, and a few mothers sorted through a heap of 'Made in China' children's clothing, red woollens with appliqué designs of teddy bears and flowers, set off by characters. I noticed that the nan bread had a more elaborate floral design here, that the women were taller than in Kashgar and wore white flowing headscarves, and the men wore almost conical fur hats.

Xinjiang is a land of stories, fairy-tales and music. Mountains, rivers, ancient sites are all endowed with their own tales. Propagated by story-tellers or told at home, sung, and often accompanied by music, these stories have been passed down through generations. My guide pointed to an old man with a rough woven shirt below a gaping *chapan* and a white embroidered pillbox hat on his shaven head, squatting in a corner of the market. A group of children sat in a semicircle around him, and a few laughing adults stood within earshot. We edged closer. The children listened intently to his melodic sing-song.

'It's the story of the brave donkey,' Rishat told me, familiar with the tale.

A pretty girl with long braids and red cheeks plucked a *dutar*, a long-necked lute strung with silk. Everyone in Xinjiang seemed to be able to play the *dutar*, just as everyone sang and knew endless strings of songs. Legend tells that Khezr, who was a friend of

God, was the first to discover how to sing. He taught the water, and the water taught the people.

Rishat had to go and said goodbye in a sweet, shy way. I went back to the hotel, tired out. Tomorrow I would try to get a ticket to Qiemo, I told myself out loud as I fell on to my bed. The Chinese girl was not there.

Hunger drove me back out in the evening. I followed the glow of a few *kavabchi* lining the street. Four shadows hunched over a table, eating, periodically illuminated with red, blue, and green lights escaping from a first floor window of a disco across the road. They turned out to be Kitagawa and three other Japanese travellers, one of whom introduced himself as 'Xinjiang'.

'As a boy I had fantasies about the Silk Road, and read every book I could find about it,' he explained his peculiar nickname. Xinjiang was round, wore glasses and was friendly. I liked him. He planned to visit Yotkan the next day, and invited me to come along.

After a few heavily spiced kebabs, nan and a bottle of beer, I turned in for the night. The Chinese girl sat on the bed watching television. She seemed mesmerized by the flickering images, eating peanuts, mechanically dropping the empty shells on the floor. She barely seemed aware of my presence, or maybe she had decided that it was better not to talk to the *waiguoren*. I thought of the story-teller in the market, and wondered how long it would be until he was made obsolete by the box.

Was it really this easy? I queued in front of the ticket counter and when it was my turn I asked for a ticket to Qiemo. The Uighur girl stapled a few pieces of paper together, and asked for 28 renminbi. I handed her the money, she handed me the ticket. I thanked her and hurried from the station.

That day didn't seem to get off the ground. It was cold and oppressive. The air was dusty, and everyone coughed and spat. I didn't care. Despite the weather, a peculiar warmth resulting from the adrenalin pumping, in anticipation of my departure, had spread through my body. I could have screamed: 'Yes! It's going to work.'

I returned to the hotel for some breakfast and ran into Kitagawa and his new friends. They were discussing a sightseeing tour, and Xinjiang, friendly, fiddling with his glasses, asked me once more to come along. Our first stop was to be the museum.

It lay just a block down from the hotel, an old building under renovation which also served as a library. The archaeological collection was closed.

We walked next door to the jade factory, a series of small workshops and a flashy exhibition room with a glass counter displaying beautiful Chinese-style carvings, ridiculously overpriced for the tourist market. A Chinese girl offered tea and cookies and a man asked us if we wanted to see the production of the carvings. The workrooms lay just behind the exhibition area. Four or five craftsmen sat crammed next to each other grinding away at the jade with electric drills and saws. It sounded and looked like a dentist's surgery. Our tour was quickly brought to an end when it became clear that none of us was interested in buying. The man asked if we had been to the museum. I said it was closed. 'Ring the bell,' he said.

He was right. We rang a bell and the door was opened by an old curator with the face and belly of someone who enjoyed his drink and food. He apologized for the mess, but graciously led us into the exhibition rooms. The place was in disarray and the showcases covered with fine dust from the walls which were being stripped and re-painted. I walked from case to case, lifting dust-sheets, cursing the inadequate lighting. There were heads of Buddhas and Bodhisattvas, devis, some portraits of patrons and monsters, made of clay, many painted. Most of them probably came from Rawak, and were from the sixth and seventh centuries, but there were no labels. There were some bronze Tibetan religious implements and small sculptures, some fragments of wall paintings, and lots and lots of clay sherds from Yotkan. In one case there lay a strip of cloth, cotton with some indigo print with a chequerboard pattern to one side. It looked familiar, and I realized that the fragment belonged to another I had seen in the Urumqi museum. I called the curator and told him about the piece in Urumqi, a textile which, according to the label, was excavated from Niya, one of the desert sites on the southern road.

It was of the same cotton weave, but depicted a figure. Framed in a square in the lower left-hand corner was the torso of an 'indianized' figure of Tyche, the Greek personification of good fortune, holding a cornucopia. Nude, heavily bejewelled, her smiling comic-book face was surrounded by a halo. Next to it, framed in a separate register, were shallowly undulating leaf-garlands and birds, terminating in the mouth of a fantastic creature. The image synthesized two different artistic traditions, in which the Greek Tyche had taken on the voluptuousness of an Indian fertility goddess, reflecting the different artistic currents present in Xinjiang during the early days of Silk Road traffic. I guessed it to be from about the second century AD.

The curator smiled at my story, but didn't say anything.

It was almost noon and I suggested we move on to Yotkan, a site which most authorities considered the ancient capital of the Khotan kingdom from before the beginning of the millennium to the Muslim conquest of the oasis in the tenth century. The Japanese weren't sure for a moment; it was too late, it was too cold, and maybe we should hire a car after all, best postpone it till tomorrow. I said I was leaving tomorrow and started walking west. Xinjiang took one look over his shoulder, left his group and followed me. Kitagawa and the others stood for a moment in indecision, then fell back.

Just outside the city limits we flagged down a bus. After a few kilometres we got off near an inn, in a village made up of a few houses which hugged the main road. We asked for Yotkan. Some kids screamed, 'Yotkan bazaar, Yotkan bazaar,' and pointed to a lane disappearing between fields and trees.

Hiking through empty fields we caught up with two girls leading a donkey and cart which was heavily loaded with cobblestones, probably used to line irrigation channels.

'Yotkan?' we asked. The girls giggled and waved us to follow them. They were dressed in local Uighur fashion, with long braids hanging down under floral headscarves. Yotkan was their home. They didn't speak Chinese but smiled a lot. After an hour's walk below the cold sulphur sun, we arrived at a homestead, built high on a bank above a shallow depression traversed by a deep muddy channel, the Yotkan Yar. Mounds overgrown with grass rose from the field. Nothing pointed to an archaeological site.

The girls invited us into their home for some tea, introducing us to their many brothers and sisters, nine in all. There was a courtyard spanned with trellises for grapes, but they had all been harvested. Against the back wall leaned farming implements. The family lived in a typical Uighur farmhouse, fashioned of mud and wood with a carved veranda and painted eaves, the main room taken up by a long sleeping platform padded with colourful carpets.

The eldest daughter brought out a brick of pressed tea, broke some off and crumbled the lump into a teapot. She ceremoniously cleaned two bowls with a few drops of water, sprayed some on to the shiny, stamped mud floor and poured some tea. It tasted slightly salty.

They had guessed the purpose of our visit. A boy of maybe eight, with a dirty face and runny nose, brought out a little box and showed off some reddish clay sherds and coins. He gestured that we could buy them: five renminbi for the sherd, a moulded piece of terracotta, perhaps part of a pot, more for the coins. Where did they come from? I tried to ask him. He grinned and pulled on my hand. Xinjiang followed. We went back down to the Yar, and watched the child skid down the muddy bank. He looked around for a moment, then fished a sherd from the water. He threw it on to the bank. It was of the same red terracotta, shaped as a camel's head, and looked very much like the material I had seen in the British Museum, deposited there by Stein who had spent several days at Yotkan in 1901. Stein had also found gold flakes, worked jade, gems, and coins spanning a period of almost a millennium.

A year later I saw a series of similar clay objects in the National Museum, Helsinki, brought back by Baron Mannerheim, the adventurous military man who acted as commander-in-chief of the notorious White army during the Finnish civil war of 1918. Mannerheim had joined the Russian military as a young man, and at the time of Russian expansion towards Central Asia, was ordered to participate in an archaeological mission led by Paul Pelliot, with the aim of collecting military intelligence. Disguised as a scientist, Mannerheim in effect acted as a spy. Pelliot, who needed Russia's goodwill for easy access to the region, fully supported the young Baron's secret mission. George Macartney, the British representative in Kashgar, duly recorded the arrival of Pelliot's party there in January 1907 as 'including a Finn named Baron Mannerheim, who is to make an archaeological collection for the Helsingfors Museum'; he was obviously taken in.

Mannerheim's idiosyncratic taste was reflected in the eclectic collection he brought back to Helsinki; most of the clay pieces had explicit sexual overtones, and included a large number of copulating monkeys.

The sun was getting low. It was time to leave. The two girls who had led us to their home took us some way down the path, then stood and waved until we disappeared around a bend. Just before sunset we came upon a farmhouse. I had not remembered the way as being so long. Some people loading melons on to a tractor agreed to give us a lift, and we tuck-tucked back to the hamlet where the bus had dropped us off, balancing above the large tractor wheels. From there we hitched a ride with a truck, back to Khotan. Xinjiang climbed in the back, while I squeezed between two Chinese men in the cab.

'How old are you?' asked one of them.

'*Er shi* . . . twenty,' I said, mistakenly. I tend to mix up the numbers twenty and thirty in Chinese.

The driver grabbed my leg. 'They make them big where you come from,' he chuckled.

The Chinese girl had packed and gone. I sorted out my gear and packed myself. Tomorrow, with some luck, I would be on my way to Miran.

NINE

Two Uighur Fairy-tales

A LONG TIME AGO, in the woods at the edge of the oasis lived a man, whose name was Däna, and his beautiful wife, who was called Güli Räna. Däna cut and collected firewood for a living, and Güli Räna kept house. She also possessed great magic.

One day, around the time of the midday meal, a Baj (rich man) drove by the house. He had been hunting in the foothills of the Tekilik mountain, where his arrow had pierced the hearts of several quails. Now he was hungry. Pointing at Güli Räna's door, he ordered his servant to go to her house and cook one of the quails. The servant, a young man, entered the house and saw Güli Räna standing by the fireplace. Her exceptional beauty made him swoon. Bewildered, he sat down to talk with her, forgetting all about the bird, which he had placed on a spit over the open fire. Not until black smoke filled the room did he remember the bird, which by now had burnt to charcoal. Fearing his master's wrath, he started to cry. Güli Räna was astonished and asked him why he was crying.

'I will be punished if I return without the meal,' the young man sighed.

Güli Räna felt pity for him, reflected for a moment, then told him not to worry. Swiftly, she kneaded some noodle dough and moulded it into the shape of two birds, with tail feathers and eyes, expertly sculpting every detail. Then she moved her lips and whispered a magic formula. Miraculously, the birds came alive. They were much bigger and fatter than the one the young man had brought. Güli Räna prepared a delicious meal from one of them and sent the young man on his way.

The Baj tasted the food and asked how he had cooked the bird; never had he had such good quail. The servant did not answer. But the Baj insisted and finally the young man told the whole story.

The Baj became angry, and began to have evil thoughts about Güli Räna. He sent his servant to fetch Däna, and spoke to him: 'You have a quail, and so do I. We shall let them fight each other. If you win I give you my quail, and some gold. If I win, you give me your quail and your wife.'

To refuse the powerful Baj was impossible. Däna returned home and fretted over the situation with Güli Räna. She pondered for a moment, then said to Däna:

'Go to my father's house. We have three quails, bring them to me.'

Däna complied and hurried away. Even though Güli Räna's father lived at a distance of four *potaj* (about sixteen kilometres), he went at an incredible speed, and soon returned with the birds. But he was doubtful.

'Look at those skinny birds, how can they win against the Baj's?'

'Be quiet,' Güli Räna said calmly, 'and take them.'

Däna took one of the birds and, wearily, went to the Baj. The Baj laughed when he saw the scrawny bird, and in good spirits presented his own fat bird. But as soon as the fight started, Däna's bird jumped on the fat one, who was too sluggish to move, pecked, one-two-three, and killed it.

The Baj ground his teeth in anger. Däna, surprised but victorious, asked the Baj to pay up.

'Baj-Khan, where is the gold and silver?' he laughed. But the Baj angrily shooed him away with threats. Dana went back home to his normal life, working in the woods and making love to Güli Räna.

But the Baj was seething. He could not forget the humiliation. He called together his servants, soldiers and companions and set out to kidnap Güli Räna. Däna, who was working on a hill near the house, saw them approach from a distance, and ran home to warn his wife. Again Güli Räna was calm. She told Däna to climb on to the roof of their house, fetched a chest her father had given her as a wedding present and joined him there.

The Baj drove at the head of his troop, firing the horse with loud calls of '*posh, posh*'. He arrived at the homestead, ready to fight Däna, looked up and for the first time glimpsed Güli Räna. 'How beautiful she is,' he thought, and at that moment he fell hopelessly in love with her. Now more than before, he wanted to steal her away. He ordered a ladder to be put against the roof. Just when he got ready to climb it, his troop behind him at attention, Güli Räna pulled out the first drawer from the chest. Suddenly, from the depth of the Taklamakan a wild storm rose, sand filled the air, and the temperature dropped to an icy cold, like winter. The water in the canals and irrigation ditches turned to ice. The Baj and his troops also began to ice up, white frost stiffening their hair and beards.

Güli laughed and screamed from the roof: 'Baj, will you ever rob again?'

Full of fear, the Baj, who could barely move his frozen mouth, whispered a desperate promise: 'Never again!'

But Güli Räna only laughed, pretending not to have heard.

'Well, then, we'll just have to behead you,' she said, and pulled the third drawer from the chest, and out of thin air, men appeared. They were carrying battle-axes, and without hesitation, they beheaded the Baj and his whole troop.

For the people of Khotan, a better life started.

A long time ago a man went with his donkey in the direction of the southern mountains to collect firewood. When he arrived at a spot where there was much wood, he took his skin filled with *qatyk* (a drink of soured milk) and the rope he would use later to tie up the firewood, dug a shallow hole, and covered them with earth and leaves. Then he went off, leaving his donkey to graze.

Along came a tiger. It crept up to the donkey and spoke to it.

'Hey, donkey,' the tiger growled, 'what are you doing here all alone? Are you not afraid?'

The donkey, trying not to show his fear, replied: 'Why should I be afraid? I'm not here to fear.'

The tiger glanced slyly at the donkey and said: 'If you are not afraid, we shall have a fight.'

'Agreed,' said the donkey, 'but let's first measure our strength in a competition.'

This suited the tiger, who liked to show off. Walking to a thick poplar, the tiger shook the tree and, with a swipe of the paw, felled it.

'Now it's your turn,' he said to the donkey.

The donkey was desperate, knowing he could not match the tiger in strength. Head held high as though he had not a worry in the world, he strode over to the spot where his master had buried the rope and the skin filled with *qatyk,* scraped the earth with his hoof and dug up the rope.

The tiger in turn threw a large boulder.

'Watch me,' said the donkey, and jumped on to the *qatyk* skin. White liquid shot from the ground.

Then the donkey cried out boldly: 'With one hit I ruptured the intestines of the earth, and shattered its marrow . . . What in comparison did you do?' And with the bravest, loudest 'Iahh' he could muster, the donkey stamped about some more.

The tiger became afraid. 'Anyone who could spill the guts of the earth can also kill me,' he thought. He bolted in fear..

In the midst of his escape, he almost collided with a fox.

'Hey tiger, friend, why are you running away? Stop!' the fox cried out.

'No, my friend, and if you value your life, you must run too. There is a donkey over there, who wanted to kill me, and I escaped at the last moment.'

'A donkey?' said the fox, astonished. 'Ha, I will work him over, he'll be afraid of me. I tell you what, let's go back together.'

'No, I'm afraid,' said the tiger. He was still shaking. 'And anyway, as you are a tricky fox, I can't trust you.'

'You can trust me,' said the fox, 'but if you are really so afraid, we can tie our tails together.'

The tiger agreed. The two tied their tails together and, side by side, went back to the clearing where the donkey was.

The donkey saw them approaching. Afraid for his life, he screamed an earth-shattering 'Iahh.'

This panicked the tiger. 'Now you see, he wants to kill us,' he screamed to the fox, and he turned and ran, dragging the fox behind him. They were still tied together by their tails. The fox's head shattered on a boulder, but the tiger did not notice. He kept running. After some distance, catching his breath, he turned around and saw the fox's mouth pulled into a ghastly grimace, like an enormous grinning mask.

'Ha,' said the tiger, 'how can you laugh at a time when I'm so afraid my heart almost stopped?'

Again, he dragged along the dead fox, then he threw him on to some stones and pulled his tail out.

That was the end of the fox.

TEN

Forbidden Road

WHEN I ARRIVED AT THE BUS STATION, I found the bay for the Qiemo departure deserted and for a split second the fear that I could have missed my bus hit my stomach. Then I caught myself, confident that I had come early enough, no matter which time they were using.

There were only going to be five of us; myself, the driver, his child-apprentice and the young couple warming each other in a dark corner. I half-expected Kitagawa to join us and, abandoning any hope of hiding in a crowd, I wrapped my shawl tightly around my head and climbed into the bus. But he didn't appear. Our paths had crossed before dawn on the way to the bathhouse, where he snubbed me with a jerk of his head. As I sat waiting I was experiencing a bad case of second thoughts, accompanied by paralysing panic. Mentally reprimanding myself for feeling a coward, I breathed deeply, but felt no better for it.

With a few rough words to the little girl crouching next to him, the driver ground the transmission into gear. Khotan was still asleep. The two fingers of headlights felt their way through silent streets, lighting up shapes and buildings for fractions of a moment. As it had been in most towns, the electricity was turned off for the night. I had dressed by the flicker of the thin, foul-smelling paraffin candles I had bought in Kuqa for this purpose. The kind that gave you cancer if you lit a cigarette from them.

Paved road ceased shortly after we passed the first eastern bridge, and the surface deteriorated instantly. Perhaps Ahmet had spoken the truth when he claimed that the only reason the southern road wasn't open to tourists was the dismal state it was in. By sunrise we were travelling along a gravel trail with the consistency of a washboard. Accompanied by ear-splitting noise, very much like children's bicycles with playing cards stuck between the spokes, every single component of the bus vibrated with agonizing intensity, forcing my teeth into an involuntary chatter. I had the image of a vital organ rupturing, and felt like screaming. The others, wiser to the conditions, had packed thick layers of padded coats under their behinds. Relief came only occasionally, when we slowed for a sand dune which, overnight, had obliterated the road.

In the early afternoon we reached the small oasis of Keriya. As we pulled into the characteristic compound at the edge of town, the bus driver announced that we would be staying until the next morning. There weren't enough passengers for the journey to Qiemo, he complained, and he would go around drumming up more business here. My guess was that he sold tickets privately, lining his own pocket a bit. Who could blame him? As a government employee, he probably didn't make more then 100 yuan a month, and with the steady price rises, that was no longer enough to feed a family.

Feeling paranoid, I walked into the village, which was laid out in a precise grid of shady roads, strikingly clean and tidy. One-storey brick buildings were neatly arranged next to one another, set back to leave room for sandy sidewalks. A white monolith praising the revolution rose in the centre of a crossroads. Too neat. There were the grey loudspeakers again, perched high in clusters of four on poles spaced closely together. Mercifully, they were silent.

I entered a restaurant, identifiable as such by the skinned carcass of a sheep suspended from a lintel over the gate. It was frozen solid. Hiding in a dark corner, I called out for an order of noodles and tea. An older woman who had eyed me suspiciously when I stepped through the door let out a cackling laugh when I pulled off my cap and shoulder-length blond hair spilled out from underneath. She hurried over with a shallow bowl and a tin kettle, addressing me in gun-fire rapid Uighur, which I failed to understand. I could only reply with a smile, and felt secretly pleased that she had thought I was a man. At least my disguise worked.

The tea was good and fragrant, spiced with cardamom. The short, fat noodles were unlike the spaghetti-long pasta common on the northern road. She made them with little snaps of her thumb, shooting bits of dough into the boiling water.

While refilling my plate, the lady leaned over and stroked my cheek. Her hand felt cool and left a lonely pang in my heart. I paid up, went back to the caravanserai and crawled between heavy covers, hoping to cure my cold and the rising blues. There was a residual hum from the road in my body.

The Chinese call it Yutian, the ancient name for Khotan, even though Keriya is not an old settlement. It was founded in the late nineteenth century to serve as the headquarters for the Khotan ambanship under Chinese administration. The allusion to history was probably intended to provide political legitimacy. These days it is infamous as the site of the Yutian Labour Reform Disciplinary Production Detachment 15–06 with over 10,000 inmates. In China 87 per cent of prisons are of this type – slave labour camps.

We reached the oasis of Niya, the Chinese Minfeng, around noon the following day. It did not seem much bigger then Keriya, though the streets looked more alive. Tall women with long blue skirts and flowing white headscarves hurried down the road together, carrying roughly woven baskets of vegetables; the men's fur hats were cut-off cones, instead of the flat, wide-brimmed *tumak* I had seen along the western edge of the Taklamakan.

I was still existing in a cloud of sensitized nerves, expecting to be picked up at any moment by the authorities, though the acute panic had gone. I figured that I had to pass a magic point somewhere along the road, from which I would be sent east rather than back the way I had come. Still, the horror stories about electric cattle prods and vicious policemen, which had circulated in the Qinibagh, kept surfacing.

The driver had announced a two-hour rest-stop. Gülli and Aberchan, the couple from Khotan, invited me to come along to the bazaar for some food. They placed me between them, shielding me with their bodies as though they were aware of my illegal presence in this village. We ducked into a little restaurant serving coarse food and salty tea.

Sparkly-eyed Gül, with her broad face and broad hips, and big Aberchan were in love. They had been mooning over each other since I first met them. She shook her long braids, and told me they had just got married. They were modern newlyweds, she said, *xiandaide*, stressing the 'modern', and tweaked Aberchan's arm, making him grunt in agreement.

'What do you mean by modern?' I asked.

Instead of having their union arranged for them by their families, they had chosen each other and married in a small circle of friends. She seemed at once proud of their behaviour, and at the same time somewhat ambivalent. Tomorrow she would meet her husband's parents for the first time and she hoped they would be kind. It scared her, she admitted, laughing behind an up-held hand. From the money they saved by not having the traditional ceremony and feast, they had bought lots of presents. Her family, from a village south of Khotan, had already given their blessing.

'Do you have a husband?' she wanted to know.

'No.'

'How old are you?' she gasped in a surprised voice.

'Thirty.'

She looked shocked, and squeezed my arm pityingly. I assured her that I was single by choice, and that I did not lack suitors.

I asked what they did for a living.

Her work unit was attached to the carpet factory, and Aberchan had recently found a job with a Han Chinese who had started a private enterprise and made lots of money. I couldn't quite find out what kind of enterprise, but it was clear that the money was good. To underline the last statement, Gül showed off her new velvet jacket, maroon with a fur border and pewter buttons. It was a bit tight across her breasts. Accompanied by Gülli's appreciative laughter, Aberchan imitated the Chinese drawn-out vocals, a mocking 'Look at her!'

'I'm lucky,' he said, 'I found a good job.'

In demonstration of his fortune, he called out to a young boy hanging around the inn for just this purpose, to go to a store and buy a few beers. The boy eagerly snatched up the ten-renminbi note and brought back three large bottles of *Xinjiang Pijiu*. He beamed as Aberchan told him to keep the change.

A feeling of wellbeing spread through my body. Here I was, at the western edge of the kingdom of Shanshan; at least so it became after the death of Xian, the dreaded king of Yarkant, in AD 61 when Khotan and Shanshan agreed to share power on the southern route. At its apogee, during the first few centuries of the Christian era, Shanshan reached along the caravan route from the Lopnur all the way west to the borders of Khotan somewhere around the Keriya river. Within several generations it grew from a semi-nomadic society to a highly organized authoritarian monarchy with a frightening bureaucratic system. Niya, or the ancient Niña, was the capital of one of the five *rayas* or provinces of the kingdom. The king of Khotan placed the guards of his eastern frontier near here.

There is a ruined city some 60 kilometres north of where I was sitting, and I longed to attempt to reach it: Cadota, another rich province of the kingdom, where Stein had excavated a large number of documents written in a local version of the Gandhari Prakrit language and in Kharosthi script. The documents are mainly of a bureaucratic nature, business transactions, court judgements, even a divorce agreement, and date from around the third century. Stein had called the site Niya, after the modern oasis nearest to it.

I felt a sneeze coming on and pulled my handkerchief out of a pocket, turned my head and honked into it. Gül blanched.

'No, don't do this, it's very bad . . . *bu hao*,' she scolded me, waving her finger in emphasis.

I was perplexed; obviously I had socially disgraced myself. It was apparently considered the height of bad manners to use your hanky in company. Apologetically I stuck the offending cloth back into my pocket, watching the slurping figure of a fellow traveller nonchalantly spitting inedible bits of food on to the floor.

We walked back to the bus. A large crowd had gathered around it, and it looked as though it was going to be a tight squeeze. The driver glowed with satisfaction.

After Niya the landscape turned more and more desolate. The Southern Mountains loomed on the right; somehow there was no comfort in them. The thermometer hovered a few degrees below zero. Whenever we were surrounded by a particularly large tract of sand or high dune, the whole bus went silent and we all stared, hypnotized. The desert gaze.

Around five we reached Ändirlänggär. My throat tightened and I swallowed violently a few times, choking back those tears which had sat too loose anyway all day. I had never before seen a town at the brink of death. There were a few mud-brick houses of the same colour as the sand licking at them, and a skeleton of a tree in the centre. Children watched us drive by with open mouths and big eyes.

An hour later we stopped for the night at what must have been the easternmost perimeter of the once prosperous oasis. Twisted dead poplars, fruit trees and tamarisk cones bobbed among dunes like the debris from a disastrous shipwreck. There was no irrigation project – maybe there was simply no water. The occasional inhabited hamlet struck the eye in amazement. North from here, another of Shanshan's illustrious *rayas* called Saca, Stein's Endere site, lies swallowed by the sand.

Shudang is what they call this large square enclosed by a ten-foot-high wall. A kitchen, a few rooms and quarters for the family who run this government stop abutted on two sides. A rusty water tank lodged in the back.

I turned to it and ladled some of the precious liquid into an enamel bowl, attempting to remove a layer of dirt from my skin. A small boy with a pretty, dimpled face and a slit in the seat of his trousers (isn't that dreadfully cold?) watched me intently as I brushed my teeth, excavated his nose with a dirty finger as I brushed my hair, and pointed in astonishment as I used a second toothbrush to remove the black rim from under my fingernails.

Pitiful screams from a goat had filled the air for the last few minutes, then stopped. I noted it abstractly, still smiling at the boy. Then suddenly, I smelled the sweet odour of fresh blood and heard a low hiss of escaping air and quickly turned around. The poor beast lay almost at my feet, its head all but severed, the body writhing with the last tremors of life. Blood was spurting from the gash in the neck and was sucked up by the sand. I watched with dismay as a crimson rivulet snaked towards my boots. Hearty laughter from the people crowding round released me – they found me hilarious. The act had obviously been dramatized for my benefit, and I had fallen for it.

It is strange, but to this day I can't remember the face of the butcher, whereas that of the goat, its scared eyes popping out of their sockets, is permanently imprinted on my memory. The laughing Gül put an arm around me and pulled me away.

'*Chi fan*,' she hooted, '. . . dinner.'

What a place, where you're introduced to your dinner before you eat it, I thought.

I shared a soot-blackened, perfectly square room with eight other women and four children. There were only seven beds, lined up against three walls, and one next to the door. The men brought a large shallow iron bowl filled with live embers which they placed on the floor in the centre of the room. We squatted around trying to keep warm. No one was comfortable.

To pass time I showed around illustrations of paintings from Miran. The beauties represented in the lunettes of the garlands received special comment. The girl with the guitar was deemed a perfect Uighur beauty, though she was painted long before the Uighurs settled in Xinjiang. But then few of the women in this room looked Uighur, and several could easily have taken their place among the maidens from Miran.

The hum of the generator stopped, the lights flickered and went off. By the glow of the embers we bade each other goodnight, squeezing close to one another for warmth and comfort and out of necessity. A baby whimpered; its mother sang to it in a low voice until it fell asleep again.

ELEVEN

Qiemo

THE MAJORITY OF THE PASSENGERS departed before we reached the centre of Qiemo; each stop was requested by loud shouts and the women's high-pitched 'Oiy'. Gül and Aberchan were among the first, alighting as the oasis came into view. Qarqan, it was called in Uighur. Aberchan's parents occupied a small plot of land on its western periphery, he had told me, which they had farmed privately for some years now. Wealthy peasants, he called them proudly. I stepped off the bus with them to say goodbye, noticing their momentary perplexity and perhaps a twinge of fear that I might want to come along. I shook their hands, and hugged Gül, wishing her good luck.

By the time we pulled up to the bus stop there were only myself, a middle-aged Chinese engineer, from whom I had kept my distance, and Sachang, a big, friendly lout in uniform who I think was a policeman. The two had told me that they were on the way to Ruoqiang to attend a meeting celebrating Han–Uighur unity. Feeling obvious and exposed in the noon light, I followed them into the government inn, and after much show of various IDs, letters and papers, was assigned a room. The next bus to leave due east was in two days, a skinny attendant informed me.

The entry in the *Han Shu* about Qiemo indicated that the oasis had kept the same name, its Chinese name that is, for a good 2,000 years. 'To the north it adjoins Weili, and to the south one reaches Xiao Yuan after some three days' journey. There are grapes and various types of fruit.' Weili, I gathered, must have been somewhere to the south of Korla, and Xiao Yuan, the little

Yuan, was incorporated into Shanshan during the great expansionist era in the first century AD; it was last cited in literature in the third century, and then just disappeared. 'To the west there is communication with Jingjue', it went on. That is the ancient Chinese designation for Cadota, the desert site north of Niya.

Stein had only found some pottery sherds strewn over a wide area in Qiemo; a few foundations but not a major site. This has always surprised me. As another important *raya* of the kingdom it was called Calmadana, and there must have once been a substantial city. It was to Calmadana that the monarch retreated during the dissolution of Shanshan in the fifth century, shortly before he capitulated and moved his subjects away from the volatile road to the safety of the north and regrouped in the vicinity of Hami. I recalled that the director in Urumqi had said that they had sent an expedition to Qiemo this summer, and I wondered what, if anything, they had discovered.

The door to my room was opened noisily, and two young men stared at me. I stuck my tongue out, got off the bed and slammed it shut again. Adolescent sniggers answered me. A kingdom for a room with a key, I grumbled to myself, cursing the splitting headache which was becoming difficult to ignore. I put my trousers back on and went down the hall to buy a bus ticket for my next destination, Ruoqiang. With the piece of paper safely in my pocket, I felt more confident and consciously put a bit of swing into my depressed shuffle. Imagine yourself several centimetres taller, my mother used to say, it'll make you walk straight. I tried to think even taller than my not exactly short one metre seventy-four, and walked into town.

A geometric network of streets was arranged around the main road, which turned abruptly south in the middle of town. There was a small airstrip on the western perimeter, where the Uighur farms also lay. Like most of the small oases I had visited, the traditional town centre had been replaced by zealous socialist architecture. Bland municipal buildings dominated; there was a hospital identifiable by the large red cross painted above the entrance and some relics from the early part of this century. A yellow brick building had an unmistakable school flavour and could just as easily have stood in a Pittsburgh suburb. Next to it was a sports field.

The thumping behind my eyes reminded me painfully of the empty aspirin bottle in my medical kit, and made me slump again. I entered the hospital in search of a remedy, bringing my problem before a small window with bars, situated opposite the entrance. A hand pushed a small slip through the opening, accompanied by a crisp '*ba mao qian . . . eight mao*', about one penny. That was for the piece of paper. I wrote my name at the top and returned it together with a few tiny bills. Monopoly money. A minute later a small woman in nurse's whites and a helmet of tightly permed curls came out of the door next to the window and disappeared through another. I waited, engulfed by institutional green walls, lots of dark brown doors, and the peculiar institutional smell I had already encountered at the academy in Urumqi, here with faint antiseptic overtones. I seemed to be the only patient. After some more minutes a third door opened and a young Chinese doctor in a too large white coat greeted me with a smattering of very polite English.

'Welcome to our hospital. Please come in.' I followed him into a sparsely decorated examination room, dominated by a modern-looking gynaecological chair.

'I would like some aspirin, please.'

'Headache?' he asked while taking out a blood pressure sleeve.

'Yes, some aspirin will do.'

'Can I do something for your cough?'

'No, just the aspirin.'

'Do you have a prescription slip?'

'No.'

'You must purchase one,' he informed me, taking my pulse.

I returned to the small window, purchased the prescription slip and took it back to the doctor. He wrote on it, handed it back to me, and called something out to the girl behind the window, who emerged once more from her door, entered another and opened yet another window with bars. I handed the slip back to her through the bars. She then stamped it and, while returning it to me, demanded '*Yi kuai wu mao qian . . . one yuan and a half*', and pointed again to the doctor's office. There the young man took the slip, signed it and handed me a small paper packet which contained five earnest-looking white tablets. My aspirin. A comment about bureaucracy on the tip of my tongue, I decided to leave as quickly as possible and without saying much of anything.

The procedure had taken a good forty minutes. My headache had eased up, probably stunned into submission. I wondered what they did in an emergency.

A few tables displaying apples were set up at the crossroads. I bought some, sorely missing the cornucopia of fruit and vegetables which had been available anywhere throughout October, and went looking for something to take care of the small signals of hunger. Since the cold weather had started I found that I lost energy quickly and needed a steady flow of carbohydrates to keep me going.

Next to the inn was a small restaurant selling freshly made *samsa*, little dough pockets filled with minced mutton. A tall, slim woman who with her long white headscarf had the air of a nun, presided over a set of cauldrons and a smoke-belching oven. She smiled at me out of large grey eyes, and beckoned me into the dark room filled with a few crude wooden benches and tables.

While serving half a dozen of the dumplings, she noticed me looking with interest at her copper bracelet. Much to my embarrassment she took it off and quickly laid it before me on the table, waving her hands vehemently at my attempt to return it. It had star-shaped flowers stencilled into a flat band with a pearl-pattern border. Native to Central Asia, these patterns are found in hundreds of paintings over hundreds of years, yet it was the first time that I had observed it in contemporary society. I thanked her profusely, touched again by her striking appearance, paid, and went north towards the bazaar. There I walked about listlessly, while my thoughts drifted impatiently ahead to Ruoqiang and Miran.

There wasn't much of a market. A few mobile stalls perched along the edge of the desert, stocked with more wrinkled apples. I bought a small hat of the peculiar type worn by the women between Niya and Qiemo: a little doll's hat of no more than eight centimetres in diameter at the opening, constructed of four triangles of goat skin, faced with black wool and a small silk top. Traditionally they are pinned somewhat rakishly to one side of the head on to the white scarves prevalent here, and are apparently unique to this area of the southern Silk Road.

I noticed that I had acquired a small following. Some children had been watching me noisily from a safe distance, and when I turned around abruptly they scattered with delighted shrieks. As they edged closer again I asked if there was a beauty salon or hairdresser in Qiemo. 'Why not?' I muttered to myself. At the inn the bath facilities consisted of two tall barrels full of water topped with a thick layer of ice, and I could not bring myself to pour some of it over my head. A small girl with a crudely shaven head and a pink dress, her matching pink sister in tow, bravely took my hand and, followed by the others, started to pull me down the road. I felt like the Pied Piper by the time we arrived at the small hole-in-the-wall shop, run by a young woman of obviously Han Chinese origin.

I entered, leaving a cluster of onlookers crowding in front of the door. Faded posters advertising perms decorated the wall; there were a couple of shelves with hair creams, combs and brushes and a hair dryer of the retro variety, one of those huge silver bomber kinds. The girl seemed to enjoy the attention and almost manhandled me into a stiff wooden chair in front of a near-blind mirror, and began to play with my hair.

'Cut,' she smiled, brandishing large rusty scissors.

'No, wash,' I demanded.

'*Jian fa* . . . cut,' she argued back, with all the force of the liberated Chinese woman.

'Wash only . . . *xi tou*, *xi tou*,' I replied anxiously, glancing at those scissors.

I finally managed to communicate to her that all I wanted was a wash and dry, much to her visible disappointment. Pouting, she poured boiling water from a large aluminium kettle into a plastic contraption on the wall, mixing it with some cold. A rubber tube extended from the bottom of the makeshift water tank. The whole thing ominously resembled an enema. Exclaiming dismay over the brown brew which came out of my hair, she soaped it up with a gooey gel that smelled like the stuff my grandmother used to clean her floors. Finally convinced of the cleanness of my hair, she gave a deep 'hao', and rubbed me with a stiff grey towel. There wasn't any electricity to work the dryer. Any moment now, I thought, the audience was going to applaud. When I finally escaped and walked back to the hotel I noticed that the itch of my scalp had intensified.

I had long suspected, but finally admitted to myself, that there was a certain species of Chinese woman that scared me. She usually worked as a bus-ticket girl, as a watchdog and key-keeper of hotel rooms, and, I concluded, as a hairdresser. The revolution seemed to have liberated her into utter confidence devoid of the slightest hint of compassion.

It was evening when I returned to my room. The engineer and Sachang called me to have dinner with them in the kitchen of the restaurant attached to the hotel. It was a warm, crammed space full of pots and pans, over-sized woks and a big smiling cook, who apparently knew Sachang.

A fight between the cashier and a customer started in the dining-room, apparently over the correctness of the bill. There were noisy shouts and the sound of crockery smashing on the floor. The fight spilled over into the kitchen as the vehement girl was pushed through the double swinging doors. The cook grabbed a large knife, firing insults at both of them. The engineer and Sachang continued to slurp their noodles, didn't look up from their plates, didn't comment or interfere. I followed their example.

Next morning I woke early, and stuffing some apples into my day-pack set out to explore the area north of the oasis. At the bazaar, the day before, I had asked for *mingoi*, hoping to find out something about an archaeological site, but got only a vague sort of sweep in a northern direction.

Walking felt good. I went at a high speed, flexing my muscles and drawing oxygen deeply into my lungs. I wanted to walk off the stiffness, the stone in my stomach, the dust of the bus ride.

I passed a succession of small settlements, quaint mud-brick houses lining the sandy road, half-hidden between supple poplars.

The river lay to my right, no more then a tired trickle in an oversized bed. Children stared from shy eyes and features so strikingly Caucasian they could have played in any European playground without attracting much attention. Soon the strip of green along the road diminished and sand dunes started to close in on both sides.

I must have wandered about ten kilometres away from Qiemo bazaar, when I came upon a group of men loading sacks on to a tractor blocking the road. I slowed, grinned a greeting into their suspicious faces and attempted to pass.

'Hey, you can't go this way, what are you doing?' screamed a stout Han Chinese in work clothes. He was obviously the leader of the squadron.

'Just taking a walk,' I informed him politely.

'Go back, you can't go this way,' he shouted and grabbed my arm.

With a strong reflex I yanked my arm back. 'Okay, okay . . . calm down,' I retorted obligingly, and with no desire or reason to step on anybody's toes, I turned and left in the direction I came from.

But why the hostility? For a long time after, the incident bothered me. I couldn't find a plausible explanation for the man's abrupt behaviour. Much later I learned that the No. 2 Industrial Division of the Xinjiang Production and Construction Military Corporation, a labour reform camp with over 10,000 prisoners, had its base in Qiemo. I wondered if I had come too near its location.

I was still pondering the mishap, slowly walking back towards Qiemo, when a rider on a camel with a second one in tow appeared on the road. People here have the habit of simply materializing out of the desert, leaving one wondering what may be hidden there. I stood aside, marvelling at the clumsy stride of the beasts. They were of the two-humped Bactrian kind, a breed which, I had read somewhere, was diminishing. The rider pulled his fur-lined cap out of his eyes and flashed me a large set of teeth.

'Want a ride?' he smiled.

Getting on a camel is an experience deeply dependent on the principles of physics and gravity. The animal gets down on its knees, the rider climbs into the saddle. That's the easy part. Then suddenly the rear end shoots upward, propelling the unsuspecting forward. The same is instantly repeated in the opposite direction, when the front comes up. I managed to stay on top. Just. I've never very much liked camels. They are vicious and unpredictable, and they have a habit of turning their heads back to bite you. But moving through the desert on one is like riding through the streets of London on the upper deck of a bus. All the way in front.

We neared the outskirts of town, when a jeep came towards us fast, stirring up lots of dust. They were looking for me, and had orders to take me back to the hotel without delay. I thanked my guide and jumped off my boat, feeling wobbly for a moment on the solid ground.

I was lying on my bed twiddling mental thumbs when, without prior warning, the door opened and three policemen came in, one after the other, and crowded the room. I had been expecting them. A minute later a fourth person entered, introducing herself as Officer Zhang. A pretty, stern face framed by short glossy hair. She couldn't have been much older than myself. Inspecting my passport, which one of the men had handed to her, Officer Zhang addressed me in English.

'This is a closed area, you have no permit.'

'I know, and I don't want to be here,' I answered, giving her a premeditated excuse. 'I'm on my way to Korla, and this was the only bus there was in Khotan.' My answer seemed to perplex her.

'Ticket,' she demanded efficiently.

Reluctantly, I pulled the thin piece of paper from my pocket. She grabbed it and waved for me to follow her. With much authority she called the proprietor of the inn, who also doubled as ticket officer, and watched me as I purchased a new ticket. Korla, it read now. Politely, but forcefully, she instructed me that I was now under house arrest and was not to leave my room until the bus arrived.

I was already asleep when the door opened and a huge Uighur woman, groaning under the weight of various bags and parcels, entered the room and with much noise occupied the other bed. A strong smell of sweat and mutton stuck to her. I lit a candle and watched her as she ripped a small rectangle from a piece of newspaper and filled it with tobacco. Exposing brown gold-framed teeth, she handed me her paraphernalia. I accepted and twisted a cigarette. Puffing away for a while, we exchanged a few smiles, and finally settled for what was left of the night.

Later I learned that I had missed the archaeological site by only a few kilometres. It lay east of the bazaar, not north as I had assumed. It had been discovered by local farmers earlier that year while extracting salt from a deposit. A series of burials were found there, complete with the pickled corpses of men and women. I saw a photograph of two of the mummies. The archaeologists had seated the couple on chairs, reinforcing their eerie reality. They were obviously Caucasian, with long brown hair, dressed in soft leather clothing. The extraordinary feature was their height: the woman measured one metre ninety-six while the man topped an impressive two metres ten. They had been buried over 2,500 years ago. I wondered whether they might not have been subjects of Herodotus' legendary Land of the Giants.

TWELVE

From Qiemo to Ruoqiang

A RUDE KNOCK ON THE DOOR roused me only a few hours later.

'Time to go!'

The woman in the other bed had already packed and sat matronly on a chair, waiting for her husband to collect her. I gathered my belongings, splashed some cold water on my face, and stepped outside.

Thick bundles of humanity huddled around the old bus, fighting the icy pre-dawn chill. Smoke from the first kebab fires, and dust stirred up by a procession of donkeys with loads piled to twice their height, blended with the foul smell of local cigarettes. Today, Tuesday, was market day in Qiemo. Groups of Uighur men in long padded coats and thick fur hats conversed quietly. Wang, the Chinese engineer, stood isolated near the door clutching his black plastic briefcase. His dark-blue Mao jacket was buttoned tightly up to the collar, and a cap pulled down over his face hid his eyes. Several layers of hand-knitted underwear were pushing their way out of his sleeves and trouser legs. He looked desperately out of place, and from the expression on his face, he felt it.

Wang had been transferred only recently to Niya to work on the new irrigation projects, he had told me over dinner. He had left a wife in the northern suburbs of Beijing and a son at university. He despised sheep, Uighurs and Xinjiang, and dismissed all three as filthy. His orders were to travel to Ruoqiang and attend a meeting to discuss Han–Uighur relations in the district. Wang had been chosen to represent his *danwei*, or work unit.

127

He seemed relieved to see me and waved a greeting.

'Good morning.'

'Did you sleep well?'

'No, the police came into my room at two-thirty to make sure I was still there,' I joked.

An uncomfortable silence followed. Wang stood staring at his shoes and drew vigorously on his cigarette.

The bus door was suddenly pushed open against the wave of padding trying to force its way inside. I scrambled for a seat, stored my gear and settled for more sleep.

Officer Zhang and her assistants watched over my departure, happy to see the last of me. An old shrivelled grandmother almost completely hidden in a large white headscarf was selling fried dough twists. The mutton grease had solidified in the cold and looked like glazed sugar coating. The bus headed east.

I tried to doze, tried to ignore the darkness, the cold, the cramped seat (built for people about twenty centimetres shorter than me), to ignore the rumble in my stomach and the sudden and desperate craving for coffee. And more than anything else, I tried to ignore the fact that the ticket in my pocket now read Korla instead of Ruoqiang, and that my chances of seeing Miran had evaporated. After the last weeks of excitement, the let-down was almost physical. Shivering, I let my mind wander around Qiemo . . . Qarqan . . . the ancient Calmadana . . . or maybe it was the lost kingdom of Xiao Yuan after all. My friend Nick was arrested there during his epic journey along the Silk Road four years earlier, and I wondered if he would ever get the postcard I had managed to send from the local post office.

A sharp elbow in my side woke me. '*Yao bu yao*', said a quivering voice. Two-thirds of my field of vision were taken up by a most beautiful apple which was attached to a dark brown wrinkled hand with dirty fingernails and nicotine stains. Above it loomed an almost toothless mouth surrounded by an angelic smile.

By now the first rays of sunshine had taken the edge off the freezing cold. Slowly, the desert took on a golden glow and the dark shadows of the night turned into the grey, crevassed foothills of the Kunlun, bathing in pink light. Crisp snow-capped peaks appeared one by one, set brilliantly against an indigo sky. It was still below zero. Despite my gloomy state of mind I smiled, thanked the old man and took a hearty bite from my breakfast.

This gesture was enough to set off the questioning: 'German? Really? hey, listen everybody, he's from Germany! *hao, hao!*'

'No, I'm a student. London, London University.'

'Is it true there's no more Berlin Wall?'

Before I could answer any more questions the bus pulled into a walled compound for the long-awaited piss stop and a second breakfast of mutton-grease-pepper-noodles.

I walked towards the conveniences, a low mud-brick shack surrounded by a minefield of dried turds, and entered the section marked for women. Almost immediately, a hostile surge of shouts and angry faces hit me, and a thick-set woman with a big red scarf tied over her long braids tried to push me back out of the door. I instantly realized that my masquerade had fooled the world too well. I took off my cap and, pointing at my crotch, frantically shouted back '*meiyou, meiyou* . . . I don't have one!' Crude, but it worked. Everyone collapsed with laughter, but I was watched very closely while squatting over the open pit.

I was leaning against the wall of the small adobe shack, facing the pale disc of the yellow sun, when a tall figure in fashionable red Arctic explorer gear and with a large camera round his neck approached me. He'd got off the bus heading in the opposite direction.

'Who are you, what are you doing here?' he asked in flawless Oxford English.

'Who wants to know?'

'Don't you know that this road is closed to foreigners?', he informed me indignantly, obviously not intent on answering my question.

'You don't seem to be exactly local yourself,' I pointed out.

'Hong Kong.' he answered, '*I* made a special deal with the government' – stressing the 'I'.

'Germany,' I smiled. '*I* didn't.'

He looked like a little boy whose candy had just been taken away by the classroom bully.

'East, I presume?'

'No, south,' I answered, turned and went indoors to get some more noodles, leaving him fuming on the steps. I had met his type before. The I-want-to-be-first type, who will never understand that 'first' happened here a long, long time ago.

Twenty minutes later we were on the road again.

I had stopped in a small village somewhere between Kashgar and Yarkant when I learned that the wall dividing Berlin had fallen – three weeks after the event. A Uighur man, wearing a dark-brown suit and a blue flat cap, one of the people crowding around the noodle-shop, overheard that I was German, sat down next to me and bought me a beer to celebrate.

For the first time I heard a local using the word Turkestan. 'There are many Turkish people in Germany?' he had asked.

'Yes, at least in the West,' I answered absent-mindedly.

'There is no West, no East any more,' he said.

I hadn't read a paper since July and the news came as a total surprise. Although I had been away from Germany for thirteen years, I was deeply moved and walked around in a daze for half the week, unsuccessful in finding an international telephone exchange. It still filled me with disbelief every time someone mentioned it.

News travels fast in China. The estimate is that any major story not covered by Beijing broadcasting takes three days to spread throughout the country. That's almost village time.

The revelation that I was female rekindled the interest of my fellow travellers. 'Far away from home, far away from your parents,' a young girl whispered, shaking her head sadly. Her beautiful brown eyes glistened with genuine empathy. My hair, bleached blond by the sun, was stroked, and a woman poked at my chest to see if I really had breasts.

The engineer was chosen to test my academic abilities. He pulled out a small pad and wrote on it CO and thrust it towards me.

'Do you know what it means?'

Lacking the proper Chinese vocabulary, I imitated the noises of a car, waved my hand to indicate smoke, and pretended to choke. The sun-burned faces around me looked startled. But Wang beamed a big smile, 'She's right, she's right', and wrote another, FE. I knocked on the side of the bus, *Na*, and indicated salty food on my tongue. Wang acted like a professor who had discovered a genius among his students. A little tired of the game, I took the pad from him and with the flair becoming the young genius wrote $E=mc^2$. The others looked impressed, Wang shook his head, and asked for an explanation.

A sudden commotion in the front of the bus saved me, just in time, from certain embarrassment.

'*Xia che, xia che* . . . get off the bus,' screamed a high-pitched female voice.

This was at least the fifth fight I had been close to since I started travelling in Xinjiang. Twice, my glasses had been broken. I immediately ducked and covered my head in the aeroplane crash-landing position.

When I surfaced, I saw a tall, dark figure, dressed in Levis and black leather jacket, holding apart an irate Uighur woman and a Chinese man in workman's blues, both wriggling to escape his grip. Quickly, other passengers stepped in and the fight subsided.

The argument was over a seat. The bus had taken on more passengers than was comfortable and people, padding and luggage, stored in bulky rice-cloth sacks, congested the gangway. Tensions between locals and Han rise quickly. Anywhere. A false move, a look, or the wrong word can set off an eruption of emotions. And all Uighur men conspicuously wear a knife at their belts.

For the rest of the journey, the tall young man stood leaning against the vertical iron bar next to the bus door. A cigarette in the corner of his mouth, his arms casually crossed, he regarded the bus with an air of nonchalant arrogance.

He's not Chinese, I thought.

We were moving into the heartland of the kingdom of Shanshan and the mountains towards the south changed their name from Kunlun to Altyn Tagh. Dunes obstructed our view to the left and right and swallowed whole stretches of the road. The afternoon sun threw long shadows and created intricate textures in the sand.

Up front, near the engine, there was a hole in the floor, and fine golden sand filtered into the bus. It also got into our shoes and our luggage, sand ground between our teeth and filled our ears. We had all taken on a grey, spectral look, and the dust glistened like diamonds in the rays of the sun.

Large grids of twisted straw were laid out like giant carpets at the side of the road. A solitary worker dressed in rags of no particular colour and a large sun hat was planting geometrically precise rows of marram grass, intended to bind and stabilize the sand. His lone fight against nature struck me as pathetic and hopeless. Behind him stood a forlorn shanty of corrugated metal, drifting on the sand like a raft lost at sea. The desert was slowly advancing with the relentlessness of a glacier.

In antiquity, the road followed the Qarqan river, which flowed about 60 kilometres to the north, and which they say was named after the old kingdom of Shanshan. It emptied into the wastes of the Karakoshun marshes, which once spread east all the way to the edges of the great salt lake Lopnur. Now these were dry, and oases like the old Calmadana, or the ancient sites north of Endere and Niya, were in ruins. The desert had expanded southwards and the road had edged closer to the mountains. In the eighth century this was mainly caused by a dramatic increase in agricultural production which drained the water supply. In Khotan during the Tang dynasty, for example, agriculture developed so rapidly that the upper course of the river ran dry and dozens of Buddhist communities had to be abandoned. More recently, the same had happened to the Lopnur, Sven Hedin's fabled wandering lake. That had dried up completely only within the last few decades, when Xinjiang's population tripled, and the rivers which fed it were harnessed for irrigation long before the water could reach the lake.

In the bus everyone had become still. Then someone started to chant a melancholy dirge that seemed to have no end.

I reflected that the original name of the kingdom of Shanshan was Kroraina, which the Chinese pronounced Loulan, and that it had surrendered to the Han for the first time in 108 BC. Along with the other kingdoms of the Tarim basin it had fallen to the vision of the Han Emperor Wu, and to the desire of his generals to eradicate the nomadic Xiongnu, the Hun tribes against whom the Great Wall had been constructed.

During the following decades Xiongnu and Han struggled for the mastery of the Silk Road, and Kroraina was caught between the two superpowers. Both expected loyalty and tribute – but while the Xiongnu made no territorial demands, the Chinese had come to settle. Their caravans brought the military, which established communication points and agricultural colonies, and levied taxes. In a last attempt to prevent the colonization of their oases, the people of Kroraina aligned themselves with the Xiongnu. In retaliation, their king was kidnapped and brought before the Han court on charges of conspiracy.

'Your Majesty must understand,' the king said in his own defence, 'we are only a small state among large empires'; then he cleverly proposed to resettle all his subjects inside the boundaries of Han China. 'That would solve the problem!' He was sent back home unharmed and a prince was brought as hostage to Changan.

After the death of the king in 92 BC the family requested the return of the hostage son to take his father's place, only to discover that, as punishment for some offence, he had been 'sent down to the silkworm house'. In other words, he now served as a eunuch in the Imperial Palace.

A potent prince was put in his place, and hostages were once again sent to the Xiongnu and the Han. This king, whose name was never recorded in the histories, died soon after, and the Xiongnu sent their hostage, a young man called Angui, to be crowned ruler of Kroraina. Immediately after his coronation, the new king was summoned to the Han court. But his wife, who was also his stepmother, warned him against going: neither his uncle nor his brother had ever returned. He decided to defy the summons. His younger brother, Weituqi, saw the king's refusal as his opportunity to seize power, and himself submitted to the Han, agreeing to a devious plan to kill his brother.

A group of mercenaries was sent to assassinate the king of Kroraina. He was stabbed to death and decapitated; his head was sent by mounted messenger to the Han capital, where it was nailed over the Northern Gate. Weituqi, now vassal to the Han, assumed the throne in 77 BC; at the same time the name of the kingdom was changed in the Chinese books from Loulan to Shanshan.

And that is how the river got its name.

I was brought back to the present by the fat young man in uniform with greasy shoulder-length hair and acne, who had managed to sit next to me since the last rest-stop. I eyed him suspiciously.

'Postman,' he grinned, pulling on the circular badge on his breast pocket. It was a five-pointed golden star on a red background, the centre of which was formed by an abstraction of the characters *Dian Bao*, Telegraph.

The first crippled poplars were appearing down the road. We were about to reach Ruoqiang.

'We'll be stopping here for the night,' shouted the driver's assistant. 'Bus leaves for Korla tomorrow at seven o'clock.'

'Beijing time or Xinjiang time?' I asked.

'Beijing time!'

Someone groaned.

We pulled into the walled compound at the edge of town and disembarked. On an impulse, I grabbed my luggage from the roof of the bus and followed the engineer, the postman, and the tall stranger in Levis down the main street.

'See you tomorrow,' I called out loudly to the other passengers who were already fighting for sleeping spaces in the caravanserai.

With a show of authority, I checked into the government hotel, left my passport at the counter and went to my room.

It took the policeman only two minutes to get there.

'Welcome to Ruoqiang. Welcome to China!' he repeated several times in broken English.

THIRTEEN

Ruoqiang

THE INDIGNANT-LOOKING GIRL who had occupied the other half of my room when I arrived had requested to be moved, leaving me to appreciate my stroke of luck. I sat back, barely able to contain my jubilation. I was only 78 kilometres south of Miran. I was at a clean hotel, in a clean room, with a clean bed, and had access to a large washroom a few doors down the hall. And for the moment at least I had the rare pleasure of being alone. A pump thermos with hot water stood on the side table, and several sachets of jasmine tea were nicely arranged around a ceramic mug with a lid. Forgetting all about dinner, I slid between the sheets and slept, soundly and dreamlessly.

Next morning at eight (ten o'clock Beijing time), certain that I had already missed the bus, I shouldered my bags and walked back to the empty depot. Cocooned forms wandered through the dusty streets like somnambulists through moonlit nights. White fog-flowers bloomed in front of our faces, disintegrated, and fell to the ground. The frozen sand and gravel creaked like dry snow beneath my feet. For once I hardly felt the cold.

An old man was sweeping the abandoned yard. When he saw me approach, he stammered something about another bus in ten days, shook his head, and mumbled, '*Waiguoren*', before resuming his task. I thought it best to inform the police, and set out for the Public Security Bureau.

The Ruoqiang PSB was a one-and-a-half-room affair housed in a low building to the west of town. Two Uighur men sat huddled round a tall iron stove slurping tea from marmalade jars. A young

135

Han officer, pretty in a hard-edged manner, eyed me with surprise and suspicion. She could have been the sister of Officer Zhang in Qiemo. I looked about in vain for the chief who had welcomed me in such a friendly way the previous night .

'Permit?' she asked sharply instead of a greeting.

'No . . . I missed the bus to Korla,' I tried to explain. I felt she did not believe me.

'Ticket, passport,' she demanded without looking at my face.

'I'll just take the next bus . . .' I tried to interject, stumbling over my words.

'No bus,' she said coldly, commanding me with an authoritative gesture to sit on a chair before her desk. I quietly added policewomen to my list of fear-inspiring females in China. After some minutes of silence, then heated deliberation with the two officers, too fast for me to understand, she indicated I should follow her. We returned to the hotel, where she handed over my passport to the not-so-friendly proprietor, a fat, bald man who looked like W. C. Fields *sans* cigar. I was under house arrest again.

The whole procedure was observed with unabashed curiosity by a few shadows slumped in the semi-darkness of the reception area. The engineer scuttled away, avoiding eye contact. What was he afraid of? Then I saw the young man from the bus leaning against the wall smoking a cigarette. I walked over to him.

'Hi,' I said in English. No reaction.

'*Nihongjin desuka?*' I tried in Japanese. The same.

'*Chi fan?*' I asked in Chinese where I could find something to eat. Without a word or change of expression, he jerked a nod in the direction of some curtained glass doors. I shrugged and went into a large, empty canteen. So he was Chinese after all.

Remnants of breakfast and scattered chopsticks suggested that mealtime was already over. A few women, dressed like nurses, worked in a raised kitchen area in one corner of the hall. I went over to ask for food. They ignored me.

Without my noticing, the young man had stepped up from behind me and handed them several paper tickets in exchange for a few stale steamed buns and a bowl of watery rice.

'You're late,' he said, pointing at my bowl, and asked, 'Where are you from?' while watching me eat. He spoke distinctly for my benefit.

His face had changed; it was animated and smiling. Two intelligent brown eyes sparkled behind tight slits. A small scar in the shape of a half-moon was outlined pale against the tanned skin of the right cheekbone. It gave him a look at once daring and vulnerable; a Chinese James Dean. His name was Chang and he came from Sichuan province. He had been travelling in Xinjiang for the last two months. In Qiemo, where he was visiting friends of friends and rode horses three days south of the road, he'd heard that they had arrested a foreigner. And then he saw me, he said, during the fight in the bus, protecting my face against possible blows. He laughed a low, throaty laugh and threw his head back, and it was then that I noticed that his black hair was wavy with glints of brown highlights.

Two officials in uniform came through the doors. Chang's face went immediately blank, and without excusing himself he disappeared as fast as he came. I didn't have time to tell him about Miran.

On the map Ruoqiang, or Qarkilik, gives the impression of an important town. A crossroads on the southern route, it is connected to Korla and the east; a new road leads over the Altyn Tagh which splits to go on into Qinghai and Gansu, and to Da Qaidam and Golmud, the terminus for travellers to and from Tibet. The old road from Qiemo along the river also stops here, before continuing further down to Miran and into the desert.

Grey, dusty Ruoqiang seemed to be unaware of the image it conveyed on the maps. Built in the socialist style of all the government structures in China, with a large red star over the entrance and a dejected courtyard with a burnt-out bus, the hotel dominated the sad town. Twenty-five metres to the north-east the desert started. A concrete school, a store (which sold wonderful home-made honey), a post office and a few other indeterminate buildings made up the centre. A slab of pavement between a few buildings was the dismal excuse for a market place. Missing was the smell of kebab fires and fresh *girda*, the large bagels. Missing were chatting groups of men, the coloured eggs sold by women stuffing their earnings into rubber garters . . . missing was life. If there had ever been a local village, it had been wiped out by progress.

In history the area had been as important as its appearance on paper. Colonel Przhevalsky, ostensibly in search of a route to Lhasa, wintered here in 1876. Near the town he found some ancient watch-towers and a mud wall of about two miles in circumference, called *Ottugush-shari* in memory of a former Khan of the city. Maybe he saw the ruins of Wuni, the capital of the kingdom of Shanshan which was located somewhere in the vicinity. Or perhaps the remnants of *Nob-ched Po*, the capital of the region during the Tibetan occupation in the seventh and eighth centuries. He probably set foot in Marco Polo's Lop, the last town before the Great Desert of Lop where travellers rested before entering the sands.

Remains of an old city wall still rose near the outskirts of town. A few dilapidated Muslim burials nestled into it; but broken glass, empty beer bottles and black scars from bonfires had long desecrated the holy site.

The postman from Qiemo occupied a room on the same floor. He busily waved a friendly greeting through his open door as I walked to the bathroom, eager for conversation. His round face was aglow with grease and perspiration.

He had been born and raised in Ruoqiang, he said, son of an immigrant couple who had been sent to Xinjiang with the first wave of Maoist zealousness in the fifties to help develop the frontiers, and stayed. He had come back for a ten-day training course, happy to be close to his family. I told him that I was looking for transport to Miran.

'Sometimes there is a bus.'

'When?' I asked with interest.

'Sometimes!'

'Can I rent a car, or maybe a bicycle?'

'I don't think so,' he answered thoughtfully. Then his face brightened.

'I'll take you on my motorbike.'

'Really?' I smiled at the possibility. 'When?'

'Sometimes!'

I have to stop having these conversations, I told myself, and went to the loo.

I had not yet learned about the conflict I caused amongst Han Chinese, between their earnest desire to fulfil their own wishes (hospitality), their obligations (family), and the no-can-do's (imposed by society and politics). These restrictions are the volatile component, and in the end they override all others. Ignorance about those basic facts made me a complete outsider, a *waiguoren* and a liability. But I didn't know that then.

I went to my room to relax and take account of the situation. Never had I been closer to Miran . . . and yet it felt so far away. Yesterday's euphoria was giving way to stark realism. There appeared to be no private transport; all jeeps and cars seemed to be in the hands of officials. I considered walking or going by bicycle, but discarded it as impractical. Much of the terrain was desert, a military zone, and temperatures rarely hit 0° Celsius. I began feeling more anxious and trapped. Without my passport I could not leave Ruoqiang and without certified transport destined for an open town the document would not be released. Thus, my movements were restricted, although there was surprisingly little enforcement of the house arrest. Because of the Han–Uighur unity conference, security had been stepped up and very obvious plain-clothes policemen in trench coats and sunglasses patrolled the streets, leaving an ostentatious trail of Mild Seven cigarettes in their wake.

Without warning the door to my room opened and, before I could protest, the postman's moon-face appeared in the frame, inviting me to eat at his family's home. He'd fetch me in an hour or so, he said, and closed the door again with a friendly '*hao ba?*', before I could formulate a refusal. I put the *Jungle Book* into my Walkman and tried not to think at all.

The postman's family lived in a small, squalid mud-house of the sort I had so far only associated with the poorer of the Uighur dwellings. A few skinny chickens cackled in a wire enclosure in a front garden. From the entrance, hidden behind a thick green carpet, appeared a slim man in his forties, and welcomed us graciously.

We were escorted to a T-shaped room filled with oversized furniture solidly arranged on a concrete floor polished to a shiny slate grey. A television set covered with lacy material occupied the focal point opposite the mastodon of a couch. Five or six men sat around a low table smoking, presided over by a distinguished-looking grandfather.

'*Qing zuo, qing zuo* . . . sit down,' said the postman's older brother, indicating that dinner was about to commence. I sank into an overstuffed chair; someone handed me a drink.

I had been invited to a feast celebrating the postman's home visit. Considering the meagre displays of food in the markets, the riches being dished up here were remarkable. Included were all types of meat: pork, beef, chicken, even fish. But there was no mutton. There was rice and vegetables and clear soup, washed down with plenty of *Xinjiang Pijiu* and thimblefuls of foul-tasting clear liquor, *Baijiu*. After weeks of noodles and kebabs, I felt as if I were at a king's table, tasting morsels comparable to a Saturday lunch at a smart restaurant in London.

The postman brought up my wish to visit Miran. He was listened to carefully by the men.

'We have a sister-in-law there,' said the older brother, and then to the group, 'perhaps younger brother could take her.' Almost imperceptibly the grandfather in the corner shook his head. That concluded the subject. Soon after I thanked my host and went back to the hotel, feeling a bit of a heel for having dismissed the postman earlier in the day. Regrets didn't make me feel a lot better.

All day people had been arriving in town and by nightfall the hotel was booked full. Many of the newcomers were officials of some sort, most of them Han Chinese. I was requested to change my room and moved into a smaller one a floor up. There was a double-happiness sign embroidered on my pillow-cover and someone had already brought tea and a plate of fruit. Also, for the first time there was hot water, and I enjoyed a long overdue bath.

A knock on the door. It was the postman again. He said there was a party this evening, in anticipation of a two-day CCP conference. He said the drummer of the band was a friend and he had extra tickets. He said he was meeting some others in his room at seven, and if I'd like to come . . . ? I said I'd think about it.

Trying to tell myself that he did what he could, and that really I ought to be thankful, and anyhow, there was always another way, I forced myself to pull out of the depression threatening to engulf me. At seven I went downstairs and joined a circle of four beer-drinkers. I was introduced to two schoolfriends, with the same dusty hair and broad faces as the postman. Chang was also present. He had strategically positioned himself on the corner of a bed, smoking and cracking peanuts.

'What's your name?', he asked, staring at me directly. 'Tough ass,' was the term that crossed my mind. 'Thinks he's cool.'

'Christa.'

'*Kissa?*'

'No, Christa,' I repeated slowly. Han Chinese have problems in pronouncing my name.

'I think this woman needs a new name, a Chinese name,' he laughed, addressing the others.

'Gül,' snickered the postman, the common Uighur name meaning flower. I tried to say that I knew someone with that name.

'*Bu shi, bu shi* . . . no, that doesn't suit her,' argued Chang flirtatiously. I guessed it wasn't going to be Gül.

'Some people call me Charley,' I said. I'd used that name before in Pakistan.

'*Jia Li, Jia Li*,' Chang repeated a few times, trying it on for size. Then he pulled out a piece of paper and an ink pen and started playing around with characters, scratching them out, drawing more. Finally he circled a set, and showed them to the postman. The postman approved. Thus, I was settled with a new name and two characters to prove it. Both meant good and beautiful. The baptism was celebrated with liberal toasts of beer.

'*Zou ba Jiali* . . . let's go!'

I could live with that name, I thought, as we went off into the night to join the dance.

As we neared the local headquarters of the Communist Party, the sound of 'Edelweiss', the melody made famous by *The Sound of Music*, drifted towards us. The lyrics were in Chinese.

The makeshift ballroom was decorated with streamers and large posters displaying slogans. Metal folding chairs, three rows deep, were arranged around a large rectangular dance floor. Uniforms and women in their finery congregated in groups of their own gender, observing each other with excited whispers. I looked somewhat self-consciously down at my own outfit. The big brown trousers were showing their four months of travel. My boots had taken on an undefined grey sheen. Though I had tied my hair back with a bandana and put some lipstick on, I looked like the poor cousin from the country. The postman came back with some beers and handed them to us.

The lights flickered twice. With much commotion, couples paired off quickly and gathered in the centre of the floor. Then the lights dimmed and the dance began. Stiff and prim they moved, counter-clockwise, in exaggerated tango steps. When one song was over the lights turned bright again and the whole procedure was repeated.

A middle-aged man bowed in front of me, asking for a dance. To the cheers of the bystanders I took his arm and tried, clumsily, to follow his large strides. I wasn't too good at it, and hiking boots are not exactly proper dancing gear. From out of the corner of my eye I saw Chang's laughing face toasting me.

For the next dance several young men hurried towards me. They must all have gone to the same dance school. My back and shoulder were soon aching from the uncomfortable position. There were well-meant jokes about my lack of skill, as I was being pulled round and round.

'Hello,' said an unlikely English voice next to me. It belonged to a well-dressed Chinese, who had come up to me smiling.

'I'm a journalist,' he explained himself. 'The *Korla Ribao*. I would like to know what you are doing here?' There was a timbre of superiority in his voice, instantly repelling me. 'None of your business,' I thought.

'I'm a spy, of course,' I answered flippantly, but immediately regretted my wisecrack when I saw him grimace. Then he laughed hollowly, accepting it as a joke. He left me standing and sat down next to a man with a frozen visage wearing a tightly belted beige trench coat. I received a glare from cold eyes, hitting the uncomfortable spot in my stomach. I returned to my companions and a moment later the chief of police appeared beside us. Ignoring my greetings, he regarded my new friends with a stern expression. They went quiet.

'She can watch, but she can't dance,' he commanded, looking at them rather than me.

Had it not been for the fear visible in the faces of the postman and his buddies and Chang's rigid countenance, marked by just a trace of contempt, I would have laughed out loud at his farcical statement. I also remembered I was under arrest, and held my tongue. The mood was spoiled and we left subdued. Chang said nothing all the way back to the hotel. The postman and his friends walked ahead, consciously keeping their distance. Quietly, we all went off to our respective rooms.

A commotion in the hallway woke me early the next morning. I had slept uneasily and woken several times, dazed with nightmarish images. Red, swollen eyes and a pale face stared back at me from the mirror. I dressed and went downstairs for breakfast.

The hall buzzed with polished uniforms and suppressed excitement. From a distance the pulsating beat of military music and drum rolls came closer. Ruoqiang was celebrating. In the unexpected sunshine, embellished with flowers and laughter, the atmosphere reminded me of the Corpus Christi Day parades of my childhood. Dressed in white with garlands in our hair, throwing blossoms from small baskets and feeling very religious, we marched in front of the canopy to the drone of 'Our Father'. There was not much doubt about the nature of this occasion. The walls were lined with familiar posters preaching the harmonious coexistence of a multitude of nationalities.

From across the street Chang waved to me and drew me into the crowd already lining the kerb.

'"Han–Uighur Unity",' he read out loud from the large banner levitating in front of the long snake of approaching bodies. '"Togetherness",' from another.

Then came the children: first the Chinese boys and girls in blue and white uniforms like little scouts, drilled to perfection; five rows of drummers, then those bearing red flags with all the seriousness of young soldiers. Following this tight group were the local kids dressed in pseudo-ethnic clothing, the girls with headscarves, the boys in embroidered white shirts. Their faces had been painted with garish colours, bright red cheeks and thick black eyebrows and outlined eyes, mocking the delicate make-up of traditional dancers. Instead of flags or drums they carried large paper flowers.

The parade was obviously put on in honour of the conference. I noticed that the stores were closed and even the baker had not lit his oven today. They must have recruited the entire town to create a spectacle this big.

A laughing Uighur woman waved to her child of no more than four, stumbling along with the group. She turned to me, and touching my hair, told me that her son too had golden hair when he was born.

'We are not Chinese, you see,' she continued, almost as though she had been reading my mind.

The disparity between the two groups had become more and more noticeable even to me, the outsider, as I travelled along the southern route. In most towns the old centres had been eradicated and replaced with standard concrete buildings and nationalistic street names. Along with their mud-brick houses and bazaars the Uighurs were being pushed to the outskirts. In many areas, satellite towns round the now predominantly Han centres had popped up. Ever since the democracy demonstrations in June, when students marched in Urumqi, smashing the windows of government buildings and screaming slogans like *Give Us Back Our Time . . . Give Us Back Our Land*', the atmosphere had chilled noticeably throughout the province. More and more painted posters had appeared in the towns showing local people and Han hand in hand, preaching a unity that wasn't. The situation was being exacerbated by some crass policy misjudgements, such as forbidding formal religious education and stepping up the one-child-only campaign among the Muslims, at the same time as a temporary economic downturn was affecting the whole nation. Somehow this parade reflected the sorry state of relations in all of Xinjiang.

Chang looked bored and asked me if I wanted some lunch.

'Hm, maybe we can find a *kavabchi* . . . you know,' I suggested, while imitating pulling barbecued mutton bits from long iron skewers with my teeth. His exaggerated theatrical grimace told me that he would never dream of eating such foul-smelling flesh. Rather, he had discovered a restaurant which served the food of his home province.

Once there he informed me that he was leaving for Dunhuang. He picked his way through chilli peppers and the occasional slice of beef. 'You can come along, if you want,' he said hesitantly, afraid that I would say yes, afraid that I would say no. It was only later that I fully understood the risks he was taking.

'When are you going?'

'Don't know, there are some trucks leaving. Maybe tomorrow, day after. I'll know soon.'

I thought about it. Five days in this town and as many packs of cigarettes had worn down my optimism about ever making it to Miran. Low temperatures and the fine sand blowing continuously from the desert had exhausted my spirit for exploration. All I could do was to wait for the next bus to Korla, which wasn't due for another five days. A trip over the mountains, completing the southern road to Dunhuang, might be better than nothing.

'I don't have my passport, but let me know when you leave,' I said finally.

Chang threw some notes on the table and sent a volley of words in the direction of the kitchen, hardly resembling the careful Mandarin he'd been using with me.

'Sichuan,' he explained, and added, 'there are lots of people from Sichuan here.'

We parted outside the restaurant.

'I'll knock on your door before I leave,' he threw over his shoulder, and disappeared into an alley. I stood nonplussed for a moment or two.

On the way back to the hotel I ran into the postman, who stood among a crowd staring at a bus which had halted by the side of the road. The people inside stared back solemnly. I noticed that they were all men, all dressed in grey with thick black coats, all Han Chinese.

'What's going on?'

'They are from the desert, from one of the towns which isn't on the map,' he answered.

'What do you mean?'

'There are some towns which have no names . . .' he said vaguely.

'Where are they going?'

'Korla, probably.' I moved on. The postman caught up with me.

'Have you seen Chang?' he asked.

'Yeah, why?'

'I was looking for him and he has checked out of the hotel.' I shrugged, and wished him goodbye.

'I'm sorry I couldn't help you, Jiali,' he called after me.

'Never mind,' I called back, and sketched a wave. '*Zaijian*.'

I walked back contemplating the news. Chang hadn't told me he had checked out. Perhaps the run-in with the chief last night had disconcerted him. Or perhaps he was more sure of his departure then he had let on.

Contemplate the devil and he will appear. The chief was waiting for me in the lobby when I returned.

'I'm trying to put you on a jeep to Korla with some of the people returning there,' he informed me.

'You know, there's a bus to Korla tomorrow,' I said.

He only glanced at me, and left. I was genuinely sorry to have caused him grief. He seemed like a decent man.

I went over to the desk to find the proprietor. He wasn't there, but I could see the girl who sometimes worked as *furen* on the first floor sitting by the stove knitting what looked like long underwear. I signalled her.

'I'd like to pay, please. I'm leaving tomorrow on the bus,' I told her. She couldn't care less. And when I asked for my passport, she handed it over without a murmur.

Then I joined a few guests in front of the television for the local news. Lots of beautiful people in beautiful fields with beautiful tractors. Irrigation projects, and a conference in Urumqi with lots of smiling men. Then a scene which struck me. A huge bonfire in the market area of Kashgar. An unemotional voice commented on the smuggling of goods and the increasing frequency of illegal private enterprises. I stayed for some Made-in-Japan children's animation about space wars and mutant soldiers. Then I went upstairs to get my gear into shape and pack.

FOURTEEN

Mountains and Asbestos

I SAT UP IN BED, covered with sweat, not knowing for a moment who or where I was. The room was pitch black.

There was the sound of faint scratching at the door.

'Jiali, psst, Jiali.'

'Chang,' my fogged brain flashed in recognition: he was leaving today as I had suspected. I glanced at my watch. It was four. Groping for the candle and lighter on the bed stand, I called out for him to come in. The doors are never locked anyway.

He'd rather be on the look-out, he hissed, urging me to hurry up.

'*Congmangba!*' he whispered, '. . . hurry!'

I was ready. Having slept in most of my clothing, I quickly threw on trousers, thick sweater and grey Norwegian jacket. I stuffed candle and lighter into my blue day-pack, grabbed my bag and followed him into the silence of the corridors, disturbed only by the occasional rumble of a snore.

In the reception area Chang leapt behind the counter. He had a knife, ready to break open the small wooden cabinet where our assorted documents were kept.

'Got to get your passport,' he grunted.

'No, I've already got it. I've got it. Let's go!' I called back. I had almost forgotten about my foresight yesterday. He nodded a pleased '*hao de*', grabbed my bag and we left.

We crossed town in the stiff coldness, our way lit by an unbelievable brilliance of stars and a small wedge of a moon.

'Hurry!' Chang broke into a light trot. I followed blindly, asking no questions.

Twenty minutes later we arrived at a small enclosure illuminated by the headlights of four trucks. The engines coughed softly. There was a shed to the left. Chang told me he had slept there last night. A tall figure dislodged itself from the swarm of fireflies which I guessed to be the glow of cigarettes, and moved towards us.

'*Xin Yi*,' Chang panted, '*ta jiao Jiali*', introducing me with a flick of the head. Xin Yi flashed some teeth, gave me a nod, and took my bag from Chang.

'*Zou ba, zou ba* . . . let's go!'

Chang shoved me into an overcrowded cab next to a large driver, banged the door shut and beat on the side twice. I saw him climb into the vehicle behind me, then the driver slammed into first and, leading the caravan of four, we left Ruoqiang. I noticed the heating wasn't working, and drifted back to sleep.

When I came to again, drowsily rubbing my stiff neck, the stars were fading and a cool light pushed away the last of the night sky. Dawn had painted the stark landscape pastel powdery blue. We must have been on the road for nearly two hours. The phantom behind the wheel metamorphosed into a swarthy round face with high cheekbones covered with pockmarks. He noticed I was awake and smiled, causing his eyes to disappear completely behind the folds of the lids. We crossed a bridge and headed into a gorge, cut deep into the rock.

'*Milan he* . . . the Miran river,' he pointed out.

I felt wretched. He couldn't have known. I managed a muffled '*shi ah*', and tried not to appear impolite.

The disc of the new sun added some warm hues to the cold palette. Boulders enclosed us on both sides, we were about to climb the massif of the Altyn Tagh . . . the Altun Shan, as the Chinese say. The vehicle made sudden clanking noises. Metal grinding on metal. The driver cursed low beneath his breath, '*tamade*', signalled the others, and pulled over to the side of the road. His head vanished under the bonnet and he mumbled something about it taking a few minutes.

Chang came prancing up to the truck and held the door as I clambered down. He wore a mischievous expression and threw a huge laugh and an incomprehensible avalanche of words at me.

I can get around in Chinese. I can even make a phone call or get a decent bed at a local rate, but my vocabulary is limited to one and a half terms of school Mandarin. With the Uighurs it hadn't mattered that much – their proficiency and accent was in many cases worse than mine; anyway, for them, perfect diction would immediately have put me in the other camp.

I asked Chang to slow down. Reverting to baby-talk he told me that the vehicles were headed for Golmud. They would take us to a town somewhere near the Xinjiang–Qinghai border where we would have a chance of finding a ride to Dunhuang. I aked him about yesterday. The chief had caught up with him and checked his papers, he said. That made him feel very uncomfortable. He didn't like policemen. And anyway, it was better that our disappearances from town shouldn't be connected to one another.

I was astonished. So he had planned to take me along after all.

'I'd be worried, too, with those documents,' interrupted a joking voice.

'They are fake . . . well sort of fake, you know, a favour from a friend of mine,' Chang explained.

Of course, I had noticed countless times during my journey that any sort of movement of Chinese people in China was accompanied by thin pieces of paper and impressive-looking red stamps. Recommendations, permits, introductions, and indicators of status, they are supplied by work units or other official bureaus to justify a person's presence in a specific place. Without them it was apparently difficult to buy a train ticket or get a room. Chang seemed to have somehow side-stepped the system.

'Isn't that dangerous?' I enquired.

'That's China,' said Chang. 'You can get anything and do anything, if you know how.'

'And I suppose you know how?' I countered facetiously.

'*Dangran, wo xiaode*', of course he did, he stated, without so much as batting an eyelid and with more than a tinge of arrogance.

Despite myself, I felt a growing admiration; as well as a rising doubt as to his sanity.

He introduced me to the other three passengers. The joker was Che Tao, a sturdy, squat man with a funny face and a large black mole sprouting a few long black hairs on the lower right cheek. He held out a very welcome steaming cup of tea towards me. 'A comrade from work,' Chang said; they had been travelling together for two months now.

I had already met Xin Yi, the one who had fastened my bag on top of the loaded truck so it looked like a bright-red police siren. He was the oldest in the bunch, mid-forties, I guessed, with an elegant demeanour and an aristocratic shape to the head. He held out a hand with long slender fingers. An unexpectedly hearty grip made me wince.

'How do you do?' he addressed me in English, bowing gracefully.

'Oh, you speak English?'

'*Bu hui . . . bu hui*,' he laughed shyly, and waved his hands in negation. He had joined Chang and Che Tao in Kashgar, and was now on his way back to Chengdu where he worked on the railway. What was he doing here? Just travelling, like the rest of them. Visiting relatives and friends. A holiday. I thought that he was an unlikely candidate for a railway worker.

The fourth in the group was Zhong Yuan. He was standing with his back to us, talking to the drivers who were blowing smoke into each other's face next to the last truck. They kept to themselves. For them, we were extra business, cargo. Fifty renminbi a head, a bit more for me. Danger money.

Chang called out to him and he turned and walked towards us. You could imagine God saying, 'Let there be all kinds' – and making Zhong Yuan. He could have passed as a relative to prehistoric Peking man: sloping forehead, prominent chin, and a flat nose which looked as if a donkey had sat on it. One of his pupils kept wandering off to the left, giving him a slightly retarded gaze. As is often the case with ugly people, a smile transformed his face and made him beautiful.

Zhong Yuan stuttered something and pointed up towards a rocky ledge. There, immovable as a sculpture, hovered the backlit shape of a mountain goat. Che Tao held up his hand mocking a pistol and went '*peng*', breaking the magic. The animal came alive and scuttled out of sight.

A bleating horn called us back to the vehicles.

We chewed into the mountain, climbing hairpin-turn after hairpin-turn. Snow, wind-packed into small drifts, lined the sides of the precarious path. It was 4,800 metres, the height of the Kunjerab, the driver told me. The road was impeccably kept, a one-lane strip of compressed gravel, scarring its way through the barren rock. Blue, blue alpine sky, accentuated by a few frayed clouds, immersed us as we reached the top of the pass. Below lay the endless and silent rosary of peaks which made up the Southern Mountains.

We stopped and the driver took out his camera. I followed suit. He wore the same glazed look on his face as I imagined I had, that stunned expression that comes from realizing your own insignificance perching on top of the immensity of your own planet, and trying to dismiss it with clichés and finding that you can't. Then you tell your mind to go to hell and just feel, with your heart and your body, and bathe in the knowledge of being close to some higher force. Talking was superfluous or maybe even sacrilege, but we found ourselves grinning a silly grin.

Descent was rapid. To save fuel the driver turned off the engine and we burned round the turns at neck-breaking speed. It's something my father told me never to do, because your control of the vehicle is not very good that way. In fact, beyond a certain speed, it's impossible to get the thing back into gear. What it amounts to in the end is a little game with death; and it doesn't save very much petrol anyhow. Jaw clenched, knuckles white, I held on for dear life, damned if I'd make a comment.

It had passed noon when we stopped and I was not certain whether the touch of nausea had resulted from lack of food or the ride. In either case, I felt grateful for solid ground beneath my feet.

We parked close to a mud-brick building with a flat roof and peeling whitewash. Two chimneys puffed cotton-wool balls.

Laundry fluttered in the breeze, casting sharply contrasting shadows. A clear creek murmured across the road, the dead summer grass on its banks sheathed with ice. Three or four weathered wooden doors were painted with crude linear graffiti of men and women. There was a naïve nude with outsized breasts and an exaggerated erect penis.

We were ushered through a foyer smelling of stale socks into a murky back room. A day bed, a coarse wooden table and a few dilapidated stools made up the furnishings. The dark wooden walls, low ceiling with protruding beams, and metal bars on the tiny window recalled the interiors of the mountain huts in my native Bavaria. But then our altitude couldn't be much below 4,000 metres. I wondered how anyone gets a job in places like these, lonely truck stops and desert caravanserai. Not more then a handful of vehicles came through here every ten days.

'Government,' explained the driver. 'You get assigned here.'

'I asked to be here,' asserted the proprietor, who had just entered the room with an armful of kindling. 'I love the mountains, the quiet . . . not much bother here,' he added hesitantly. I could only agree with him.

I squeezed close to a small iron stove, crouching on my haunches, warming my hands. The drivers paid for our noodles.

The road continued straight as though drawn with a ruler across a high plateau reaching up to the Qinghai border. The driver pointed out a small lake, lapis blue, offset by the white strip of a saline beach. A herd of Bactrians with thick black pelts and humps heavy with winter rations was outlined against a hazy landscape fading with the first signs of dusk. He said they were wild camels.

A little further on the road became littered with debris, gravel and fist-sized rocks. We were nearing our dropping-off point. We pulled over and the other trucks followed. My four travelling companions were ordered to climb up behind. With Chang and his friends holding on to the white tarpaulin covering the cargo, we entered a moonscape of crushed boulders, man-made gravel hills and a confusing maze of small roads. I noticed green stones, large as children's heads, and thought how very much they looked like dark jade, similar to the piece Ahmet gave me in Khotan.

'We make them big here,' the driver chuckled, reading my mind.

'What is that stuff?' I inquired, concluding that it couldn't be jade.

'*Shimian*,' he explained.

What the hell is *shimian*, I wondered, and asked him to draw the characters. It took him a while to write them on the pad I held out to him and it took me a while to find the word in my dictionary. When I finally found it, I drew in air with surprise: asbestos? The green rock was serpentine, hydrated magnesium silicate, which in its more benign form is often carved into sculptures or decorative objects.

Suddenly there was a big explosion, the earth rocked, and an eruption of pebbles and dust rained down on us. With uncanny timing we were being shown how the material was mined! The driver floored the accelerator, screaming out to his human load on top, were they all right? Coughing and cursing was interpreted as a positive reply. When the dust cleared we were facing a small valley, a sort of cauldron surrounded by mountains. It was spanned by an improbable sky. Four dust-covered humanoids climbed from the truck and we paid off the driver, who left hurriedly without getting out of his cab.

We stood stunned for a moment at the edge of town, dwarfed by the spectacle of nuclear colours above us. Not even Pittsburgh had ever produced anything this magnificent. Saffron, magenta and violent purple swathes cradled the sickly red disc of a plunging sun. Ripped crimson sheets with citrus edges fingered the jagged lavender shapes of rock. A neon sky brought to you by your friendly neighbourhood asbestos factory.

The town below the bubbling firmament was in contrast bland and grey. Mud-brick barracks were arranged in rows at right angles to the main street. They were sunk to three-quarters below ground level, the roofs weighted down with boulders. A large hospital, newly built or freshly painted, conspicuous with its two oversized red crosses on the wall, lay opposite a truck stop and a small restaurant and shop. Further on more subterranean houses. The far end of the avenue was dominated by a grey metal cube with a tall chimney jutting into the air. The sun had fallen behind it, and the factory looked as though it had been constructed from giant children's building blocks.

A woman dressed in a white coat, a white cap and a white mouth-covering screeched by on a rusty bicycle. A child in a padded one-piece suit, a miniature Michelin man, held on to her like a little monkey to its mother. White flakes covered the road and the houses, and I gathered it wasn't snow. I rummaged in my bag for a bandana and tied it over my nose and mouth.

Chang sprang back into action to do what he did best: organize. He hustled us into the dark of the shop, found that we could occupy a back room and ordered some food. When in doubt, eat. A jolly fat woman brought some enamel bowls and hot water. Heat emanated from a stove, and slowly we thawed again. There was some space at the truck stop, Chang reported, and he'd reserved us some rooms. It would be best for me to wait until it was dark, then I could move in, he said. Have a beer. He filled the air with chatter. Comforting rather than annoying. The town was called Mangai Zhen. It lay at about 3,800 metres, and it didn't appear on my map. My feet had been numb all day from the cold, and the blood flowing back into them caused a painful, prickly feeling.

Opposite the stove stood a large square table upon which some-one had drawn a geometric design and some numbers in green felt tip marker. There were two fields of squares, separated by an empty space. The four centre bottom fields were crossed out.

'*Jiancha*,' said Chang, noticing my interest. Some form of chess, I gathered. It served as a dinner table.

The beer acted like liquid lead. I kept nodding off, and hardly remember being taken to a room. I was asleep before I hit the mattress.

For the last two hours I had resisted opening my eyes. Throughout the morning there had been comings and goings and voices drift-ing into the grey fabric of semi-sleep. Through a thicket of grainy lashes I watched a tall Chinese girl put on an anonymous green uniform over utilitarian grey underwear. Nineteen, maybe twenty, with long, sinewy thighs and high haunches. She frowned at me as she left, holding the door for a girl attendant who threw a few shovels full of brown coal into the stove. The wind howled outside, rattling the tiny windows blinded by ice-flora. A thunderclap, and the small earthquake which followed, reminded me that I had landed in an altogether inhospitable place.

The door opened to Chang's Cheshire Cat grin wishing me good morning.

'*Zhayao* . . . dynamite,' he explained the earthquake.

'When are we leaving?' I asked a bit too eagerly. He said nothing.

'Are you saying we have to stay here?' I shouted. 'It's not exactly healthy . . . *shi bu shi.*'

He shrugged, 'There aren't any trucks right now,' and I apologized. The cold and circumstances were wearing me a bit thin.

'Che Tao is making breakfast,' Chang added, softening. 'Come on over when you are ready. Room number seven,' and left.

This was not going to be a good day. I dressed and crossed the frozen compound to number seven. It was larger than my room, with four beds and a table. A brick furnace, a ground oven similar to the alpine tiled stove, gave off quiet heat. Xin Yi and Che Tao were busy laying out food, while Zhong Yuan sat on his bed humming to himself. Some sing-song about Xinjiang being a good place. His ugly face brightened into a sweet smile as I entered. I was offered a chair, some tea and some raisins.

'Are you travelling all alone?' he asked me.

I thought about it. It's a question I'm often asked. All alone? As a woman, moreover? Actually, I pondered, it is rare to find oneself travelling alone. The world is crammed full with people, and one has to make an effort to be alone. Perhaps if you climbed one of those because-it's-there mountains or crossed the Gobi on a tricycle, you would get the chance. But with a bit of bad luck you could find yourself squeezed between the Osaka climbing club and the French women's all-star hiking team on the mountain and meet an expedition in gleaming new Toyota trucks in the desert. These days, I would settle for a room with a key.

'Yes, I am,' I answered correctly.

'What are you doing here?' he enquired further. The standard set of questions.

Being mad, I thought, trying to break the laws of a foreign country to visit a lot of old mud–bricks.

'I study the antiquity of Xinjiang.'

'Ah, the history of our glorious motherland,' I heard Zhong Yuan say from the other side of the room.

'Well, not really, I study Xinjiang,' I explained.

'She means the Buddhist antiquities, like Kuqa, Turfan,' Xin Yi interjected.

'Yes, and specifically Miran,' I added.

'Ah, Miran,' Xin Yi pronounced the name dreamily. 'I've just come from Miran. The father of my wife lives there. I've seen the old site. Beautiful. These raisins, they are from Miran. You know, they have the best raisins in Xinjiang there?'

I managed a 'Really?', and wished I could stop feeling so bloody sorry for myself.

'How much for the Miran raisins?' Che Tao wanted to know.

'Four-fifty a kilo,' Xin Yi told him, holding his fingers up in a curious gesture, and turned back to me enthusiastically.

'Archaeology is my hobby,' he continued. 'I heard they made some new finds at Miran. Figures with wings and crowns. And a bronze mirror. Some of the locals deal in the stuff they find there. As cheap as thirty yuan. Most of it is sold to Pakistanis. You wanna buy some Miran antiquities? I can set you up a good deal!'

I felt as though I had just been punched in the stomach. Despite my effort to gain some self-control, hot tears shot into my eyes. I got up abruptly, mumbled an irrelevant explanation, and left the room. Outside I sucked the air deep into my lungs, shaking myself like a wet dog. No reason to make a fool of myself just because someone stepped on my dream. I padded back to the shop, to the empty back room where we'd eaten dinner the previous evening, and tried to calm the storm brewing in my heart. I bought a beer, nursed it slowly and thoughtfully. Perhaps the new finds were the reason for my exclusion from the expedition. Third time lucky, I finally told myself, and made a resolution to give it one last try.

The mention of Pakistanis was interesting, though. In recent years there had been a lot of illicit art trade, mainly in Gandhara sculpture. Mujahedeen had been plundering the cultural heritage of Afghanistan to finance the ongoing war. The area of the Swat valley in northern Pakistan, with its hundreds of unprotected sites, was another well-known source. Smuggled via Peshawar and Karachi, a lot of material had found its way on to the international market. A substantial amount ended up in Japanese private collections. It wasn't surprising that there was a spill-over into Xinjiang, where sculptures and other artefacts remained easily accessible. My experience at Yotkan had shown just how eager locals were to add a little income to their deflated wallets.

Chang entered, flushed. He'd obviously been looking for me. 'Jiali; don't cry, Jiali. It hurts me when you are hurt, and I feel like crying when you cry.'

I looked at him, startled at the strong emotion behind his words, and noticed that there really was a tear gleaming in the corner of his eye. I felt strangely drawn to his enigmatic and forceful personality. How could I explain to him that maybe it was easier in the West to cry than in China? That all it meant was a touch of self-pity and frazzled nerves. I told him about my attempts to make it to Miran.

'I didn't know it was so important,' he said finally, looking at me as if he understood for the first time what I was doing here.

I watched him, thinking how unlike my mental picture of a typical Chinese man he was. Charismatic, argumentative, full of laughter, he commanded attention from every group of people he met. Fastidious about his looks, he dressed well, cashmere sweaters, Levis, good shoes. The only luggage he carried was a toothbrush and a wad of money. I knew very little about him. Except that he travelled. Every year, with the money hustled as a taxi driver, 'the best-paying job in China', he called it, he journeyed to a different part of the country. And I knew that I trusted him.

'Teach me this game,' I changed the subject, pointing to the table I had noticed yesterday. I wanted to keep my mind occupied with anything which would distract my attention from myself.

'Ah, *Jiancha*, but you need to understand the characters,' he said, pulling open a box full of heavy black disks engraved with various characters, some green, some red.

'So I'll learn them.'

He shrugged his shoulders doubtfully, but set up the board.

Like a chess board, *Jiancha* is made up of sixty-four squares, and each player has sixteen pieces at his disposal. In contrast, however, it is divided into two camps, each eight squares wide and four deep. And rather then being chequered, it works on the principle of opposing colours, red and green. The lines, or their junctions, are numbered, one to nine across, and one to five down. Patiently Chang named each piece and explained its role.

I was glad to use the brain muscle again, and quickly memorized the counters and their function. After some time I was able to place them correctly, calling out their names and moves. In the early afternoon we played a trial game. *Jiancha* is faster and less complicated than chess. I made a timid start, then gained confidence and attacked aggressively. I took his central *shuai* with a *pao* and followed with *ma*, a stone similar to the knight. To my astonishment I won the game. Beginner's luck.

'So you're a smart one, eh?' Chang mumbled to himself, visibly baffled, and congratulated me with a lopsided grin.

The hours had passed quickly. Finally we left our retreat to return to the others, first crossing the road to use the loo in the hospital compound. We noticed that the temperature had dropped again drastically.

I am truly no friend of Chinese toilets, which consist of open holes in a concrete or wooden floor over a cavernous receptacle. You squat above it, trying not to breathe in and not to lose your balance. This one was clean and whitewashed, though, and the cold had eliminated all smell. It had one unusual feature, none the less: because of the frigid climate, the human waste, which usually spread out at the bottom of the pit, had grown into faecal stalagmites, slim columns of frozen shit which peaked through the openings. Decorated with bits of coarse pink toilet paper, they looked like Christmas trees from Mars.

I re-emerged at the same time as Chang appeared from his side. We looked at each other and broke into the laughter of mutual recognition.

'Three metres, at least three metres,' he howled.

'Must be really cold.'

'Yeah, really cold.'

I went to my room to fetch the thermometer fastened to the

zipper of my day-pack and laid it out for a few minutes. Minus 18° Celsius, it read, and that didn't allow for the knife-edge wind cutting across the compound.

We joined the others waiting in the warm nest of a room and had something to talk about. There was concern in Xin Yi's eyes, which Chang set right with a few explanatory words.

To alleviate boredom, Chang led us into a hilarious competition of songs and poetry. Everyone took their turn in an attempt to outdo the others. I was unimpressive with a rendition of 'Bare Necessities' – no one here knew Disney. Chang performed a nasal falsetto piece from the Chinese opera, shaking his hips effeminately, waving an imaginary fan.

'Shudada,' he exhaled sweetly.

Zhong Yuan began singing in a beautiful voice: 'Mei you gong chan dang, jiu mei you xin zhong guo . . . without the Communist Party there won't be a new China.'

'Sing that when you get to Taiwan,' Xin Yi joked, and the others laughed appreciatively. Zhong Yuan repeated the lyrics until I'd memorized them.

The frequency of the dynamite blasts had escalated over the course of the afternoon, and now they came at fifteen-minute intervals. At nightfall they suddenly stopped, leaving an eerie silence filled with imaginary echoes. Dusk turned the air in the room an umber dark, warmed by the glow from the stove. There was nothing else to do but go to bed.

On my final trip past the hospital I saw a few small children carrying coal, disappearing below the ground like moles. The image generated a startling and painful awareness that they might not reach adulthood.

FIFTEEN

Dunhuang

I LEANED IN THE DOORWAY of number seven, hands wrapped around a hot mug of tea, impatiently waiting to leave this miserable town. Behind me, the attendant was already sweeping out the room, chattering softly with Che Tao, who was packing up the left-overs. The courtyard between the L of the building and the outer walls was congested with four trucks loaded high with plump rice-cloth sacks; one of them had burst open, spilling white flakes. The cargo was going to Liuyuan, the railhead near Dunhuang, to be shipped east, they had told us. Chang was darting about, still trying to negotiate a ride. There was a lot of discussion and frequent glances in my direction. The drivers seemed reluctant to take me along and one of them enquired about a permit. Finally, Chang pulled out a small stack of bills which quickly disappeared in the jacket of a man leaning against his engine, and by late morning I was positioned between my friend and a heavy, short driver with the drooping moustache of a Mongol warlord.

Blasting Hong Kong pop at deafening decibels we left Mangai Zhen towards Youshashan, a sprawl on the salty shores of Gas lake. With loony gestures Chang acted out the lyrics to a tune. It was one of his favourites. The melody was western and faintly familiar to me from a Eurovision Song Contest. His mood was infectious. '*Oh bu yao bu yao bu yao beisam, wo bu yao bu yao kuqi . . .*' we sang, '. . . oh I don't wanna be sad, I don't wanna to cry, but momma, tell me, where I'm gonna sleep tonight . . . tam tam tam . . .' It was to become our theme song.

Without stopping we cut down into the underbelly of the Qai-dam desert, and swapped the mountains for huge ochre sand-dunes. Unexpectedly, the crushed gravel road switched to tarmac and we made rapid progress. At Dingzikou the driver informed us that he had to deliver some papers in Lenghu, and turned sharply south towards the grey flatlands studded with industrial plants and fire-spitting iron towers. Lenghu was one of those towns which had appeared with the natural gas and oil fever dur-ing the 'Great Leap Forward' movement in the late fifties. It was the terminus of a pipeline which traversed the Danhe Nanshan mountains and went north-east. The pipeline was indicated on my map, which surprised both Chang and the driver.

'Are you a spy?' the driver asked me half-seriously.

'No,' I laughed, 'but they make good maps in Germany.'

'Must do,' he mumbled.

We halted beside a chain-link fence containing nothing. The town looked abandoned. There were some low buildings con-structed with concrete blocks and corrugated flat metal roofs. Wind hurled dust into the air, twirling it like miniature twisters. Across the street was a department store. To pass the time, I decided to take a look.

The store was well-stocked, albeit with the most chaotic and unlikely array of goods. Tennis rackets perched next to galoshes and a tricycle; on the wall hung a fishing rod. Behind a glass counter hunched a sallow-looking youth, clicking the beads of an abacus swiftly and with utter concentration. His lips moved rapidly, adding up inaudible numbers. When he saw me, his eyes widened and his thin body leapt spontaneously a step backward. He pushed his thick glasses back on to the bridge of his nose and blinked at me. I gave him a moment to catch himself, then told him I was looking for a good cream for my chapped hands. With a broad sweep across the counter he pointed to the cosmetics. Silently I looked at the display. The small boxes and tubes meant nothing to me. I finally picked a round red one because the wrap-ping reminded me of something from home. It was expensive for Chinese conditions, almost 40 yuan, or half a month's pay for a woman.

We met our driver again at a two-table restaurant. He had

ordered a large plate of *jiaozi*, dumplings filled with minced pork and heavily spiced with ginger.

I unwrapped the cream and applied some of it to my hands. It was thick and chalky and didn't absorb into the skin. Chang grabbed the box and read the back, then chortled.

'It's a bleaching cream,' he said, and dabbed a bit on my nose. 'It'll turn you nice and pale.'

'I like my tan, thank you,' I grumbled, and tried to wipe the stuff off my hands. My skin, browned by the sun, had noticeably lightened a shade, and I looked as though I was wearing gloves.

'Chinese girls prefer porcelain skin,' the driver said.

'I'm not Chinese,' I answered.

Chang laughed, chucking me under the chin, and broke into song. '*Hei toufa, hei yanjing* . . . black hair, black eyes, red lips, pale skin . . .'

These were, I supposed, Chinese ideals of beauty. Well, I didn't pass.

At nightfall the driver pulled into a truck stop. Looking at me he told Chang to be careful. He didn't think it was a very safe place.

'You have to be a man now,' Chang ordered, before we walked into a smoke-filled dormitory occupied by a half a dozen drivers. I stuffed my hair under my cap and lit a cigarette. He motioned for me to sit on an empty bed, half-shielding me with his body.

'Uighur,' he explained to the men; 'doesn't speak *Hanyu*.' There was a joke about the stupidity of Uighurs, followed by raucous laughter. I fell asleep on a bunk, aware of Chang's physical presence protectively keeping watch.

A rough shake on the shoulder woke me, what seemed only a few minutes later. Time to go already. I stumbled out into the freezing air with chattering teeth and took my place again between Chang and the driver. The red balloon of the rising sun hovered at the end of the road like a flaming gate; we were heading right for it. Chang put his arm around me and I fell heavily against his shoulder, breathing in the musk-sweet odour of his leather jacket. The driver threw us a lascivious look and turned up the music.

I must have dozed for a few hours, when Chang dislodged

me gently, whispering, 'You're almost legal again.' We'd been climbing up the Danjin Pass and were about to descend into the sandy Dunhuang plain.

By late noon the poplars of the oasis came into view. The driver let us off near the main road and honked his horn a few times for goodbye.

Dunhuang, western outpost of the Chinese empire, was settled by the first century BC in the wake of bloody military campaigns against the Xiongnu. It profited immensely from Silk Road traffic, and by the second century the population was five and a half times that of the present 14,000. Nowadays there is little reason to visit Dunhuang other then to see the famous Mogao caves, cut into the cliff face of the Mingsha hills 25 kilometres to the south-east.

Dunhuang caters for tourists seasonally, and now during the cold months the centre was buttoned up like an English seaside town in January. The walls of hotels and municipal buildings were covered with murals of gandharvas and apsaras, those playful musicians of the Buddhist pantheon often mistakenly called angels. A gaggle of schoolgirls, rosy-cheeked, pony-tailed and ear-muffed, raced down the broad avenue on bicycles, weaving patterns into the sand. I noticed that the telephone lines hung low from the poles, and that there were no loudspeakers. Chang had passed through Dunhuang two months ago on his way to Xinjiang and knew his way around. There was a hotel where, he thought, we might find a cheap room.

He turned into an alley between two large concrete buildings. Behind an iron gate hid a small inn with a glass front. A friendly young woman, holding some knitting, answered the door and invited us into the warm foyer. Inside the tiny space, a grandfather reclined on a day bed staring with an open, empty mouth at a black and white television. We asked for some rooms.

'No foreigners,' she said, not very forcefully.

'She's a fellow student,' Chang lied, flashing his most charming smile.

The lady seemed satisfied with that explanation and for some reason didn't ask to see the mandatory white card, identification for foreigners studying in the PRC. I signed my new name, Jiali, on the registration slip. Dangling a bunch of keys she opened two adjacent rooms, and said she'd bring some hot water in a moment. It looked as though we were the only guests in her establishment.

The bay window of my room overlooked a hallway and a dank courtyard paved with slabs of concrete. Three beds were neatly arranged along the remaining three walls, there was a table and an enamel washing bowl. While unpacking my gear I noticed that the dreaded asbestos had stuck to my bag and had got into the luggage.

Pushing away images of cancer, I reclined on one of the beds and started reading about the Mogao caves. The text abounded with statistics: the caves stretched over a distance of 1.6 kilometres north to south, hewn into the eastern cliff of Mingsha mountain along the Dachuan river. In the time of the Empress Wu (684–705) there must have been more than a thousand caves; 492 of these are extant. The paintings cover a surface area of 45,000 square metres, and were created in a time frame of over a thousand years.

I was trying to imagine 45 square kilometres of painting when Chang came in and, noticing the pamphlet, said he would come along to the caves tomorrow. He asked if I'd like to grab some food somewhere. I said fine, but I'd have to change some money first. I was low on renminbi; FEC were not a useful commodity on the southern road.

We headed for the market in the south-western part of town, where I'd have the best chance of finding a money-changer. A row of *kavabchi* spread the familiar smell of burnt mutton as we neared the stalls; they were surrounded by a few Uighurs with fur hats hunching over metal skewers. I knew I had come to the right place. Chang was eyed suspiciously as we joined them and ordered two samples.

'Change some money?' I asked the man tending the meat. He was leisurely excavating his teeth with a match. Spitting a precisely placed glob between Chang's feet, he asked: 'Dollar?'

'No, FEC.'

'One-thirty.'

'That's not very much,' I argued, 'I get one-sixty in Urumqi.'

'This isn't Urumqi.'

'One-forty,' I bargained.

'One-thirty-five,' he agreed finally.

The black market value of money had been dropping drastically over the last months. At Kashgar I still exchanged at one-eighty, at Urumqi it was already twenty *mao* lower. There was talk about a devaluation of the renminbi by 20 per cent, as the rapidly expanding Chinese economy was experiencing some growing pains. The black money market was in Uighur hands, I learned, anywhere in China, and the well-being of Xinjiang's native population was tied to the flourishing of an alternative economy. There were hard times ahead.

I pulled out 300 crisp Foreign Exchange Certificates, and watched him flip through a big stack of renminbi draped expertly between his fingers. We exchanged the money and I ordered another kebab. Chang chewed the tough meat with such visible distaste that I broke out in a fit of giggles. We left in search of a restaurant.

Bouncing along, I felt the paranoia of the last weeks lifting from me. I was a tourist again. And for the first time I felt that I was in China. Playfully, I slipped my hand into Chang's pocket and found his; perplexed at first, he did nothing but stare straight ahead, warming my cold hand between his fingers.

In front of the department store we bumped into Che Tao, who greeted us with a big smile and winked at Chang. He said that they had found some trucks going all the way to Chengdu, departing in the morning at first light. Chang stared at the ground for a moment deliberating the news, then threw up his head decisively. He'd follow later by train, he announced, and asked his friend to inform their boss that he'd be a little late. With a hearty handshake, he took leave of Che Tao who stood rooted to the same spot, following us with his eyes, quietly nodding his head.

There were a number of small eateries along the main street. Poking into a few of them, we finally chose a brightly lit restaurant with a large menu advertising a variety of Chinese dishes. I entered the crammed dining-room, and was instantly greeted by some friendly shouts of 'Hello!' Around a big table, laden with plates and beer bottles, sat familiar faces from Kashgar and the bunch I had met in Khotan. Kitagawa was also there, deliberating over his rice bowl.

'Hey, I made it,' I shouted at him happily, and shoved Chang up to the table introducing him enthusiastically as my saviour and guide. Steve, an American with shoulder-length blond hair and a scraggle of a reddish beard, turned around and, looking Chang up and down, asked him directly: 'You're from Hong Kong?'

'No, he's from Sichuan province,' I answered for him.

'Student?' it came back, a bit coldly.

'No, he's a taxi driver.'

'Hm.' Steve looked away from him, slowly rolling a cigarette. 'How come a Chinese taxi driver is travelling around the country with you?' he questioned slyly, addressing the table.

Chang surveyed the crowd, then tugged at my sleeve, looking pale and angry. He didn't understand the language but had certainly picked up the hostility.

'*Zouba*,' he said quietly, '. . . I don't like them.'

We turned and left. Xinjiang, the chubby Japanese with whom I had explored Yotkan, followed us out into the street. He bowed deeply to Chang and apologized.

'They are just jealous,' he tried to explain awkwardly, 'please, let's talk later,' and went back indoors.

I was incredulous and, perhaps naïvely, baffled. Perhaps jealousy played a part; many of the travellers I had met in Kashgar and Khotan dreamt of 'doing' the southern Silk Road. And most of them, me included, identified with the lifestyle and struggle of the Uighurs, considering most Chinese as 'the enemy', a somewhat Manichaean view, I had learned. But Chang was a fellow wanderer, although, as I had experienced during the last weeks, he moved in a parallel travel universe. Rarely did the paths of the primarily western globetrotter and the local tourists meet. There were different hotels and different means of transport, even different money. I recalled my own surprise to find Chang and his friends moving about the country for pleasure – undeniably it had shaken my picture of the system.

'Xinjiang,' Chang said, 'that Japanese, he's all right,' and then added after a moment of silence, 'Have you read Maupassant?'

'No, I haven't,' I said, looking up at him in surprise.

We finally settled for a small inn and a bowl of *mian kuai*, noodles the shape of 50-mao bills mixed with a hot hot sauce, and relaxed a bit.

'They will never understand China,' Chang started talking slowly. 'We've had Chairman Mao, we've had the Cultural Revolution and we've had thousands and thousands of years of history.'

'And you've had Tiananmen Square,' I interrupted.

'Bah, forget Tiananmen, it was a mistake.'

'Whose mistake?' I persisted.

'The students, of course. People don't want a revolution, people want videos, stereos and cars. They want money, not politics.'

'Many got killed,' I reminded him in a small voice.

'One thing we've got plenty of,' Chang said coldly, 'is people.'

'I don't understand China either,' I said. 'Let's drink.'

We walked back to the hotel through dimly lit streets, cut off from each other in our own thoughts. I felt the gap widening.

'Hug,' I said abruptly, 'this is a hug.' I put my arms around him, and wished him goodnight. He was not used to this. For a moment he dropped his head on to my shoulder and held me, then pulled back sharply. In my room I performed the ritual cat-wash and went to bed feeling lonely.

A few minutes later the door opened and Chang came in.

'Jiali,' he whispered in a hoarse, excited voice.

Without speaking, I lifted the covers and watched him strip hurriedly in the faint, freezing light. We lay for a long time engulfed in warmth and closeness, tentatively exploring each other's body. In becoming a traveller and sometimes having to be a man I had forgotten what it felt like to be a woman. I touched the smooth limbs and buttocks of an adolescent. Chang did not have body hair. Suddenly I was acutely conscious of my own. I had not shaved my legs and armpits for months. To make matters worse, I felt voluptuous, out of all proportion in this land of small-framed, flat-chested women. Chang cupped my breasts, astonished and a little clumsy. We made love tenderly, sweetly. For him it was a kind of first time.

★ ★ ★

I woke late the next morning, alone. He must have left some time during the night. I dressed, and went to get some hot water from the boiler outside the office, feeling ambivalent. I walked up and saw Chang chatting with the proprietor. As he saw me he smiled and blushed, asking if I'd slept well. Deflecting my own embarrassment, I said I was dying for some coffee and that I'd buy some from the department store down the road. I had seen an advertisement for Nescafé in the window the day before.

I returned ten minutes later with a large glass jar of instant coffee. For the first time in what seemed ages, I enjoyed a morning cup, while Chang told me about his enquiries. The normal tourist bus to the caves wasn't running; there was a private taxi-service we might be able to use, he said, but we had better leave soon. I gathered my notebooks, fetched my coat and we left.

Opposite the flash New Dunhuang Hotel, next to a stack of frozen melons, waited a 'taxi', a small delivery cart with a lawn-mower motor. We climbed in the back and slowly putted into the desert. Some men were shovelling sand and gravel through large sieves, leaving small dust flags. Half an hour later, we screeched to a bumpy halt in front of the entrance to the caves, where a big sign informed us that the next tour would be held at one o'clock. To pass time we climbed the small hill facing the caves.

Before us rose the sandy wall of the Mingsha, gouged out by the river below. Into this cliff, stretching left and right until the bend of the river denied us further visibility, had been hewn a city. Cave upon cave, stacked in levels of two, three and even four, connected by stairs and balconies, had been excavated by hand. *Qianfodong*, the Thousand Buddha Caves. A nine-storey pagoda appeared over the trees on the far left. The first grotto, I had read, had been created in 366, while the earliest ones extant were from the time of the Northern Wei Dynasty (386–534). With every century, more were added. The faithful had paid homage – and money – to this building frenzy. More than an expression of piety, it appeared to me a monument to wealth and political power. A ninth-century topographical text from the so-called *Dunhuanglu* stated as much. 'Considering all these caves,' an unknown geographer had commented, 'they must have cost a lot of money.'

And money flowed to the Gateway to China. Here the roads, skirting the southern and northern edges of the Taklamakan, came together. And the roads brought an international clientele: merchants from Sogdiana, princes from Shanshan and Khotan, Tocharian soldiers and Nestorian priests, Confucian scholars and Jewish traders, Tibetan invaders and finally Mongol hordes. Now there were tourists.

At one o'clock we clustered together with an eager Japanese tour group in front of the red metal gate. Large flashlights in hand, we were led by a bored-looking Chinese guide, holding the keys. She opened the first cave. Expectantly we entered, only to behold an empty hole and a big sign in English and Chinese lamenting the theft of art-treasures by European explorers in the early part of this century. I asked her about cave 17, the so-called walled library, where a repository of old texts had been discovered by the Daoist Abbot Wang Guolu around 1900. In order to finance restorations to the then almost forgotten paintings, he had sold them off to Stein, Pelliot and others. It is said the library had contained some 50,000 documents and objets d'art spanning from the fourth to the tenth century. She shrugged and said that cave wasn't part of the tour.

As she opened door upon door, our group went quiet with astonishment and awe. Every square centimetre of the walls was covered with decoration. Buddhas and Bodhisattvas sat, smiling gently, surrounded by a myriad of figures, worshippers, devis, gandharvas. There were illustrations from Jataka tales, sutras, and scenes from everyday life. Rich earth colours gave way to blues and greens. There were portraits of kings and queens, pictures of palaces, soldiers and farmers. Some caves were large and spacious, other, like those at Kizil, featured the central column representing the world axis.

I had made some preliminary notes for comparison of specific motifs with those I knew from the Miran paintings, but quickly gave up. It would take a lifetime to study the Mogao treasures.

By the end of the afternoon the caves closed up; our heads crammed with images, we found a taxi to take us back to town. Did we want to climb the famous Mingsha sand dune, the driver asked? Chang and I looked at each other, and almost simultaneously said we had seen enough dunes to last a while.

I left Chang at the hotel and went to find Xinjiang. He was packing his suitcase as I walked into his room and told me he was afraid to go back to Japan.

'I've been travelling for a year now,' he said, 'I don't know if I'll fit in again.' Without discussing the incident of the evening before, I left him to go and pack my own things.

'Tomorrow,' I decided, 'I'll go back on the road to Miran.'

SIXTEEN

Chang

A FAINT PALLOR along the eastern horizon hinted at the beginning of a new day. Our feet rested on the exhaust pipe, which lay exposed in the aisle of the early morning bus to Liuyuan. Chang was going to catch the Chengdu train to take him home, and I was heading back west to Xinjiang, planning to visit some of the ancient sites around Turfan, before resuming my journey.

Chang sat next to me impassively, wearing that stone face again. As always, it made me feel a little uneasy. I had to admit that, while part of me was sad at seeing him go, another part of me looked forward to moving on alone. We'd shared an adventure, and had had moments of real tenderness, yet I was starting to miss my independence. Typically Catholic, I was also feeling guilty about my boyfriend in Italy. But I didn't let this stop the warmth from radiating through me.

I tried to arrange the fragments of what I knew of him into a coherent picture, and had to admit that I knew very little. In conversations, here and there, I had glimpsed pieces of it, and had found that his life, like that of many Chinese, was inextricably bound to the political history of his country.

His father was born into the revisionist milieu of the first decade of this century. Influenced by an elder brother, who had trained in the famous Whampoa military academy and later became closely aligned to Chiang Kaishek, he joined the press corps of the Nationalist Party. Reporting for the Guomingdang, he covered the Northern Expedition on his first assignment, and later, during the Sino-Japanese war, spent much time in Manchuria. After he returned from the field he met and married a young novelist of land-owning background. When the Nationalists retreated to Chongqing, the couple made a home there. Then the Communist troops closed in, and the family, aided by Chang's influential uncle, decided to leave along with the whole of the Guomingdang echelon to what was then still known as Formosa, the island of Taiwan. That was in 1949. Chang's mother, pregnant with her fifth child, however, was physically unable to travel. Her husband stayed with her to keep the family together, delaying departure until after the birth of the child. But within a few weeks China closed up, making escape impossible. The father was arrested and interned, and in a botched execution he was hanged, an ordeal which he miraculously survived. But it left him a broken and anxious man, Chang said.

Chang came along as an afterthought, well into the turbulent days of the Cultural Revolution. His mother's mild books were found to contain counter-revolutionary messages; then her family background was criticized. She too disappeared into a camp. Chang was brought up by his sister, fifteen years his senior. For some reason he left high school and never made it to university. But he was bright, embarrassingly well acquainted with literature, and had a particular weakness for French romantic novels. He said he had spent some time in the army and worked on the railway, but was vague on the details. Now he hustled, trying his hand at anything which could make money, usually by driving private cars. He was 28 and he wanted to see Australia.

A penetrating smell of burnt rubber hit my nose. It came from my shoes. The exhaust pipe had heated up during the ride, and had slowly melted a deep ridge into the soles. I cursed heartily. My only other footwear was a worn-out pair of sneakers.

We pulled up to the small railway station of Liuyuan. Chang had been quiet during the ride. Suddenly he asked me, 'You'll try to go to Miran again, won't you?'

'Yes,' I answered.

Liuyuan was waking up. Shop owners were sprinkling water into the dust of the pavement, the smell of fresh steamed buns wafted through the air. Chang dashed into a store and came back with a new set of underwear, fresh socks and a game of *Jiancha*.

We entered the tall doors to the station and moved up to the ticket counter.

'Two tickets to Turfan,' Chang demanded to my astonishment. 'I'll help you get there,' he said, turning round.

'Okay,' I said with mixed feelings, unable to rebuff him.

SEVENTEEN

Turfan

'BU SHI WO BU MING BAI . . . I see blocks and blocks of build-ings, I see acres and acres of harvest, I see oceans of people, I see millions of cars, I look left and right, and front and back, this and that, and it all looks mad . . . *Bu Shi Wo Bu Ming Bai*', a lanky Chinese youth chanted softly. It almost sounded like rap. Crouched in the corner of the railway station waiting-room, clutching his guitar with fingerless gloves, hair tied into a pony-tail trailing over the black leather jacket, he looked like a busker on the London Underground. Chang joined in the refrain: '. . . it's not that I don't see, this world is changing fast . . . *Bu Shi Wo Bu Ming Bai* . . .' then walked over and offered him a cigarette.

The song was written by a Beijing artist called Cui Jian, they explained, who was gaining fame so quickly that the government couldn't touch him. 'He speaks my heart,' Chang exclaimed, beat-ing his chest. The busker grimaced an agreement, tucking the cigarette away between the strings and the neck of his instrument.

'Are you travelling with her?' he asked Chang, who nodded.

'*Hao* . . . good,' he answered and said his biggest dream was to travel around the world. Shanghai was the furthest from home he had ever been. But he was still a child then, and barely remembered the trip. Now he was on his way to Xian to see friends. I asked him what he did for a living and he said nothing. There wasn't much chance for someone like him in Hami. Then he carefully packed up his guitar, shook hands with us and left for his train. I made a note to buy a cassette of the singer Cui Jian.

Draped over my bag, Chang nodded off. Gravity pulled his head on to his chest. He could sleep anywhere. I looked down on him, studying his face, the high cheekbones, the arrogant chin, and wondered about the coming weeks. His spur-of-the-moment decision to travel on with me worried me; and what about his job? Secretly, I had looked forward to returning to the world of Uighurs, a simpler world, less harsh, or perhaps only more familiar. With him that would be impossible. I wasn't sure if I liked 'his China', as he had called it, the China of the Han Chinese.

A group of five well-dressed students, with heavy new back-packs, came into the hall.

'*Xianggang ren* . . . they're from Hong Kong,' Chang observed, rousing from his nap. He was able to wake to full consciousness as though he had all along been sleeping with one eye open. He was right. Though certainly Chinese, they were too well-groomed, their hair too much in place, the clothing too fashionable.

'They treat us like shit when they travel in China. Wishing away the people, wanting to keep the landscape and the history. Think they are something better. But we'll show them. In ten years, we'll be doing the laughing. Then we will own Hong Kong,' Chang said in a low voice.

'That's mean,' I replied.

'But true.'

One of the collegiate-looking young men had noticed my 'westernness' and approached us. Ignoring Chang, he addressed me in English, enquiring if I was, by chance, going to Turfan. I told him I was.

'Could you take care of those girls?' he asked, pointing at two young women with too much luggage. 'Perhaps you could buy their tickets.'

I passed on the request to Chang, who had followed the exchange through half-closed eyelids, pouting. He snarled something but bought the tickets anyway. The boys left, and the girls slumped on their bags looking distressed. They had flown to Dun-huang, and now wanted to travel the oases to Kashgar and over the Karakoram to Pakistan. I had the feeling they'd rather be back home. Neither of them seemed interested in a conversation.

At eleven the train finally arrived. We fought for seats in an overcrowded third-class carriage, among countless sacks, people and screaming babies. But it was warm, and the rhythm of the train comforting.

By evening we were passing Hami, Kumul for the Uighurs. It was difficult to believe that Hami was still famous for its honey melons, traded as early as the Tang dynasty even in the distant imperial capital. From the train window we saw smokestacks enshrouded in solid brown smog, and once again I recalled the conversation with the lone ecologist in Urumqi. The lack of concern for the environment and the degree of pollution was indeed alarming: wherever there were people there was filth. Sacks of garbage were left by the side of the road for the wind to carry paper and plastic bags into the desert. Considering that millennia-old documents written on perishable materials had been found by archaeologists, it was easy to imagine that even biodegradable matter would not disappear easily in this arid climate. Perhaps future scientists will be sorting through styrofoam lunch boxes and shopping bags, writing theses on the march of modernity: 'A Prolegomena of Imported Packaged Goods as Deposited in the Taklamakan Desert 1959–2059', or something like that.

A baby had started to scream from discomfort or hunger. The mother, a heavy woman with a ruddy complexion, held the child awkwardly away from herself, helpless and repelled by the outcry, until her husband gently took the infant into his arms and lulled it back to sleep. I drifted off myself. Chang had bought some fried fish which looked like herring, and kept spitting the bones on to the floor.

There is something cruel about waking the body at three o'clock in the morning. The metabolism is at its lowest, and the brain still hovers on the other side of the moon.

It was three when we pulled into Daheyou, the station nearest to the Turfan oasis, and I still have no clear memory about getting off the train and falling asleep on a bench in the ticket hall. At six, Chang woke me once more, and said that it was time to walk to the bus terminal. My neck was stiff, and I was disorientated.

The two Hong Kong girls followed us through the dark, foggy streets, straining under their heavy luggage. They had travelled first class and looked rested and clean. On a rough gravel incline, one of the girls crumpled under her burden and fell, face down into the dirt. Wordlessly, Chang took the pack from her and continued walking. She cried all the way to the depot, complaining that she had lost her contact lens, and asked for the nearest airport. They never thanked Chang, and when the bus arrived and they didn't get on I was almost glad.

The sun was just beginning to colour the sky a pale frosty pink when we arrived at the oasis. Chang led me to a large Chinese hotel built from yellow burnt brick. It looked like a school, with huge windows and iron bars and a walled courtyard. He negotiated with the owner who, he said, was a friend of a friend's friend and managed to get us a room to share. The *furen*, a young girl of sixteen, grinned at me as she opened the door and with an exaggerated gesture, welcomed me to the hotel. I found it unsettling that her insinuation made me feel slightly cheap.

The room was comfortable enough, with three beds, a table, and a TV, but I didn't like the hotel. The bare halls smelled of urine and disinfectant, and there was no hot water. Like many new buildings in China, it was already in an advanced state of deterioration.

'I think we should move to the Turfan Guesthouse,' I said to Chang. I had read about the Guesthouse in someone's copy of the *Lonely Planet* travel guide to China.

'That's for tourists,' he answered, drawing on his cigarette. He was switching through the channels of the television, receiving only snowstorms.

'Well, this tourist would like a hot shower,' I grumbled.

I unpacked a few things, then went out to the washroom to clean my hands and face. When I returned I found Chang had fallen asleep. Feeling exhausted myself, I lay down next to him. He mumbled a few things I didn't understand, put his arms around me and held me tight, spoon fashion, like a man drowning.

It was already dark when we woke. Both of us felt more cheerful and very hungry, and we went out to a corner restaurant near the hotel. It was a T-shaped room with a small bar to one side and reminded me of one of those tacky Italian restaurants in west London. Bottles were lined up on shelves like soldiers, there were a few instruments displayed on the wall, draped with plastic vine-leaves. But it was the small tables with their red-checked table-cloths that did it. There were a few foreigners and some Chinese.

'I know you,' someone cried from across the room. The voice was definitely American. It belonged to a fair-haired, slim young man, seated with three others four tables away. He looked familiar, but I couldn't place him.

'Justin, Justin Rudelson,' he screamed again, and laughed as embarrassment crimsoned my face.

Justin was an anthropologist from Harvard who had visited SOAS a year earlier, introducing his PhD thesis to a small group of fellow Central Asianists. Something about identity among the Turfan Uighurs, which involved handing out a large number of cameras to people. I recalled that I had criticized his methodology, perhaps somewhat too severely.

'It's working, by the way,' Justin called over, apparently remembering my comments.

'Great.'

'Come and see me tomorrow afternoon, I live at the Guesthouse,' he added and returned his attention to his dinner companions.

I explained Justin to Chang, who had been watching the exchange with wonderment.

'You know a lot of people,' he commented.

'It's a small world,' I mused.

Turfan by daylight seemed to be made up of several dusty streets, rows of poplars and low houses pushed back from sandy pavements. The road leading down towards the Guesthouse was spanned by trellises carrying a few skeletons of scraggly vines. 'Do not pick the grapes' read signs spaced intermittently along the walkway. With the cold wind and dust blowing, it was hard to imagine that in summer Turfan has the reputation of being one of the hottest places on earth. We walked through the gate of the Turfan Number One, as the guest house was also known, into a quaint courtyard covered with wooden latticework, and followed the arrow to the reception at the end of a single-storey building. Chang had reluctantly agreed to a move. Two Chinese girls greeted me in friendly English, and got out the registration forms.

'A room for the two of us,' I said, pointing to Chang, who lingered in the doorway.

'Japanese?' they smiled, addressing him.

'*Bu shi* . . . no, he's Chinese.'

Their smiles vanished, and one of the girls demanded to see his papers. Chang gave me a I-told-you-so look, and diffidently pulled out his frayed pack of documents.

We were assigned separate rooms, on opposite sides of the compound. I followed my instructions to D13, a two-section dormitory with six beds, five of which were already occupied. Gear was strewn all over the floor and laundry hung from lines crisscrossing the room. I threw my things on to the empty bed and went out to find Chang. He had been put up in the older wing near the reception. A Chinese man gawked at me from a room opposite Chang's as I knocked on the door. It was a pretty, two-bed room with a vaulted ceiling and Uighur carpets.

'I don't understand it, why can't we share a room?' I complained, flopping on to a bed.

'You need to be married in China, if you want to stay together.'

'How do people make love in this country?' I wondered, more to myself.

'With difficulty . . .' Chang laughed.

'No, seriously, what do you do . . . you must have had girlfriends?'

'I do have a girlfriend,' he admitted uncomfortably.

An irrational wave of jealousy rushed through me, but I pushed it aside.

'You make love in the car, or borrow a friend's room, there are some hotels which are okay, but they are usually very expensive . . . there isn't much privacy. And you can get into a lot of trouble if you're caught; get fined money or even thrown into jail on a prostitution charge,' he explained.

'Jesus,' I let out the air slowly, 'so much for sex in China.'

'People don't have sex in China, they procreate,' Chang joked and kissed me.

'Yeah, once in a lifetime . . .'

We decided to spend the afternoon sightseeing. The museum, a few roads up from our lodgings, was closed. An old man walking beside his donkey carrying fodder pointed us in the direction of the Emin minaret. We took the main road due east, almost to the outskirts of town, then turned south again through small shady lanes and impoverished-looking homesteads, flanked by barren maize fields studded with massive cubes of open brickwork. Chang said the towers were used for drying grapes. From a distance we could see the tall, tapering silhouette of the minaret.

Built by the Uighur architect Ibrahim in 1777 in memory of the Muslim ruler Emin Khoja, it struck me as the most beautiful building I had ever seen. There were no tiles, there was no colour but for the colour of the desert. Constructed in sun-dried mud-brick, in a filigree texture of geometric and floral designs, the minaret dominated the site. The adjoining mosque appeared plain in comparison. It sat at the edge of a ruined town and there was a brick factory nearby. The factory seemed to be utilizing the ancient settlement for raw material, thereby slowly levelling it. We climbed up a staircase, reading the many inscriptions scratched into the walls by countless visitors and lovers.

'I don't like Xinjiang,' said Chang, looking out over the fields into the desert beyond. This time I didn't believe him.

Slowly, we wandered back to the guest house, strolling along a small lane which skirted the southern rim of the oasis. Walls, surrounding crumbling buildings, lined the shady track, an irrigation canal ran along the side. A few dirty children with shaven heads played with a doll; there was an open-air bakery. The smell of fresh bread brought on pangs of hunger, and we bought some of the still hot nan. Tomatoes and chilli peppers were laid out on flat roofs to dry, contrasting brightly with the dusty, monochrome surroundings. They reminded me of Christmas.

Chang accompanied me up to my room to borrow some shampoo. Music blasted down the hall as we approached, indicating that the occupants of the other beds had returned. I knocked and opened the door. A group of Japanese, three boys and two women were seated on the floor or sprawled over the beds, submerged in smoke. They looked up languidly as I entered, then laughed with recognition. They were the same bunch I had met at the Qinibagh, meditatively kneading hashish under orders from the fat German, when I was trying to get information about the southern road.

'Did you make it?' Chiyo, the girl with henna-red hair spilling from a Pathan hat, asked.

'Well, almost,' I said, and gave a brief summary of the last weeks.

'*Wah, sugoi . . .*' they muttered appreciatively.

They had left Kashgar a few days ago, and were now on their way back home. Like most of the Japanese I had met travelling in Xinjiang, they did not seem crazy about returning to their country. I introduced Chang, but there was no common language, and he quickly felt out of place.

'This is where you're staying?' he questioned, looking at the boys.

I pulled out my dictionary and looked up the Chinese word for hypocrisy. *Weishan*.

He left to take his shower, and we agreed to meet again in a couple of hours to visit Justin.

Justin lived in the new part of the guest house, an ugly, modern building with a carpeted foyer and its own reception. A handsome Uighur woman in a well-tailored Western suit and high heels, accompanied by three officials, sauntered down the stairs as we went up. The door stood open, and a sturdy cleaning lady with headscarf and thick brown stockings was making the bed, carrying on a lively conversation in a mixture of Uighur and Chinese, kidding Justin about a girl.

'Girlfriend, hm?' I teased him, as I entered.

'Well, there is this girl who thinks . . .' Justin stumbled and blushed.

'Uighur?'

'Hm.'

'This is Chang,' I introduced my friend.

'*Ni hao*,' Justin shook hands and offered tea. The cleaning lady left with a hearty goodbye.

'How is the Miran project coming – it was Miran wasn't it?'

I told him about the frustrating time in Urumqi, and then repeated the summary I had given to the Japanese.

'I'm going to try again to get there. Chang is going to help me,' I added.

'You're crazy, do you have any idea how dangerous that will be? Maybe not so much for you, but for him . . .' he exclaimed. Switching to Mandarin, he asked Chang if he was aware of the trouble I could cause him.

Chang nodded.

'You're both crazy,' Justin muttered under his breath and offered more tea.

I liked his room. There were lots of books and carpets, trinkets one collects over time. It had a lived-in feeling, and I suddenly started missing my own rooms in London. I had been on the road for five months, and the longest time I had spent in a single place was a week.

To change the subject, I asked Justin if he had noticed the tension that I had felt building up in the province. I told him about the unity parade in Ruoqiang.

'Nothing here in Turfan, this place is quiet, and it doesn't seem to change much,' he commented. I wondered if that was really true.

After a while of pleasant conversation, oddly academic, filled with gossip about common acquaintances and Central Asian scholars, we took our leave. I felt that I had been pulled back into another world for a moment, the real world, and realized that I had been living in a bubble, sustained by this drive, this crazy notion, as Justin called it, to see Miran.

'Let's play tourist tomorrow,' I said to Chang, as we walked back to our rooms.

*　　*　　*

Chang knocked on our door in the morning, announcing brightly that he had organized a car to take us to the main archaeological sites around Turfan. Still sleepy, the seven of us crowded into a Land Rover driven by a gaunt, chain-smoking Uighur of indefinable age who informed us that our first stop was Kharakhoja, the ancient city of Gaochang – or, as it became known when the Uighur kingdom held the oasis, Xoco. The site lay to the southeast of the oasis, less than an hour's drive.

The desert and mountains were still swathed in cold morning mist, when we stopped at the base of a tall, long wall. A guard shuffled out of the side of a building and opened the gate enough for the car to pass through, saluting us military style. Beyond the gate, confined within fifteen-metre-high walls, lay the ruins of a huge, silent city. Sunlight warmed ruin upon ruin, and lit the gaping mouths in the side of mounds where treasure hunters had dug for spoils. We drove into the heart of the city, towards a palace complex dominated by a tall, partially restored building. Remnants of paintings still survived in the niches of a wall that once housed Buddhist statues. The engine noise from our car seemed an intrusion.

Gaochang took its name from a Chinese garrison which controlled the Jushi kingdom, and with it the key position on the Gansu–Hami trail to the west, until the fourth century. At the time when the Chinese commenced their infiltration into the 'Western Regions', Jushi banded together with Loulan, attacking and robbing Chinese envoys and caravans. 'They act as the eyes and ears to the Xiongnu' (China's arch-enemy the Huns), a military report complained. In 108 BC, a Chinese assault troop was dispatched to 'capture the king of Loulan and defeat Jushi'. By 48 BC, a military commander had established the first fortified camp. Turfan's plight did not stop there.

An inscription from a temple dedicated to the Bodhisattva Maitreya, the Buddha of the future, indicates the presence of a minor branch of a Turkic people, the Tujue, during the fifth century. During the sixth century it was known as the Jushi-Gaochang Kingdom and once again under the control of Han Chinese. In 640 it was occupied by the Tang army, and later overthrown by the Tibetans. Then the Uighur people migrated from the Central

Asian steppe lands into the Turfan region in the ninth century and placed their capital, Xoco, here.

Gaochang-Xoco became a meeting place of cultures, a nodal point on the east–west route, where many languages could be heard and where the world's great religions coexisted peacefully, unified by the common interest in trade. German archaeologists excavated a large number of temples during the early decades of this century, finding Buddhist, Nestorian, Christian, Manichaean and even Hindu remains. Manuscripts in sixteen different languages and twenty-four scripts were unearthed, including rare Manichaean documents written in 'Estrangelo', an alphabet derived from the Syrian script, and old Turkish texts in Uighur script, developed from Sogdian; there were writings in Brahmi, Sanskrit, Tibetan, and Chinese, all reflecting the varied cultural makeup of Turfan during its heyday.

Chang and Chiyo, who had stuck around to listen to my lecture, looked bored. The driver was already leaning on his horn, urging us to come back to the car. I took one last sweeping gaze over the ruins. Its ancient streets and avenues were covered with potsherds and 600-year-old debris. I wondered why this city, after its destruction in the fourteenth century, was never reinhabited. Perhaps too many had been killed.

We drove west to visit the necropolis of Astana, a graveyard where Chinese as well as some Sogdian merchants were buried from the third to the eighth century. The name was taken from the nearby modern Uighur village and translates as 'capital', an allusion to the proximity of the ruined city. Hundreds of tombs have yielded innumerable treasures such as wall paintings, manuscripts, silks and other textiles, and above all, the famous Astana dolls, small, carved statues representing mythical beings. Stein himself had spent time here, digging up a number of them.

We parked next to a wooden building which served as ticket office, small museum, tourist shop and home to the caretaker's family and several donkeys. A barefoot girl fetched some keys, then led us on to a vast gravel field. Mounds and flags sticking in the ground were the only sign of archaeological activity. Only a few graves were open to visitors, she informed us, as she nimbly hurried down a diagonally slanted shaft to open the door. We crowded into a claustrophobic grave chamber, decorated with Chinese-style wall paintings. Mummies and grave goods were laid out to shock the tourists, reminding me how much I disliked organized tours.

Again we were hurried along by the impatience of our driver, on to our next stop, the caves of Bezeklik to the north-east of Turfan. Bezeklik, 'Beautifully Decorated Houses' as it translates from the Uighur, was a series of shrines dug into the steep cliff-face rising from the Murtuq river. We bought some tickets and, accompanied by the caretaker's colourfully dressed children, we were ushered into the first chamber. As at Kizil, it was empty save for the inevitable sign condemning the theft of cultural treasures. Grünwedel and LeCoq had extracted most of the wall paintings from the caves, shipping them to the then Ethnographic Museum in Berlin, and for the first time I was grateful. The caves which still housed some paintings were in a sorry state. Central Buddha images were surrounded by a hierarchy of beings, recreating a Buddhist paradise in which the worshipper could transcend the cruel world outside. A guardian with hog's teeth, executed in fine linear brush work influenced by the painting masters from the Far East, was a mere footnote to the artistic splendour. But graffiti had been scratched into the vivid colours, and many of the images were defaced. Why do they always take away the eyes? Much of the devastation probably happened during the Cultural Revolution, but one inscription gave a date: 1986. If you want to see the paintings from Bezeklik, go to Berlin.

An immense sand dune slowly encroached upon the edge of the cliff, contrasting yellow sand with white rock. A donkey taxi had parked at its base, and I wondered where, in the midst of all this emptiness, it would go.

'What about Jiaohe?' I asked the driver, as soon as we were on the road again. I was looking forward to visiting the famous city on the cliffs. The driver didn't answer. Chang, in his impatient way, exchanged a few words with the man, who seemed to be on the brink of getting angry. Wordlessly, oblivious to our protest, he sped back to town.

Instead of taking us to the guest house he stopped near a mosque and some mud-brick buildings. People gathered at the entrance, there was Uighur music. A wedding was going on. The driver disappeared into the house. We edged closer. Drunken men were dancing, snapping their fingers, while some older women were handing around filled dumplings. We were drawn into the celebration, and soon started dancing ourselves. Chang stood safely at the back. Suddenly an elbow hit me between the ribs. Chiyo was getting the same treatment. We were not welcome. That evening I took a long, long shower, wondering what had happened.

We decided to leave town the next day.

Halfway between Turfan and Urumqi, a short way past the village of Baiyanhe, the driver gave in to the increasingly determined grumbles of the passengers and pulled over for a piss-stop. Like everyone else, I hurried away from the bus, eager to relieve my bursting bladder. A low gravel hill looked private enough, and I quickly scaled its side. Remnants of a mud-brick structure sat on its narrow ridge, and a ruined watch tower was guarding the grey, empty landscape. It was impossible to determine its age, but the floor of the edifice was circular and covered with straw and sheep dung; a suitable place for a toilet, indeed. As I squatted, a glint of light caught my eye and, ignoring Chang's insistent shouts, I felt compelled to investigate. What I found puzzled me. Hidden between two large boulders nestled a small, cracked, ceramic figure of a seated Buddha, covered with silver paint – the type you can buy in any Hong Kong tourist shop. A weather-worn rosary was draped over his extended hand and a few dried flowers and burnt-out joss sticks lay at the base. Someone had worshipped here only recently, though it was impossible to tell whether Uighur or Han. In a province dominated by Muslims and Mao, this image of the Compassionate One was the only evidence of devotion to Buddhism I had come across during my travels through Xinjiang. And I had obviously stumbled upon someone's secret. I added a stone to the cairn behind the solitary Buddha on the hill, raising the primitive stupa, then descended slowly, accompanied by the honking of the driver's horn.

The bus bumped along much too fast for the condition of the road. There was some good-humoured teasing of the driver and astonished exclamations about a man who had been stretched out on the back bench since Turfan, snoring consistently despite the rough ride. A large swarthy Uighur, handsome in a scruffy sort of way, lit up a joint. Smiling with the nostalgia of one who had been a student in the US before Nancy Reagan's 'Just Say No' campaign, I nudged Chang with the reflex acquired many moons ago.

'Smells good,' I said.

The Uighur had caught my smile, and passed the fat cigarette down to us. I noticed that it was rolled from local newspaper.

'*Da Ma* . . . the big horse,' said Chang.

'Have you ever tried it?'

'No, it's bad for you, it makes you impotent.'

'I don't think so,' I laughed.

Chang took the joint and puffed on it, and again.

'Take it easy,' I warned.

He started to giggle, and catching himself, put his hand over his mouth. More giggles came, uncontrolled, and there was fear in his eyes. I tried to calm him down. He fingered his face, as though not sure if it was still there, and I suddenly realized that he was fighting the feeling of being high, the feeling of losing control and, more importantly, 'face'.

The Uighur man shook with laughter, and mumbled '*Hanren* . . . Chinese,' between his chuckles. Chang, I thought, was a foreigner too.

EIGHTEEN

Back to Urumqi

THE DRIVER DIDN'T BOTHER pulling into the terminal, but discarded us at an intersection near the centre of the city. It was dark and wet, and recognizable as the afternoon only by the time displayed on the face of my watch. The low sky couldn't make up its mind whether or not to snow or rain, and suddenly decided to do both. Urumqi was about as uninviting as when I had left it. For a moment we stood disorientated, ankle deep in the dirty slush on the pavement, trying to figure out which number bus would take us to the Hong Shan hotel.

'G'day.' I heard an unmistakable Australian voice behind me. It came from inside a mess of blond beard, furs and a Uighur's thick padded coat.

'Small world,' it said. 'Kashgar, the Oasis, Alex . . . ?' it questioned into my blank face.

I remembered. The muffled face belonged to the young man with whom I had had a disagreement about the purchase of furs from endangered species sold at the Sunday market. The hunting of lynx and small leopard had increased with the tourist trade, I had argued. He had shrugged, grinned, and commented on how pretty they were. Now he pointed to his hat, which sported a broad silver fox trim.

'Nice, eh?' he said, with a mocking gesture of flicking ash from an imaginary cigar. It was difficult to keep up my air of righteousness, and I returned the smile.

'Got about a dozen of them,' he explained proudly, pointing at his bag, 'some georgous snow leopard too.'

'You know you won't be able to take them abroad; ban on endangered wild life . . . they might not even let you out of China, looking like that,' I teased back.

'Na, I'm taking the lot over to Russia,' he explained. 'They love this stuff there. Do some tradin' for caviar.'

Alex amazed me. He was a born con-man. He didn't speak a word of Chinese, nor Uighur, let alone Russian, yet he had mysteriously finagled a 'Foreign Expert Card', the Mercedes of all resident permits. It granted him privileged treatment just about anywhere in the PRC, and the right to pay for hotels and transport as a local would. It opened doors. When I first met him six weeks ago, he had in tow two young girls, who worshipped him with doe-eyed gazes. They didn't talk a lot.

'Looks like your friend is feeling the cold a bit,' he commented, nodding at Chang who had been stepping from one foot to the other. Though the temperature was a good ten degrees higher here than it had been in Turfan, the wet cold seeped deep into the bones. A London sort of chill. Chang had developed a tendency to feel exceedingly uncomfortable when I carried on a conversation in English for too long. I think it gave him a sense of losing control.

'We're on the way to the Hong Shan. Know what bus?' I enquired.

'Take that one,' Alex drawled broadly and pointed to an approaching vehicle, then turned to move on.

'By the way, the happy honeymooners are there too,' he added over his shoulder, sketching a wave.

The bus disgorged us, along with a mass of moist, steaming humanoid shapes, near the Hong Shan department store. Keeping the symbol of the city, a pagoda-studded piece of rock called Hong Shan, the red mountain, on our left, we crossed the bridge towards the hotel with the same name. Once again, I was struck by the remarkable ugliness of Urumqi's broad avenues, a few of which converged in front of the bland façade of our prospective lodgings.

The large foyer of the Hong Shan hotel, like the exterior of the building, showed blatant signs of having seen better days. The decor kept to the institutional browns, greens and plastics, augmented by the inevitable silver tinsel and red paper decorations above the entrance to the restaurant. Chang, who had been wearing a pained expression ever since our meeting with Alex, came to life again and gingerly approached the long, curved front desk. A few people immediately became busy, ignoring him. At last, a heavy-set woman in a green two-piece suit and a clashing orange headscarf approached us with the slow-motion movements peculiar to hotel employees and took Chang's order for our rooms. The prices for these differed considerably. I fell into the familiar litany of protest, but the woman cut me short, eyed me up and down, and exclaimed with not a little venom in her voice: 'You don't have any money? Then what are you doing here?' giving me to understand that the only good foreigner was a rich foreigner.

Feeling slightly whipped, I went up to the fourth floor, got the key from the *furen* and dropped my gear into the three-bedded room. A beaten-up army backpack in a corner indicated that I was sharing with an unknown other, impossible to say whether male or female, but certainly not Chinese. It was cold; the radiator beneath the window made a few miaowing noises but failed to give off heat. I decided to go back to the lobby to treat myself to a pack of foreign cigarettes. My God, how did I come to start smoking like this?

The honeymooners were slouched over their inevitable map opposite the glass counter stacked with packs of Marlboro and Mild Seven cigarettes. I desperately hoped they would not notice me, and busily studied the supply. I had decided on a visit to Marlboro country (Mild Seven are for Japanese tourists and Chinese plain-clothes policemen) when it became impossible to ignore Tom's insistent shouts of greeting. I still found him as unsympathetic as ever, and was suddenly overwhelmed by a strong desire to be elsewhere. But there was no escape. Tom had already put his many chins in motion, and launched into a verbose complaint about how, after having transported their bikes from Kashgar to Urumqi on the bus (and how beaten up they were, Linda interjected), they had been denied permission to cycle to Turfan. I suddenly had the mental image of them carrying their bikes all the way to Beijing without having cycled a single kilometre, and struggled to suppress a smirk.

'Oh, it might interest you,' Tom added to his tirade in his peculiarly stilted English, 'that Mr John has also come to Urumqi; indeed, we have had the pleasure of travelling with him.'

'You mean he's in the hotel? What's he doing here?' I wondered.

'*Harm, yars*, he appears to be aiding some frightful American woman,' Tom sneered, and pulled on his large upper lip. Using this pause, I quickly slipped in a yawn and a goodbye, nodded to Linda and returned to my room.

'My' bed was occupied by a large woman noisily exhaling clouds of smoke against the ceiling. She said she could only sleep beneath a window, and I said I didn't mind. This, I supposed, was the American Tom had referred to with distaste just a moment ago. The long black hair, a prominent nose and the pancake-face suggested some Indian blood. Her sturdy legs filled out a new pair of Levis and a tartan flannel shirt hung loosely over the belt. There was a toughness about her one might have associated with a steel-mill worker from Weirton, West Virginia, had it not been for her red-rimmed eyes, showing that she had been crying. Tears didn't seem to go with her. She continued to smoke frantically, almost hysterically, and I started to feel awkward.

'You okay?' I asked finally, just to break the silence.

'Yes!'

'You sure?'

'Worry 'bout your own fucking business!'

'Sure.'

With no desire to spend any more time in the company of this unpleasant person, I gathered up my jacket and notebook and turned to leave the room.

'Hey, wait,' she asked in a child's voice. 'You got a cigarette?'

'Sure.'

Grabbing hold of my box of Marlboros, she ripped it open exactly the way I don't like it and sat up on the bed, crossing her legs beneath her rump with some effort. Her hair hung loosely over her face, and her hand shook when she lit the cigarette.

She had come to China six months ago ('just to travel around, you know,' she said between snivels). Hitchhiking from Lanzhou to Dunhuang she met and fell in love with a truck driver. She joined him on the road for a few months, then moved into his small home on the outskirts of Kashgar. They made plans to get married, buy their own truck and go private. 'For him, I'd even take on Chinese nationality,' she said dreamily, and then, more realistically, 'anyway, I've got some USDs tucked away.' A few weeks earlier she had travelled to Pakistan to have her visa renewed, and on her return found that he had disappeared; his room was deserted, and the information from his colleagues at work had been vague. She assumed a parental plot. They had objected to the union from the beginning and had repeatedly put pressure on him to dissolve the relationship. She was here to find him, talk to him. Her anguish was leaving marks on 'my' pillow.

'Where does Mr John fit into this?' I asked nosily.

'He's helping me to talk to his parents . . . they live in Urumqi . . . Samat, that's his name, he's probably here too.'

I wondered if I ought to revise my opinion about Mr John.

Tracy looked miserable and lost and big. I had the feeling that her boyfriend's disappearance may have been of his own choosing, but refrained from communicating my thoughts to her.

She was a drifter, she admitted. She had followed the Magic Bus trail in the seventies – before the Afghans started to bash each other's heads in – and had never quite got off. With Samat, she thought she had found a home. Tracy looked wistfully at the ceiling, took another Marlboro, using the butt of the last one to light it.

Without warning, the door to our room flew open, exposing the *furen* and Chang behind her.

'*Qing jin* . . . come in,' I said to Chang, who glanced nervously at the *furen*.

'But leave the door open,' the woman demanded in a school-marmish manner. I was about to formulate a reply, but a shadow of panic on Chang's face stopped me.

'We've got to get out of this town,' he sighed, after she had safely disappeared down the hall.

'Let's have some dinner first,' I answered, grabbed my things and left Tracy alone with her misery.

'She's looking for her lover,' I answered to Chang's questioning eyebrows. He shrugged.

Just around the corner from the Hong Shan were a few hole-in-the-wall restaurants, one of which I had favoured during my first visit.

'When can we leave?' Chang urged again, after we sat down at the corner table, shifting about uncomfortably. 'The *furen* on my floor questioned me about travelling with a foreigner . . . I don't like it. And yours wasn't very nice either. I've got a bad feeling.'

'I've got to pick up my things from the Academy tomorrow, then I'll try to see my friend at the Institute and find out what the story is about those new finds Xin Yi was talking about in Mangai.'

'Day after tomorrow, then,' Chang concluded.

'Yes, probably . . .'

He nodded, and devoted himself noisily to the large bowl of steaming noodles.

The proprietor's two teenage daughters tittered, waved and cooed an English 'goodbye' in melodic unison.

When I got back to the room, 'my' bed was empty. Tracy and her backpack had vanished. I cleaned the soiled saucer and failed to open the window. The room was still cold and the radiators still sounded as though they had swallowed a litter of kittens.

The next day brought a typical Urumqi-November-morning Tuesday. The television Beijing News was shouting away in the hall. I finally reached Youyou by telephone.

'Ah, Xiao Stein,' she twittered happily. 'Did you make your goal?'

I wasn't too crazy about the nickname I had picked up.

'No, not yet. But I'm off to Korla to try again.'

'Good!'

'I'd like to drop by and see you, if possible.'

She hesitated, then proposed in her careful English that it might be better if she came to see me at my hotel.

'I think it is not a good idea for you to come to the Institute . . .'

'Okay . . . when can you come round then?'

'Today impossible, tomorrow afternoon?'

'Well, all right . . .' I said, thinking that Chang wasn't going to like this.

'I'll call your floor when I am in the lobby,' she said briskly. '*Zaijian ah.*'

'*Zaijian, zaijian.*'

Without telling Chang, I left the hotel and walked down to the post office to catch the number 2 bus to the north of the city to pick up my things from storage. I was back before he had woken, and by the time he knocked on my door I was busy rearranging my gear and wondering how it would all fit into my bag.

'We have to stay an extra day,' I informed him without looking up. 'Pan Xiaojie won't be able to meet me until tomorrow.'

The sharp vertical line between his eyes and the pursed mouth indicated that he was indeed not crazy about the new developments, but he refrained from commenting.

'Let's go and buy the bus tickets,' he suggested.

Urumqi was still grey, only more so, it seemed. It never had been a sightseeing town at its best. A few vendors were selling citrus fruits across the street from the telephone exchange which, topped with a giant plastic sculpture of a globe and an oversized phone, may be the most comic building in China. A gang of boys crowded together near the entrance of the market applying black shoe polish to each other's leather jackets, a parody of 1950s toughs. At the Bank of China I cashed some travellers cheques, and changed the FEC into the people's currency with waiting black marketeers in front of the building. The rate had fallen again; soon it would not be worth exchanging at all. Chang had retreated to a safe distance during the transaction.

'What's the matter?' I asked, when I caught up with him again.

'*Bu zhidao* . . . something's going on; there's a lot of tension.'

It had started snowing again.

A frantic sort of boredom had got hold of us. We retreated to my room. Chang picked up a book on Xinjiang art from among my things and started to read to me slowly, meticulously pronouncing each word. My Chinese was improving – his English hadn't advanced beyond 'Okay', 'really', and 'I have to pee'.

'Do you remember when I first told you I loved you?' he asked tenderly, looking up from the book.

I shook my head.

'In Mangai, I was singing to you!' he said. I suddenly realized how rarely he sang now. Is it possible to love in a country without central heating? As I wondered thus, I decided to teach him the ABC.

We were lulled into a Sunday afternoon complacency, consuming huge amounts of steaming jasmine tea. I had lit several candles, trying to create at least the illusion of warmth. The door flew open again. The *furen* stood framed by the doorway as though guarding the gates of hell, letting off a very vocal curse in Chang's direction. I only comprehended the words 'foreigner' and 'police', but understood that she would call the police if she ever saw Chang near the room of a foreign woman again. I looked at Chang. His self-control was amazing. Mask-faced he thanked me formally for tea and apologized for the inconvenience. The woman pushed him along. I stepped out into the hall still echoing with her shrill voice. A number of doors had opened, revealing mouth-gaping stares. In China, people stare.

It was getting difficult for Chang and me to travel together. We had been treated suspiciously in Turfan, and Urumqi, the capital, proved to be the pits. Chang had lost his anonymity: the opportunity to merge frozen-faced into a crowd was taken from him in my company. He became an instant suspect. And now, in the chilling post-Tiananmen atmosphere, neither Uighur nor Han trusted us, especially in urban centres. There was a violent undercurrent running through the province, which had been steadily gaining momentum over the last weeks. With the increasingly frequent crack-downs on private enterprise and the devaluation of the currency, hostility towards Han Chinese rose in local Uighur communities. There were rumours about knifings, and talk about an uprising.

Justin's warnings came back to me. It was as if I realized for the first time the extent of the danger Chang had placed himself in by travelling with me. I wondered whether I should not release him from his promise to take me to Miran and hurried off to find him.

The door of his room was open, and from what I could observe, Chang was talking with two men. Both were wearing unmistakable trench coats; the younger sat by Chang's side and was inspecting the contents of his wallet. Without drawing attention to myself, I returned to my room and lay on the bed, smoking.

That infernal woman had obviously called the police. We do have to get out of this town!

In a state of mental exhaustion we went out for some dinner. The clouds hung low between the buildings, heavy with snow. Looking for warmth and reassurance, I slipped my hand into Chang's pocket as I had done many times before. But instead of gently squeezing my fingers between his, he jerked away to put a few feet between us, gesturing towards the left with his tongue. I followed the direction with my eyes. Across the street was the younger of the two men who had interrogated him earlier. Was he really following us?

'*Wo pa jingcha*,' Chang said under his breath, '. . . I fear the police.'

Youyou's call came late in the afternoon, and was followed almost immediately by her breathless arrival on my floor. She smiled congenially to the *furen*, who greeted her politely. I was happy to see her, and asked her into my room. Pausing for a moment at the threshold, she took in the sight before her with a comic expression of wonderment. I had spread my gear over all three beds, in a final attempt to eliminate any unnecessary items. Pushing away some books, string and a box of tampons, I cleared enough space to offer her a seat and turned to make some tea.

'Sorry I didn't invite you to come to the institute,' she said kindly.

'I was about to ask you about that . . .'

'Yes . . . well . . . you tried to get to Miran, no?' she stated rather then asked.

'Yes.'

'There are reports about you . . . one from Ruoqiang . . . *Jiali* . . .' she laughed.

'That's fast,' I stalled.

'Hm,' she busied herself with the teacup.

'I'm about to try again,' I told her bluntly.

'Good. I'm all for it, but you know, officially I don't know anything. You have to realize that you are committing an illegal act . . .' she added more seriously.

'I know. But to change the subject, I heard there were new finds.'

She raised her eyebrows. 'Who told you?'

'I'm a spy, don't you know?' I laughed.

'Yes, the expedition left just when you went to Kuqa,' she admitted, 'but I haven't seen any of the results.'

Sometimes I didn't trust her. And one of those moments was now. She put down her tea cup with a clank.

'I must go . . . they'll miss me at work.'

She took my hand between her small warm ones, patted me in an almost motherly way and wished me good luck.

'Thank you.'

'Be careful.'

'I will.'

'Goodbye.'

'*Zaijian* . . . and thank you for everything.'

NINETEEN

To Korla

THE NIGHT WATCHMAN fiddled with the fist-sized padlock with agonizing slowness. Finally it snapped open and the heavy chain fell to the ground with a loud clank.

'Jiali, *congmangba*,' Chang urged me to hurry.

Both of us had overslept. In danger of missing the bus, we ran. We ran through the dark city, down the middle of the wide and empty avenue. We ran from Urumqi, and it felt good. My mind chanted in rhythm with my breathing: we were going to Miran . . . it would be easy to rent a vehicle in Korla . . . go south . . . this time it'll work . . . it must work . . . third time lucky.

'*Congmangba*, Jiali, *congmangba!*'

People were still crawling all over the bus when we arrived at the station. Thank God, departure schedules were flexible in Xinjiang. Chang climbed on to the roof, tying on Big Red, as he had nicknamed my bag, and helped an elderly man lift a large wooden cage stuffed with live geese on to the rack. The animals sat, stunned into silence, and their large eyes peeked fearfully through the wire mesh.

I was taking in the spectacle with one of those unfocused morning stares caused by lack of sleep and coffee, when suddenly I felt some weight shift on my back. Someone was messing with my pack. I jerked around to find myself inches away from a knife-blade and a pock-marked teenage face beneath an olive green cloth cap. With all the anger that had accumulated during the last days, I elbowed the young man in the stomach, and finished him off with a right hook, which I had learned during my tomboy

199

childhood in Bavaria. He buckled over backwards, then with agile movements scrambled back on to his feet, shook himself, turned on his heel, and disappeared into the building.

Chang had watched the whole incident from the roof of the bus, but it was over before he had time to act. He was unable even to shout. It had happened in seconds. Now he broke out in roaring laughter, while I started to shake with delayed shock. I am only brave when I don't have to think about it. Finally seated in the bus, I noticed a 30-centimetre slash in the nylon fabric of my pack. The blade had hit the *Jiancha* box, which had stopped other items like my compass and camera from being stolen.

We were relieved to be getting out of Urumqi, out of November fogs, and travelling back to the desert. I was both glad and scared, and even more determined that we would reach Miran. As I massaged the throbbing knuckles of my right hand, Chang recounted the incident to the people in the seat next to him. His voice was suffused with hatred. The assault had confirmed his deep-seated mistrust of Xinjiang's native population. To him Uighurs were stupid, smelly Muslims, who liked music and dance. I had heard this phrase used too often by Han Chinese, and wondered if it was part of the national curriculum. I told him to shut up. Despite my state of shock, I found myself defending my attacker. All I remembered were his eyes, brown with flecks of gold, widening in surprise and fear when my fist flew in his face.

'Tell me about Miran,' Chang interrupted my internal monologue, changing the subject. It was his way of apologizing.

Miran. What is Miran? Today it is the name of a small village which, by association or proximity, gave its name to an ancient site. As far as I knew it was first mentioned in Huntington's book in 1907; Przhevalsky had recorded it merely as *Kunia-shari* or 'Old Town' a few decades earlier, but never visited it. In my imagination Miran was a Checkpoint Charlie positioned on the southeastern frontier of Kroraina, the kingdom of Shanshan. It was the first oasis reached after crossing the desert east to west along the foothills of the Altyn Tagh; or, alternatively, for the traveller from the west it was the last inhabited place before entering the great sands on the way to Dunhuang. I pictured markets and eateries, caravans coming and going, taxes, officials, corruption – in other words, a colourful multi-national community sustained by its location on the Silk Road.

Mentally, I listed the academic arguments attached to the history of Miran. One of the main problems had been to ascribe a historical name to the site. There were two fundamental questions to be considered: first, could Miran be identified with a specific geographical name in literary sources, and second, could we gain information about the function and life-cycle of the locality from these? Stein had argued that the ruins of Miran are those of the ancient capital of the kingdom of Shanshan, Wuni, and that it was abandoned in the fourth century AD. The Japanese historian Kazuo Enoki, on the other hand, thought Miran was the capital of the region only during the sixth century. His argument was based on a questionable passage in the *Shuijing Zhu*, a treatise on waterways compiled between AD 515 and 524, which placed the capital of the kingdom of Shanshan at a town called Yixun. Though he obviously opposed Stein's view, he did not elaborate upon the character of the site before that period, nor did he comment on Stein's hypothesis about the abandonment. More recently, the Beijing scholar Feng Chengjun attempted to correlate the four major sites of the Lopnur region with geographical names in Chinese sources, placing the Yixun of the Han Dynasty at Miran, but refraining from deeper analysis. Others had aligned themselves vaguely with one of these opposing viewpoints, though none seemed to have studied the problem of Miran systematically. I was inclined to challenge both Stein's and Enoki's theories, proposing that Miran was never the capital of the kingdom of Shanshan, and that it was not completely abandoned until after the Tibetan withdrawal from Xinjiang in the ninth century.

The Tibetan empire had undertaken a series of military crusades against the Tarim basin oases in the first decades of the seventh century, and by 670 controlled most of the trade routes to the west, establishing garrisons and checkpoints in the wake of their campaigns.

During the Tibetan period, Miran and its vicinity was known as Nob-Chu-Nu or Little Nob. The name appears in a number of Tibetan documents excavated by Stein from the fort he labelled

MI. Most of them date from the eighth century, the zenith of Tibetan influence in Xinjiang. Nob-Chu-Nu had close links with Nob-Ched-Po, the Great Nob, which was Ruoqiang or Qarkilik, the capital of the entire region which was then collectively known as Nob. Nob-Chu-Nu (Miran) was apparently divided into smaller districts and/or regiments. One of these districts, Rtse-hton, is mentioned in several of the documents, specifically in connection with land allocation and agriculture.

This name, Rtse-hton, can be linked to a geographical name appearing in a manuscript found in the famous cave library of Dunhuang, discussing events between the Horse and Tiger Years of AD 635–43. The document, which records the personal history of the Tibetan princess Khri-bans, elaborates upon her marriage in 636 to a Ha-za chief in the town of Seton, and the establishment of a summer residence there in 638. Though it is uncertain exactly who the Ha-za were, they have been tentatively identified with the Tuyuhun, a nomadic tribe of Mongol origin established in the Kokonor region, and the Qsaidam, who had invaded Shanshan in the fifth century. It was not implausible that the settlement Rtse-hton in the vicinity of Nob-Chu-Nu was an eighth-century version of the seventh-century name Seton. All things considered, Miran, it seems, was neither an isolated military outpost during the eighth century, nor an abandoned desert site in the seventh.

Most of our knowledge about the Tarim oases in antiquity come from the Chinese histories, though little is revealed about the old Shanshan during this period. There is a small note in Chapter 43B of the *Xin Tangshu*, the New History of the Tang Dynasty (618–907) which tells us that: '. . . starting from the southern shore of the Puchang lake (Lopnur) and going west, one passes Qituncheng which is the Yixiucheng of the Han dynasty.' Two points are of primary importance here. First, considering the ancient geography of the southern lake shore, Qitun must be identical with the Tibetan Nob-Chu-Nu or Miran (linguistically it could also be related to Rtse-hton/Seton). Second, the information had been 'legitimized' by the reference to the Han dynasty. The text furthermore stated that: '180 *li* further west (of Qitun) one comes to Shichengzhen (i.e. Great Nob/Qarkilik or Ruoqiang) the kingdom of Loulan under Han, also called Shanshan.'

This report is clarified considerably by a ninth-century geographical text from Dunhuang in the British Museum, which enumerates landmarks and towns along the southern road from the Yang barrier (a Chinese checkpoint west of Dunhuang) as far west as Qarqan (Qiemo) before looping back along the northern route. It stated that 'Tuncheng is 180 *li* east of Shichengzhen.' Hence Qituncheng was also known as the simplified Tuncheng and lay 180 *li* (72km) east of the 'capital'. The same text said that the capital was named Shichengzhen in 675, that is, shortly before the Tibetan invasion, when it became also known as Nob-Ched-Po. Miran, it could be assumed, was known to the Chinese as Qitun or Tuncheng during the same period that it was known to the Tibetans as Rtse-hton/Seton. The text also proceeded to identify Tuncheng with the Yixiu (Yixun) of the Han dynasty and included a summary of the famous Han takeover of the kingdom in 77 BC. It went on: 'This (Yixiu) is the town in question. Because the large city of Shanshan lies to the west, the barbarians speak of it as Little Shanshan. It is the modern Tuncheng.' Shanshancheng (= Shichengzhen = Qarkilik or Ruoqiang), the manuscript also informs us, was administered by the Chinese of the Sui dynasty (AD 589–618), who abandoned it after the fall of the dynasty. Just as Little Nob was so named in parallel with Great Nob during the Tibetan period, so Little Shanshan (Miran) was probably also known by the diminutive form of the name of the town near it in the sixth and early seventh centuries.

References to Miran in the period between the later Han dynasty and the sixth century were somewhat opaque. This was primarily due to Chapter 2 of the *Shuijing Zhu*, which erroneously placed the capital of the kingdom of Shanshan at the town of Yixun, leading some scholars to argue for the location of the capital at Miran during the sixth century.

It was a turbulent time. The original kingdom had disintegrated in the middle of the fifth century when Dugui, a general of the Northern Wei, delivered a fatal blow to Shanshan, captured its last king, Zhenda, and annexed it to the Northern Wei state. The court, and presumably a large part of the population, left the homeland and founded a colony in the Hami region. It is highly questionable to speak of a 'kingdom' during this period at all, although the geo-political importance of the region, like that of the oases along the southern road, continued to attract the attention of foreign invaders.

The *Shuijing Zhu* aside, other sources, such as the *Weishu*, the history of the Northern and Eastern Wei Dynasty (386–550), place the capital of Shanshan at Wuni, which we are told was one *li* square and surrounded by barren land. There seems to be no cause to mistrust these sources. Indeed, the history devoted an entire chapter to the kingdom. The Wei were politically and militarily involved in the Western Regions in the fifth century when they brought about the collapse of the Shanshan court. They subsequently administered the region and taxed the remaining population for the better part of two decades.

Ironically, Miran was founded as a military colony by the Chinese, who had predicted its future importance long before the flourishing of international trade. According to the dynastic commentaries of the Former Han dynasty (125 BC–AD 23), the Han were 'requested' to establish themselves south of the Lopnur. It happened during the episode of 77 BC, when King Angui was killed by the Han and the name of the country was changed from Loulan to Shanshan. Weituqi, who had betrayed his brother to secure the throne for himself, is said to have pleaded with the Han to set up an agricultural colony in a fertile oasis called Yixun. 'For a long time,' he said, ' I have been in Han. Now I am returning home, deserted and weak, at a time when the sons of the former king are alive, and I fear that I may be killed. There is a town (called) Yixun in the state, whose land is fertile. I would be grateful if Han could send one leader to set up an agricultural colony there and accumulate a store of field-crops, so that I would be able to rely on the support of Han prestige.'

The Chinese had already established several of these colonies during their move west, to supply their troops; locals were notorious for heading into the desert with everything they owned on the approach of an army, leaving many a battalion stranded and starving on the way. But I suppose a deal was a deal, the colony was established, a major and 40 officers installed, Weituqi got the throne and the Chinese a foothold on the southern road.

Miran did not turn into a prosperous city, however, until the

Chinese had been expelled from the region almost a century later and Shanshan and Khotan shared power in the whole south. The country flourished under the administration of a succession of kings for almost five centuries, a period which was followed by a series of invasions and battles for its position on the trade routes until the Tibetan colonialization in the eighth century.

I was reciting a brief history of Miran as I understood it. Miran, I told Chang, carried a number of different names during its long history: during the Han dynasty it was Yixun or Yixiu, an agricultural and military colony to mark the first oasis on the southern route into the Western Regions. At some point it became known also as Little Shanshan, in contrast to the principal town in the region. It bore the names Qitun and Tun, probably at the same time that it was also known as Seton to the Tuyuhun and the Tibetans. Its last attested historic designation was that of Nob-Chu-Nu, or Little Nob, and Rtse-hton in the eighth and ninth centuries.

My Chinese still couldn't get around some of the vocabulary, and I spoke haltingly. Chang seemed to have trouble keeping his chin from falling on to his chest and he bravely fought against making sleeping noises. A deep laugh behind me commented, 'Not bad . . . for a foreigner.' I turned around and looked into the dark brown face of an old Uighur man.

'You forgot a few things,' he said.

'Yes, I know, this was the abbreviated version.'

He nodded, winked and offered me a handful of sunflower seeds.

'Are you going to Miran?' he asked me.

'Yes.'

'Good raisins there.'

'I know.'

He smiled, pulled his cap over his eyes and fell asleep too.

Korla, the capital of the Bayingolin Mongol Administrative Region, is a flat, grey sprawl of low buildings and a few ostentatious new hotels, nestled in the armpit of the Tian and Kuruktagh mountains. It is a town marked by industry. The natural gas fields have brought money since the 1950s and with it a massive influx of Han Chinese. No one nationality appears to be in the absolute majority, resulting in the undefined ugliness caused by lack of pride or urban planning. Korla is a place of transit. Everyone stops here. It is the terminus of the Urumqi–Lanzhou railway, and a nodal point for the roads from Urumqi, Kashgar, Ruoqiang and the East. Chang had spent a week here during the early part of his journey, though I wondered why.

'Let's go and see some friends,' he said, and walked quickly towards the centre of town. Near the Kunlun Hotel, he ducked into one of the low doorways in the solid wall lining the road. It was a restaurant. A woman in tight stretch trousers, and with an unusually large bosom covered with dangling gold jewellery, floated towards us, greeting Chang in his broad Sichuan dialect. She flashed me a gold-capped tooth and pulled us on to a wicker settee. I noticed that she had extremely long fingernails, painted a dark raspberry colour. Her husband, a slight grey man, peeked out of the kitchen welcoming Chang back.

'Girlfriend?' she asked Chang. He nodded.

'Where are you from?' she asked me in Mandarin.

'Germany.'

'*Ah, Hi Te La*,' she squealed with delight, tweaked my cheek roughly, and took orders for the food.

'I hate that association,' I confided in Chang after she had moved on to other customers.

'You shouldn't. If it weren't for Hitler, no one here would have ever heard of Germany,' he said matter-of-factly.

'That's one way of looking at it . . .'

Chang instinctively seemed to seek the company of people from his home province, who generally received him with open arms as 'one of their own'. He preferred Sichuan dishes over other Chinese cuisine, and never touched the local, Uighur food if he could help it. For all his love of travel and hunger for adventure, with people he displayed a clannish expatriate manner which was starting to irritate me.

Chang had found us a small, cheap hotel – Chinese only. He thought it more inconspicuous than one of the flashier tourist ones. I wasn't so sure.

ABOVE: The vast remains of Kharakhoja, capital of Uighuristan from the ninth to the thirteenth centuries.

RIGHT: Growing up Uighur still means being surrounded by a large network of family and friends. The recent policy of coercive birth control might change all that.

ABOVE: Masterpiece in brick: the Emin minaret, Turfan.

RIGHT: United colours of Benetton, courtesy of the caretaker's children at the Buddhist caves of Bezeklik.

BELOW: Bakery near the Turfan Number One Guesthouse.

A donkey taxi in front of the great sand dune at Bezeklik.

RIGHT: The daughter of a Han Chinese family sent into 'exile' in Xinjiang. The cracks in the wall are attributed to 'earthquakes'; in reality this location is less than 200 kilometres from the Lopnur, one of China's main nuclear testing sites (still in use).

BELOW: Modern caravanserai or truck stop near Argan on the road to Miran.

MAIN PICTURE: The eighth-century Tibetan fort in the centre of ancient Miran. No one could tell me the use for the wooden tower.

RIGHT: The interior of the fort.

LEFT: The famous second-century Buddhist shrine M III at Miran, from which Stein excavated the wall paintings now in New Delhi.

RIGHT: On the eastern facade of the Vihara I discovered remnants of a standing Buddha figure.

By criss-crossing Stein's exploration track, I discovered four uncharted
structures at Miran. This one I named M 1.

LEFT: Fragment of a second-century wall painting extracted by Stein from the central register of shrine M III, depicting the 'Interpretation of Maya's dream', a famous episode from the life story of the Buddha, now in New Delhi.

BELOW: The base of the interior wall of the circular shrine MV was once decorated with a garland-carrier motif and busts of men and women of different nationalities, reflecting the international milieu of the ancient Silk Road.

I was crammed in a room together with three female water specialists from Beijing University, who did not seem pleased about my intrusion. I didn't blame them. They had been living here for the last month while surveying the area around Korla for its future water potential. Files, graphs and books were stacked high on three sides of the table under the window. Each of the girls sat stiff-backed on a wooden chair, staring at the papers, intent on ignoring me. They could have been sisters: all three had their hair cut in a bob and wore black-rimmed glasses. Black stretch pants and red woollen cardigans completed the illusion of meeting triplets.

'Don't tell them about Miran,' Chang warned me before turning in for the night.

'No problem there,' I answered and went into my own dark room. The girls had undressed and slipped under the covers while I was in the washroom.

The Chinese government has had great plans for Xinjiang's natural resources for decades, and now it was stepping up the actualization process. The province swarmed with geologists, oil and water specialists, and surveyors. There was talk of parcelling out huge sections of the desert and opening it up for foreign exploitation. The Japanese, I was told, had long had stakes in fields north of Urumqi, and Exxon had been sending reconnaissance teams into the Tarim basin. Those three girls were the proud flag-bearers of a new Gold Rush. I wondered where that would leave Xinjiang, and suddenly had the depressing thought that I was clinging to the very tip of the tail of a time gone by.

We had trouble finding a car, and I was suffering from a bad case of *déjà vu*. Chang would disappear for hours on end, following leads and names and coming back empty-handed, yet amazingly he sustained a cheerful mood and an infectious enthusiasm. He was in charge again, and any place was better than Urumqi, I suppose. I spent most of the day near the stove in the Sichuan restaurant going over Stein's site plan of Miran, mapping out a route for exploring the ruined city as quickly and efficiently as possible. Completed in 1914, his was still the only detailed plan of the site to date.

Stein had visited Miran for the first time in 1906. In a letter to his close friend P. S. Allen, endearingly called 'Publius', he described his first visit to the ruins: 'I marched to Abdal on the Tarim by a route which allowed me to visit an old site close to the Miran of the maps.' He wrote further: 'I found there a much battered fort and guided by an intelligent Lop man's information hit upon a number of rubbish-filled rooms.' With the help of locally hired workers, Stein cleared away the surface accumulation of what turned out to be a Tibetan fort and, within a two-day period, excavated records identifying the ruin as the Little Nob of the eighth century.

After this first short visit, Stein headed back to Abdal and then went on to Loulan, returning to Miran in January 1907. He continued to work on the fort and explored a number of other free-standing structures of a much earlier period. Among those were 'my' shrines, which he labelled MIII and MV, from which he recovered a large quantity of material and those wall paintings I had studied in the Delhi Museum in July. I couldn't find Abdal on the map.

Finally we had a real lead. The brother of the owner of the restaurant had heard of someone who could 'fix' things, and had arranged a meeting in a smoky eatery near the bus terminal. I was gaining confidence in Chang's attitude that everything was possible in China, provided you knew how. 'Guanxi,' he told me. 'Connections. You can't do anything here without connections.' Some guanxi, however, were better than others.

The moment I laid eyes on Qian Song I mistrusted him. There was something rodent- or weasel-like about him. Maybe it was the unblinking eyes. A sallow face, the skin a sickly pallor, was cut in half by a hint of a moustache and framed by stringy hair combed on to the forehead and in front of the ears. His emaciated body was garbed in a baby-blue leisure suit with bell bottoms and black ankle-boots with extraordinarily high heels. I had seen those heels being sold in the markets. They were all the rage in Xinjiang this year. The dislike seemed to be mutual. His opaque eyes narrowed when he looked me up and down, and he made a point of negotiating exclusively with Chang in rapid, hissing whispers, his mouth only inches from Chang's expressionless face.

'Tomorrow, tomorrow morning . . . meet me at my store . . . 150 for her . . .' were some of the snatches of conversation I picked up. For a price Qian Song would take us to a town halfway between Korla and Ruoqiang from where he would arrange a car. The deal sounded precarious at best. Nevertheless, Chang and he agreed, they shook hands, and Qian Song left the restaurant.

'I don't trust him,' I repeated emphatically.

'Neither do I, but he's our only chance. But don't worry, he's only small fry,' Chang tried to reassure me.

We spent the afternoon preparing for the final assault on Miran. I had my pack sewn up again in the market, where, as in any Xinjiang town, knife-grinders, cobblers, tailors and all the other trades lined the entrance in neat rows, competing for business. Later, we searched for the local PSB in order to get my visa extended. A month had passed already since I was in Khotan. This was the last extension possible on my current visa. In another month I would have to leave China.

The Korla Public Security Bureau was located in a small, recently established office dominated by a brand-new sign in English advertising Xinjiang's 'open' areas. Behind a large, empty metal desk sat a big Uighur officer with dark-brown hair and grey-blue eyes, who looked as though ten years ago he had been extremely handsome, but had now settled down to be a good husband and father. He stared at my passport, intently studying page after colourful page. After a few moments of silence, he admitted he had never extended a visa before, and asked me to return the next day when another officer would be on duty. I implored him to try anyway. Reluctantly he placed a stamp next to the one I had received in Khotan, but filled it out incorrectly, confusing the date of issue and the extension date. As I pointed out the error, I realized that he was unable to read either the few Chinese characters or the English, which made up the visa format. Without comment, I wrote out the correct form for him on a sheet of paper. He crossed out the previous entry, stamped my document again and faithfully copied my sample. Immediately after, I wished I had cheated on the date. Perhaps in order to regain his composure, the officer threw a few hard questions at Chang.

'Where did you come from?'

'Urumqi.'

'And she?'

'Kashgar,' I answered hastily.

'What are you doing together?'

'Oh, he helped me find your office. I don't speak Chinese, you see,' I said in Chinese.

The officer found the explanation plausible, handed back our papers, and saluted us.

'You're turning Chinese,' Chang laughed, as we got back in the street. Lying was becoming second nature.

We returned to the hotel to pack. Only the most essential items would come along. Maps, camera, film, drawing and surveying equipment, a change of knickers and an extra T-shirt, some toiletries. The rest was tied up in Big Red, and stored at the restaurant. We paid our hotel bill, and turned in early.

TWENTY

The Road to Miran

WE LEFT AT SUNRISE. Jostling each other and sneaking kisses like adolescents, we walked to Qian Song's store, south of the bus station. His business sat at the edge of a depot which was made up of mountains of coal and low concrete buildings. The store was closed. A pretty Chinese girl, with long hair and a leather jacket, leaned against the door smoking a cigarette. She introduced herself as Mali. Apparently, she too had made a deal with the weasel.

'I'm going to buy some raisins in Miran,' she informed us of the purpose of her journey.

I laughed out loud. Those Miran raisins seemed to be pursuing me.

'Why?' I asked her, after I had regained my composure.

'Business. I buy them and sell them for a higher price here,' she explained, undisturbed by my comic reaction.

'Ah.'

'They are very good raisins,' she reinforced her argument.

'So I've heard.'

She took hold of my wrist and looked at my watch.

'How much?' she asked.

'Oh, quite cheap, about 300 renminbi.' It was a black Swatch.

'Very expensive . . . and it's plastic.' That seemed to disappoint her.

The three of us had been treading sand and coal dust into a neat flat circle for about an hour before Qian Song finally arrived, walking hurriedly in a nervous, jerky manner. He unlocked his

211

store and asked us in. With four people the space was completely crammed; Mali and I hoisted ourselves on to some rice sacks and lit cigarettes. Twisting a few light bulbs in their sockets, Qian Song lit up the tiny place and I could make out a mess of supplies for lorry drivers: cigarettes, alcohol, overalls, wrenches, all jumbled together and barely contained between soot-blackened walls and a dirty ceiling. Then, propping his behind on the edge of the counter, Qian Song called a conference. There were trucks going south this morning, he said staring at his boots, but there was only room for two passengers – one of whom was himself. Mali pushed forward, asserting that she had been promised a ride last week.

'But we have to leave today,' I interjected.

'Take the bus,' Qian Song voiced aggressively, bent on ignoring me.

'I can't.' He knew very well that no one would sell me a ticket for the Ruoqiang road. Then I had an idea.

'Chang can take the bus, I'll go with you . . . when is the next bus?' I addressed Qian Song.

'The bus leaves at nine,' he said. That was in fifteen minutes.

Chang did not like the suggestion, but saw the logic in the arrangement. He made a quick decision.

'Take care of her,' he cried, and ran off before Qian Song could protest. I was left alone with the two, and suddenly felt vulnerable.

'That'll cost you extra money,' the weasel said quietly and left again.

I waited. At eleven, two empty coal trucks stopped in front of Qian Song's store. He and I squeezed next to the driver of the first, and a few minutes later we were off. Mali was left behind.

We left Korla and drove south towards Yuli, or Lopnur. The road followed the course of the Tarim river, green-lined meandering channels of water, parting the great desert into the Taklamakan in the west and the Gashun Gobi in the east.

It was market day in Lopnur. As the truck slowly furrowed through the crowd, parting donkeys, sheep and people, Qian Song looked at me with dislike, then stared out of the window. Slumping deep into the seat, I pulled my cap over my face. I guessed that only greed had persuaded him to associate with a foreigner, and he seemed to be regretting it already. I glanced at his face, made ugly by ugly thoughts and cunning. Were it not for the natural antipathy between us, I would have loved to hear his story. On the outskirts of town Qian signalled the driver to pull over, took his little bag and climbed into the truck following us. There was an empty seat. Chang could easily have come with us, I noticed with some panic.

Almost simultaneously the driver and I let out a big sigh of relief.

'He's no good,' he said.

I nodded in agreement and we both laughed. That broke the ice. His name was Ma, he said, extending a hand and a friendly smile.

'Are you Christian?' he asked me.

'Of sorts,' I answered.

Ma was Hui, a Chinese Muslim minority, and originally from Gansu province. He had married a Uighur woman and moved to Korla ten years ago.

'Ten years I have been driving for the government,' he complained.

'Don't you like it?' I asked.

'Oh, I like the job. I get around. Sometimes I take long hauls to Xian or even to Chengdu. But you can't live from it any more. I make about 90 renminbi a month. That barely feeds us now.'

'So you take passengers,' I stated rather than asked.

'Sure. Everyone does. Brings some extra cash. Actually, I would like to buy a car. Get myself a private taxi business,' he added. His voice trailed off, and for a moment he was lost in his own thoughts.

Capitalism was on the march, and with it inflation. Price rises during the previous year were being bitterly felt now. I kept hearing the same lament over and over. Those employed by the government were worst hit by it. It seemed that here, in Xinjiang, the independent farmers selling produce on the markets were the only people doing well. 'Wealthy peasants,' Aertosen had called them. And then there were those who were struggling to go into private business, creaming off the tourist trade, like Tahir with his café in Kashgar.

'How much does a car cost in Germany?' Ma asked suddenly.

'Depends on the car,' I answered.

'A small one . . .'

'I don't really know,' I had to admit.

'Don't you have a car?'

'No.'

Ma didn't say anything, as though contemplating my answer. In silence I watched the buff-coloured sand and gravel desert eat into the thin strip of green around the water of the river. Half-dried stagnant pools harboured mosquitoes and a few water birds. Ma was humming a tune in minor keys, and after a while said that it was time for lunch and stopped his vehicle.

Two buildings abutted the road on either side, facing each other. They couldn't have been more different. The one on the right was a concrete bungalow with the red star of a government rest house, while the one on the left was a shambles of wooden shacks. We headed for the left one.

Ducking low, we entered a dark room with a stamped mud floor, a stove, a narrow table and a long bench, inhabited by three women. They represented three generations: an old woman sat by the stove while her daughter and grandchild attended to the noodles. The manageress, a tall, slender Uighur, came towards us with a big smile. Ma introduced her as his wife's cousin and started a lively discussion with her in Uighur. He had brought a large bag of wet salted peanuts for the little girl, who obviously adored him. The four of us sat next to each other on the long bench, facing them. Qian Song had squeezed uncomfortably into the corner clutching his bag tightly to his chest. I watched him eye the table, the chopsticks and the women with open distaste. They ignored him. The mother and daughter started making noodles from scratch, kneading dough and gracefully drawing it out into long thin strands. Both of them had their hair done in ten long braids that reached almost to the floor. I told Ma that I thought them very beautiful, a comment which he immediately translated, causing some blushing and pleased giggles. The girl stared at me, and addressed a question to Ma.

'She wants to know if all the women in the west cut their hair short.'

'No, not really . . . just some,' I answered, and ran my fingers self-consciously through my ungroomed blond mop. I wasn't feeling too beautiful these days. The grandmother let out a cackle, and started humming a sing-song. A few minutes later we were served huge bowls of steaming noodles, the best I had had in Xinjiang so far. Qian refused to eat them. Instead he leaned over and muttered something into Ma's ear.

'He wants his money,' Ma informed me.

'What money?' I asked between slurps.

Ma winked and slapped me on the shoulder, then, getting up rapidly, indicated that it was time to go. The little girl and her mother escorted us to the vehicles, pleased with my promise to return to eat here again on the way back.

We were on the road for barely half an hour, when Ma came to a halt and said that he would have to turn off here.

'Where are we?' I asked stunned.

'Near station number 31.'

'But I have to go to 34,' I argued helplessly. Cursing Qian Song, I climbed out of the truck. Ma seemed to be waiting for something.

'How much for the ride?' I asked.

'Ten for you and ten for him,' him meaning Qian Song.

I dug into my pocket and handed over two bills.

'Let me give you my address,' Ma said suddenly. 'When you come to Korla you must stay with us. My wife is a good cook.' He scribbled a few lines of Chinese characters into my diary, then said kindly: 'Be careful little sister . . . good luck,' and patted my head from above.

I found myself alone in the middle of the desert, sunset approaching, with a long uninterrupted stretch of road in front of me. Only I wasn't quite alone. Qian Song the weasel crouched next to me, looking as though he was about to burst into tears. At the moment he seemed to be a liability rather than an asset.

'*Tamade,*' I swore in Chinese. For lack of anything better to do, I picked up my pack and started walking south.

Fifteen minutes later there was the noise of an engine. A dust cloud appeared in the distance, which turned into a pick-up truck.

Qian Song placed himself in the centre of the road and waved frantically. The pick-up stopped. In the cab were three Chinese kids, two boys flanking a teenage girl with pigtails. Qian Song was begging for a ride, and I saw contempt in the eyes of the boy behind the wheel. But they agreed to take us for some of the distance.

We climbed into the bed of the pick-up, a flat shallow rectangle with not much to hold on to. The driver accelerated, then increased speed again, flying over the bumps of the dirt road. It was impossible to sit down, and at that speed one severe bump could have easily thrown us off. Watching the laughing faces of the three kids, so close through the rear window, I realized that they were enjoying their dangerous game. Eventually I managed to arrange myself into a crouching position holding on to the edge of the truck bed with difficulty, taking the bumps with my leg muscles very much like skiing a rough piste. At some point the driver stopped, took an air gun, aimed, and shot at a few ducks in the marsh. One of the birds was hit and flapped helplessly in shallow, brackish water. Not wanting to soil his shoes, the boy shrugged, threw the gun back behind the seat and the ride continued. At the turn-off point to station number 32 he stopped and told us to get off. Qian pleaded with him to take us on to number 34.

'Five hundred renminbi,' the kid demanded ludicrously.

'Come on, you have money, pay them,' Qian urged me. It was the first time he had addressed me directly.

'Forget it. I'd rather walk, these assholes could have killed us,' I screamed at the top of my lungs, and a few things more – but in English. I was livid, and slightly in shock; I needed to scream the shakes out of my bones. There were some damning remarks; Qian Song cursed my inability to speak Chinese (my verbal eruption had just re-confirmed his belief that I did not understand a single word of *Hanyu*), and the pick-up drove off, skilfully spraying us with sand and gravel.

The landscape had become more desolate. The Tarim was nearly spent, its water used up for irrigating too many fields for too many people further upstream. There was a Uighur mud house by the side of the road and beside it a stack of firewood. I sat down on an ancient tree-trunk, lit a cigarette, and felt surprisingly calm. Station number 34 was not indicated on my map, but I guessed it was another 85 kilometres away. An old man and a few children stared at me with wide-open mouths. I waved a greeting, '*Yakshimusis*,' and laughed at them.

The old man laughed back and gestured, inviting me into his house. I thanked him, but decided to keep vigil for transport. The light was fading, and the sky lit up in a spectacular display of colours. I loved this late afternoon winter light in Xinjiang. It came at a low angle and threw long shadows, but had a warmth like no other light during the day. Magically, it turned the desert golden. Night came with its usual speed, never failing to overwhelm with its rapid approach. I watched the lights go on in the Uighur's house. It was getting uncomfortably chilly.

There was a cloud on the horizon. A ride? No, just the last rays of a distant sun playing with some dust carried into the air by a gust of wind. I took my seat by the side of the road again, and finally, half a pack of cigarettes later, some headlights appeared in the distance. I jumped up and down, in the centre of the road. The vehicle materialized into an army jeep, which came to a halt at my side.

'Are you going south? Can you take me to station number 34?' I shouted into the darkened jeep. The driver opened the door, lighting up the interior. The vehicle was occupied by four uniformed men and a woman.

'Please,' I urged them.

'No, take me,' Qian pushed me out of the way.

'We don't have space for two,' said the driver.

'I don't need much,' I argued.

'Let's take her along,' the woman decided in my favour.

There were some grumbles and rearranging of packages. A makeshift seat was constructed from padded coats. I squeezed uncomfortably between the two front seats, facing the three people in the back. We drove off, leaving Qian Song standing forlornly at the side of the road. I almost felt sorry for him.

The four men were police officers on the way to a meeting in Ruoqiang. The woman had the groomed crispness of a party cadre. She immediately started questioning me about my business on the road. I had missed the bus in Korla, I told her, and was on the way to meet my archaeological team to go on a dig. I was glad of the dark interior, otherwise she would have noticed that I was spinning a yarn. I lied. They bought the story. In order to avoid more questions, I feigned sleep. Eventually I did drift off, bits of conversation entering my semi-consciousness. They were debating whether to ask me about my papers.

Two hours later we came to the turn-off point for station number 34. I had arrived a good six hours behind schedule. Chang stormed out of the local bar, ran towards me and to the utter astonishment of the bystanders hugged me. There were tears in his eyes.

'You're turning European,' I smiled.

Sanshisituan, station number 34, was a former prison camp, inhabited almost exclusively by victims of the Cultural Revolution from Sichuan. Chang had spent the afternoon talking to former writers, artists, teachers, members of an intellectual élite who had been sent during the 1960s to the gulags of Xinjiang to do penance for their so-called counter-revolutionary behaviour. The experience had moved him. One man, he said, knew of his father, and had read his mother's essays many years ago. This man, Mr Liu, had offered to put us up for the night.

The Lius lived in a small shack, a patchwork of wood, bricks, mud and corrugated metal. Mr Liu, a tall, slim man with a ravaged face, and his wife, a red-cheeked, competent-looking woman, ushered us into their tiny, crowded living-room and offered us jasmine tea. Chang and I sank into the depths of an overstuffed sofa, and I worried about soiling the lace antimacassars draped over the back and arms.

'She brought it back from Fujian,' Mr Liu introduced the tea. His wife, he told us, came from Xiamen, a large city in the southern part of that province. She had been allowed to visit her home for the first time in twenty years.

'It's not very good,' the wife said proudly.

'No, it's wonderful, really,' we praised the fragrant and obviously precious tea.

Mrs Liu smiled and bowed slightly, reciting hospitable formulas. There was a surreal afternoon tea-time formality about the scene, and I almost expected to be offered some scones and little triangular cucumber sandwiches.

There was a commotion outside, and shouts. Seconds later, Qian Song invaded the room in his rude manner, and from the expression on his face he was not pleased. Mrs Liu continued to smile amiably.

'She owes me 150 renminbi,' Qian pointed at me. Chang had jumped up and moved his body protectively between us. Gently pushing him aside, I looked down at Qian and asked him what he thought I owed him money for. 'For the ride.'

'I already paid the driver.'

'She doesn't understand Chinese, she owes me money . . .' Qian argued.

Chang looked back and forth between us, unsure for a moment as to whom he should believe.

'Why don't you ring Ma tomorrow, and ask him,' I said a bit too smugly, and explained to Chang that Ma was the driver who had taken us from Korla to station number 31. In support of my statement I brought out my diary and showed the address to Chang. Chang grinned, straightened himself a bit and told Qian that he believed me. Qian Song turned and with a curse about foreigners left in defeat.

'Don't trust him,' said Mr Liu.

'I never did, but he was our only chance to get a car,' Chang sighed wearily.

'Worry about that in the morning,' Mr Liu replied kindly and patted him on the arm.

There were two bedrooms: a tiny space patched on to the outside of the house, two by two metres filled completely by three beds, was their children's room. The other, no bigger, was taken up by a large marital bed. Politely, they offered us the latter. I was embarrassed and realized that I did not know the correct form of reply. But Chang thanked them kindly for their offer, then praised the small room in front. We settled in there.

After a few moments, Mr Liu entered with a large bowl of fruit and straddled a three-legged stool facing us. Mr Liu had come to talk. The candlelight emphasized the hollows and lines on his face. He looked like someone who had spent many years being starved.

I noticed that Chang was using exceptionally courteous and meticulous speech in addressing him.

Sanshisituan, station number 34, Mr Liu told us, was one of those camps left over from the great campaign to expand the frontiers in the 1950s. It started out as an army agricultural colony (*tuan* actually means regiment, and is a suffix used for military terms) and was turned into a work camp in the sixties. *Laogai*, he called it, re-education through labour. He had come out here with hundreds of other men in 1968. They were supposed to make the desert green and at the same time become good Communists. Now it was almost like a village, with some big communal fields, and in the last years land had been parcelled out to families to farm privately.

'Life is much better now,' he added in emphasis.

'Why were you sent here?' I asked him.

'I loved western things. Literature, philosophy . . . Hegel, Kant . . .' he laughed a strikingly youthful laugh. 'I used to dream about the west, dream about America . . . I was very foolish in those days,' he added dutifully.

I pulled a crisp dollar bill out of my money belt and handed it to him. He looked at it, turned it front to back, and handed it back to me.

'Keep it,' I said.

'No, no, I couldn't.'

'Please do, it's not worth much. It's just to look at.'

'How much?'

'About six renminbi.'

'Ah.'

The candle had burnt down to a stump by the time Mr Liu left us, pulling the curtain closed behind him. His story, Chang said, was like that of many. Too many.

'Every family in China is haunted by the past. We have all suffered.'

'Tell me about it?' I asked him, wanting to hear more about Chang. The meeting with the Lius had obviously stirred up strong personal memories, relating to, I guessed, his parents' ordeal.

'Some other time,' he mumbled and pulled me towards him.

We found ourselves alone in a room for the first time since

Turfan. We were unaccustomed to such freedom. Slowly, with quiet passion we embraced. It struck me once again that China was not an ideal country for lovers.

I woke late the next morning, with a strong urge to have a pee and a bath. Chang's bed was empty. The room was in semi-darkness; someone had draped a towel over the tiny window to keep the light out. I picked at some grapes, slipped a sweater over my head, pulled on my jeans and stepped outside into the bright sunshine. Mrs Liu was feeding the chickens, cackling at them while throwing some seeds through the wire mesh. I called out a greeting.

'Inside, go back inside,' she shouted, shooing me back as though I was one of her chickens. It was too dangerous for me to be seen outdoors during the day, she explained.

'I need to use the toilet.' Chang had told me about the communal toilets near the shop yesterday.

'Go behind the shed.'

I did.

Finally, Chang returned. He was accompanied by a tall, muscular teenager, with a blue cloth cap and a work jacket buttoned tightly around his throat. His flat, round face was pulled into a permanent frown, and he didn't talk a lot. Chang introduced him as the Lius' youngest son.

Qian, they reported, had gone back on his promise as expected. In fact he seemed to have disappeared from the village altogether. Chang and Xiao Liu had been scouting for an alternative ride and had got hold of an old coal truck. The only problem was that the tank was empty, and the next official depot selling petrol lay about 80 kilometres down the road. There was someone in the village with a store of fuel, but the man wasn't sure he wanted to sell. Mr Liu had gone off to negotiate.

We settled back into waiting mode. I pulled out my map, which was unexpectedly incomplete in regards to the Korla–Ruoqiang road. None of the stations I had passed yesterday was indicated. Xiao Liu looked at it intently.

'There is an airport here,' he commented, pointing to a spot east of station number 34. 'And a town here, and another here and there.'

'That's in the Lopnur,' I said, remembering the grey people in the bus in Ruoqiang.

'Hm,' he nodded, and suddenly went 'boom', throwing his arms into the air, laughing maniacally. I drew a caricature of a mushroom cloud on the spot where he had indicated the site of the experiments.

'Take that away,' Chang said sharply, looking at the drawing.

'Come on . . .' I attempted a rebuttal.

'I thought you were getting to know China!' His voice was serious. I erased the drawing.

The Lopnur, the desert and the arid salt wastes to the east, has long been known to house the Chinese nuclear experimental installations, as well as missile sites pointing warheads in the direction of the Soviet Union. When relations with Russia deteriorated, and were finally cut altogether in 1977, most of the more sensitive equipment was removed to remoter valleys in Tibet. Or so the propaganda machinery says. But a friend of mine, who had travelled through Korla in 1979, had found himself at the perimeter of a nuclear blast. It was a crisp, blue-skied day, he told me, and the first thing he noticed when the bus arrived in town was that the streets were deserted, doors and shutters closed. Then from one moment to another, the earth quaked and a strong wind bent the poplars, stirring up dust and sand, and forcing him to crouch behind a wall until it calmed again. The source of the gale, unmistakably, lay in the Lopnur. No one had bothered to inform bus drivers or travellers. Another explosion was registered in 1986, only a few months after thousands of students demonstrated in Urumqi against above-ground experiments; there had been fallout in the whole Lop area. Deadly snow.

By midday everything was set. Xiao Liu and his best friend, a boy of similar stature and wearing the same frozen frown, would drive us to Miran. The deal was 400 renminbi, in addition to fuel, food and board for the two friends. Once more I dressed up as a man, then took leave of the Lius. Flanked by the three, I ran outside to the waiting truck. For a moment I stared at the thing in disbelief. The body had been painted in a high-chroma turquoise, giving it a marine flavour; a desert boat. Of Russian manufacture, the vehicle looked at least 50 years old, and smelled as though it had been used for hauling manure. A moth-eaten mattress had replaced the seat and the entire dashboard was gone. Xiao Liu took out a crank, lifted one wing of the bonnet and turned. Miraculously, it started.

The noise of the engine made it almost impossible to carry on a conversation. Each lost in private thought, we moved south. The landscape changed rapidly. There was less and less water, less and less green. Dead vegetation, a reminder of a time when the Tarim still flowed as far as Ruoqiang, stuck empty branches into the sky. We passed the ruin of a mud-brick fortress, but neither of the two boys knew anything about it.

'I think it's very old,' shouted Xiao Liu.

An hour before sunset, we stopped at a caravanserai near Argan. A few neglected mud-brick buildings huddled in on themselves, protecting a courtyard and a collection of gnarled trees. The desert broke at the walls of this compound in the middle of nowhere. Golden afternoon light tinged everything with its deceptive warm hues. A sharp wind blew from the north, chasing clouds like torn pieces of tissue paper across the blue sky.

The rest-stop was run by a middle-aged Chinese couple, resembling the Lius. To Chang's delight, they too had come from Sichuan province, and he entered into an animated conversation, using his home dialect.

The boys, it became clear, had another motive for halting at this isolated place: the couple's shy, fifteen-year-old daughter. Stalking away on long skinny legs, the girl had disappeared into another building when we arrived. She now joined us, offering a plate of fruit. She had run off to make herself pretty. Her black hair was combed and held together on one side of the head in a single pigtail; a clean jacket, neatly buttoned up, hugged her pubescent body. She sat in a corner, playing with the red scarf which was tied at her neck in a large bow, and blushed every time one of the boys addressed her.

There are surprisingly few girls of the 'right' age and type in this region. Han and Uighur tend not to intermarry, and unions of people from the same home province are preferred. Young girls like this one have become a desired commodity.

Chang was getting edgy, and urged us to eat up quickly. We

left with the last light of the day and drove on into the night.

The road had become more difficult and the engine ground through shallow sand dunes. Xiao Liu and his friend shared the task of driving, and changed at the wheel every hour. The lights on the truck barely illuminated the desert in front of us, and more than once we moved off the road, in danger of getting lost. By midnight we had reached the outskirts of Ruoqiang. Chang had fallen asleep on my shoulder, overcome by extreme exhaustion. I suggested to Xiao Liu that we spend the rest of the night at an inn outside town and go on to Miran early in the morning. He was all in favour of this idea, and pulled into a truck stop.

Chang woke with a start and was not pleased with the change of plan, but none the less checked us into some rooms. I had barely settled next to the iron stove, heating some water to wash my face, when I heard shouts outside. Seconds later, Chang entered my room.

'Pack your things together, we're going!' he ordered.

'What's the matter?'

'The proprietor's been asking too many questions. It's not safe here . . . have you any idea what will happen if the police catch us near Ruoqiang?'

Reluctantly I agreed, and a few minutes later we were back on the road to Miran, now a bare 80 kilometres away.

We turned off in a north-easterly direction, on to an ancient road constructed of boulders. The banks rose high to the left and right, as though the road had sunk. We came to a checkpoint, with a barrier across the road. I feigned sleep, but could almost physically sense the probing beam of a flashlight moving over my face. It was nearly four when we arrived in a neatly swept town square. Chang got the proprietor of the government rest-stop out of bed, and smuggled me into a room. It was cold and damp, and the bed felt as though it had not been slept in for years. I was in Miran.

TWENTY-ONE

Miran

THREE HOURS LATER I sat up with a jolt. The adrenalin humming through my veins had eliminated every trace of fatigue. I threw on my clothes and poked my head into the dark, silent hallway. Restrained shouts came from next door. Chang was trying to wake Xiao Liu and his friend, who were dug deep into their sheets; only their boots, and a hand clutching a blue cloth cap, were visible. They had been too tired even to undress.

'Get back to your room,' Chang ordered frantically, when I walked in. 'If anyone sees you, there will be trouble.' I complied.

After half an hour of studying the pastel-green walls, the green beds covered with stained quilts, the rusty enamel wash bowl, my door was gently opened. Finger to his lips, Chang escorted me to our truck, coughing noisily out front. Xiao Liu and his friend were waiting, looking sleepy and cross; Chang cracked his knuckles tensely; I was elated, and couldn't wipe a grin from my face.

Ancient Miran, the Yixun of the Han dynasty, was seven kilometres north-east of the modern village. We passed a farm and fields, crossed a dry river-bed and skirted a few struggling trees, then abruptly entered a large gravel plain. A sunken road, carved deep into the level ground, crossed it in a straight and narrow line, disappearing beyond an elevation.

'Behind that rise,' Xiao Liu pointed ahead, 'old Miran starts.'

There had been rumours of armed guards patrolling the site, and though we had all agreed that these stories were planted to deter treasure hunters, we were apprehensive about them. You

225

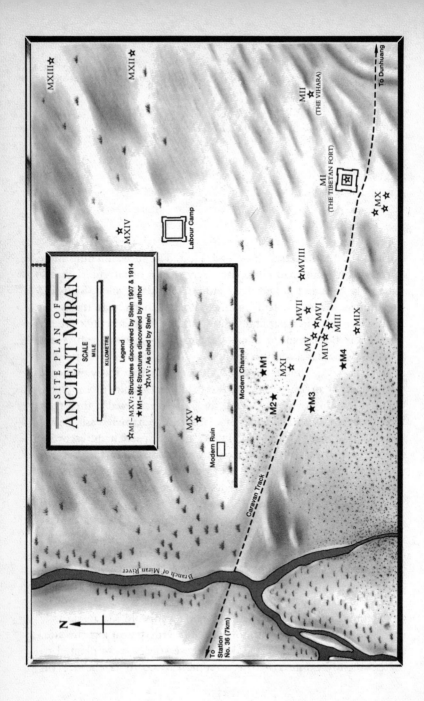

SITE PLAN OF
ANCIENT MIRAN

SCALE

MILE

KILOMETRE

Legend

☆ MI–MXV: Structures discovered by Stein 1907 & 1914
★ M1–M4: Structures discovered by author
☆MV: As cited by Stein

MXIII☆

MXII☆

MII☆
(THE VIHARA)

MI
(THE TIBETAN FORT)

MX
☆☆

MXIV☆

Labour Camp

☆MVIII

MVII
MVI
MV☆ ☆☆
MIV☆
MIII☆
★M4 ☆MIX

MXI☆
★M1
M2★

M3★

MXV☆

Modern Channel

Modern Ruin

Caravan Track

Branch of Miran River

To Dunhuang

To
Station
No. 36 (7km)

N

never knew. Xiao Liu suggested that he should drop us at the perimeter, drive for a kilometre or so into the site and, hopefully, come back with an all-clear sign.

Chang and I climbed off the truck and squatted in a shallow depression. It was freezing cold, and I felt my hands and feet go numb again. I pulled out the plan to discuss my strategy for exploration. Miran was huge, almost four kilometres east to west and two and a half kilometres north to south, though in comparison with cities like Gaochang, or even Subashi, not many imposing buildings were left. Stein had recorded fifteen ruins which he labelled MI–XV, including a Tibetan fort, and a survey conducted by the archaeologist Huang Xiaojiang in the 1970s mentioned fourteen of them in addition to some living areas and tombs. Most of the remains were apparently located relatively close to the ancient caravan track to Dunhuang, which cut the city approximately in half on a west–east axis; they should be easily accessible. There was little time and we would have to work economically and be selective about what to study more closely. My mind raced at a million miles an hour. My teeth chattered uncontrollably, and for a moment I didn't know if it was caused by the cold or nerves.

There was the cluster of buildings which included MIII and MV, the second-century Buddhist shrines from which Stein had extracted the wall paintings; at the centre of the site lay the Tibetan fort, and according to Stein's map, the vihara MII was situated on the eastern perimeter. These were our prime targets.

First I wanted to see MXV, a structure discovered by Stein in January 1914. When he examined it, he had found walls still standing up to three metres, a circular interior and traces of paintings. His entries on this mound were sparse, and for some reason he did not photograph the paintings. I wondered if anything had survived.

The truck reappeared over the ridge. Xiao Liu honked the horn: all clear. He would pick us up again at sunset. It had taken me three months to get to Miran, and I had one day to explore the site.

Chang and I crossed the track and headed north-east, along an

ancient river-bed swept clean by wind and water. There were a
few compressed dunes, and scraggly tamarisks. In the near distance we saw the wall of a ruined building, constructed of sun-
dried mud-brick. MXV? Looking at the plan, it seemed a bit too
near. We hurried towards it. The ruin sat on the opposite side of
a deep, man-made canal, faced with concrete. Large window holes
and modern construction showed that it was a contemporary
building, abandoned fairly recently.

But the canal was intriguing. Where did it go? We set out to
follow it. It continued in a straight line due east, then made a
90-degree turn north. We walked further. Then, over the horizon,
a modern tower came into view, then another. It was a prison
camp! For a moment, we stood staring at grey walls and barbed
wire. Red and yellow flags studded the ground near it. Chang
grabbed my arm and turned back.

'Those were the guards people were talking about,' he
whispered.

So much for MXV, and the whole northern sector of the site.
Assuming that if we could see them they could see us, we rapidly
hiked south, then headed east again up a gravel ridge which delineated the entrance to the site proper.

Below us lay a vast and desolate expanse interrupted only by
sand-coloured mounds, bobbing like buoys on the grey Atlantic.
To the south loomed the shadows of the Altyn Tagh, the mountain range we had crossed less than a month ago. In the distance
rose the Tibetan fort, topped by an enigmatic tower which, from
here, looked like wooden scaffolding. Telegraph wires ran alongside the track, in jarring contrast to the antiquity of the site. An
icy wind drove us on.

On a level area, high on the ridge, stood some remains consisting of nothing more than a single wall, about two metres in
width, reaching a height of about four and a half metres. The base
and half the wall were covered by debris of clay, fragments of brick
and gravel. The upper section was pierced by an opening.

Chang pointed to Stein's plan and suggested that it might be
MXI. I doubted it. MXI had been described as a square-based
votive stupa, and ought to be situated about 300 metres south-east
of here.

'This isn't on the plan, it's a new one,' I shouted in excitement, and wrote it down as M1.

'Ah, Xiao Stein,' Chang kidded, laughing at my enthusiasm.

I couldn't make out what the function of the structure might once have been and was tempted to dig into the debris.

'We're too visible here, come on,' Chang urged after a few minutes, and headed down into a depression west of the ridge, studded with eroded clay terraces. *Yardang*, Stein calls them in his book. I followed and went on to examine a curious formation which looked like a large, solid cube, and to my eyes appeared to be man-made. A perforation on the eastern side confirmed my suspicion. There, in the smooth surface of hard wind-pressed clay dust was a hole which revealed a core of mud brick. M2, as I called it, was the remains of a square-based votive stupa. Stein had discovered a large number of them, and considered them common to the site.

The desert silence was abruptly broken by the rough noise of an engine, a truck or perhaps a jeep. Chang panicked and shouted, 'Run,' while sprinting off towards the south. We crossed the road again, and dived behind a large rubble heap. The noise had ceased. When we had caught our breath, we cautiously peeked about, but there was nothing. Then I remembered the stories in the Chinese histories, and Marco Polo's tales of the desert of Lop, which talk about the ghostly sounds of imaginary armies leading travellers astray and to certain death. Only now the winds which once carried the noise of caravans moving rhythmically across the grey plains, whine with the hornet-like voices of lorries and military jeeps. Eerie none the less.

Something had caught Chang's attention and he started to dig into the rubble heap that had sheltered us from the phantom engine. Beneath the debris of masonry, clay and reed, he uncovered part of a wall, painted white at the top, and the traditional red on the bottom register. A simple geometric design of repeating white rectangles could be made out along the border of the red area. We had found another uncharted structure, and Chang ceremoniously wrote M3 on the map.

'I'm starting to like this game,' he said, grinning from ear to ear.

'Well, if you're ever out of a job as a taxi driver, you could try you hand at archaeology.'

'Not enough money,' he laughed.

'Too true,' I replied.

We photographed and measured our new find, then rushed on. The sun was moving towards its zenith. The sky hung above us, cloudless, its colour a deep polarized blue, but the temperature still hovered around zero.

'MIX is next,' said Chang pointing east, to a feature similar to the one we had just labelled M3. It was another rubble heap, and could barely be identified as a building. Yet it still reached over three metres in height, and was thickly coated with compressed clay dust. Holes in the upper part of the south side still contained remains of wooden structural supports. Debris of sun-dried bricks, together with quantities of red pottery sherds, were strewn in the vicinity.

There was just one problem: it didn't look like the MIX of Stein's descriptions. I pulled out my notes and read: 'MIX, situated on a steep clay terrace 15–17 feet; wall about five feet in height; small structure, six feet square inside.'

'This is not MIX, or anything else Stein excavated,' I said to Chang.

'Another new one?' He raised his eyebrows, doubting me.

'I think so . . . let's call it M4.'

'Are you sure we are in Miran?' Chang teased me.

'Yes,' I said pointing east again. Less then a hundred metres away rose the eroded clay platform described by Stein. Two oblique walls still stood precariously balanced on a steep cliff. Like Stein, I had no idea what the building might originally have looked like. We climbed the mound, which afforded us a wonderful view of the area. To the north we could make out a cluster of structures, floating on the sand-like islands. Even from a distance I could identify the rather phallic-looking shape as the stupa rising from the cella of shrine MIII. Judging from Stein's photographs, it seemed to have deteriorated little over half a century, despite the fact that it had seen intensive archaeological activity by Stein and Tachibana and, judging by the disturbed ground around it, had been examined by the Chinese expedition the previous month.

The structural features of MIII, along with its near twin MV, are unique to Miran and have no analogy among caves or free-standing sites around the Taklamakan. They are archaic building forms, with their origin in early Indian cult architecture. When Stein excavated it, he found a circular cella with a tall stupa in the centre, surrounded by a square outer wall of some nine metres on each side. A narrow terrace continued round the outer base of the wall.

The concave cella wall had been decorated with paintings by the artist Tita. At eye-level was a narrative illustrating the life of the Buddha. On the dado, at the bottom of the wall, were painted 24 busts of youths with large wings, their heads turned in three-quarter view. Their eyes were reinforced by white impasto, thickly applied to the area around the pupil, and must have resulted in a heightened visual impact especially striking in the semi-dark, narrow space of the circumambulatory. Seeing them just below eye-level, the devotee must have experienced the strange sensation of being followed around the path by the glances of the solemn, winged creatures.

The cella was filled in with sand, but the stupa rose from it, as in Stein's days. We got to work photographing and measuring it; time was passing much too fast, and we had not seen half the site yet.

I turned to find MV, which according to Stein's site description ought to lie some 60 yards to the north-west of MIII, that is, just across the caravan track. Well known to have been built on the same principle, with a circular cella and a stupa in its centre, it was in contrast supposedly elevated above the original ground level by means of a solid brick platform. It was described as larger than MIII and once housed the Vessantara Jataka, a version of which I had seen in one of the caves at Kizil.

When we crossed the track and confronted a series of mounds, we were presented with an enigma. There certainly was a ruin in the place marked MV on the map, but in no way did the remains resemble the feature described and photographed by Stein. Nor did any of the mounds nearest to it correspond to the shrine, which ought to have been a substantial ruin.

In its place stood a structure of almost solid brick, five by five

metres, obviously a votive stupa of the type we had seen before.
A tunnel had been dug into the centre on the south-west side,
revealing the inner stupa chamber, with an intact cupola blackened
by smoke. It was large enough for two persons to crouch around
a small fire, and judging from the empty beer bottles had been
used for less holy purposes than Buddhist chants. Near it was a
similar structure of about the same size which had been dug into
on the west side. I didn't have time to solve this riddle just then; we
photographed the cluster, including a two-storey building labelled
MIV, and hurried on to the centre of the site.

We followed the caravan track further to the east, towards the
Tibetan fort, which sat like a huge skeleton of a dinosaur in the
centre of Miran. It was shaped as an irregular rectangle of roughly
seventy metres from east to west and about sixty metres from
north to south. Some of the outer walls still reached heights of
between six and thirteen metres. Here Stein had excavated the
Tibetan documents which referred to Miran and its vicinity as
Nob-Chu-Nu or Little Nob, long after the kingdom of Shanshan
had ceased to exist as such. The contents of these manuscripts,
which are mainly of a bureaucratic nature, describe Miran as an
active administrative and military centre. Nob-Chu-Nu had a *rtse-
rje* or chief lord, a *dgra-blon* or foreign councillor, *nos-pon* or
regional chiefs, a chief lama and a chief physician. It was referred
to as a town (*mkhar*) and a mart (*khrom*), which means that it
probably functioned as a central market town.

We entered the fortress through a breach in the wall on its
western side; deep grooves had been cut into the slope by a vehicle.
Perhaps the guards from the prison camp had gone for a joyride
here. Flimsily constructed but remarkably well-preserved living
quarters lined the north wall, interconnected by a network of
steps. There were no doorways to the rooms, and I assumed that
they had to be entered from above with the aid of ladders. A
two-storey platform of solid pounded earth, surmounted by the
mysterious wooden scaffolding, probably built at one time to aid
in triangulation, took up the south-east corner of the interior. We
climbed on to the platform and were looking out over the whole
of the site when some dark specks appeared in the distance.

'Someone is coming,' I warned Chang.

We hid behind the thin curtain walls and watched a procession of donkeys packed high with firewood, driven by a stooped old Uighur man, pass below us and disappear in the distance. I wondered where he lived.

We returned to poke about again in the rooms. Chang was pulling dirty pieces of cloth from a wall, then dropped them. Their stink was disgusting, and I remembered Stein's comment about the 'peculiar age-persisting smelliness' he had found at the Miran fort. This odour was over a thousand years old.

Chang was complaining of hunger and exhaustion. I promised a rest when we reached the monastery, the vihara MII, located according to Stein roughly two and a half kilometres to the north-east. He spouted some words I didn't understand, but I guessed that the meaning came close to 'slave driver'.

Wooden stakes stuck out intermittently from a shallow pebble dune, placed there, I surmised, by the Chinese archaeological team. Considering the 'new' finds I had made, during such a short exploration, it was not unlikely that more of old Miran was buried deep under drifts of sand and gravel.

We had not walked for more then ten minutes – 'one kilometre', Chang guessed, with military accuracy – when we sighted MII. Stein's distance indication was out by a good one and a half kilometres. Immediately recognizable, the oblong building of sun-dried brick consisted of two major parts: a lower storey, about fourteen metres in length and eleven metres in width, was surmounted on the north-east by a smaller oblong structure resembling a stupa. It was an odd sight and nothing I had seen in Xinjiang compared to it. The closest analogy I could come up with were the post-Gupta tower temples in Southern India, like those at Aihole and Nagral. There also, rectangular or apsidal structures were topped with a stupa or tower at one end. But these generally had an interior, while MII looked solid.

Chang had put down the backpack with a clank and a sigh. He opened it and brought out a few bottles of beer, some canned pears and cookies. I was already worrying about the light, which was fading quickly, and set about exploring the north-eastern façade while Chang was still leisurely smoking a cigarette.

There the projecting surfaces between the niches were once

decorated with reliefs of pilasters which Stein had termed of an 'Indo-Persian' style 'descended from Persepolitan models'. Not much was left. I moved round to the south-east face, where the niches were deeper and taller. Some of them had retained a rough shape outlining the human figure, attesting the sculptures which once occupied them.

The third niche from the east corner brought a surprise, and I called for Chang to hurry over and bring the camera. Buried under clay dust and rubble I had found the remains of a low-relief figure of a standing Buddha, still preserved from the ankles to above the waist, to about one metre. A concave cut in the wall outlined the head, indicating that the relief once reached a height of over one metre seventy-five, life-size. There still survived the widely spread legs, and drapery from an upper and lower garment, clinging closely to the body in a style common in the fourth or fifth century. We took measurements and pictures, then carefully covered the niche once more with sand.

According to Stein, a passage once extended from the north-east wall which was lined with a row of colossal stucco images. When he found them, six of the eight bases had still retained the torsos, legs and hands of seated Buddha figures. The large head I had seen at the institute in Urumqi had come from here. Of these absolutely nothing remained. Since they have presumably not been excavated, and environmental factors could not have eradicated them so completely, it is not unlikely that they may have been destroyed wilfully.

A second wall ran parallel to the wall against which the figures were once situated, continuing north-east where it joined a small building. According to the plan it ought to have been circular in shape, though to my eye it was constructed on a square plan. This was all that remained of a monastic complex at Miran, hardly sufficient to have housed the large number of monks Faxian told us resided in Shanshan.

Faxian, a Buddhist monk living in Changan, had set out in the closing years of the fourth century to travel to India to obtain Buddhist scriptures. He journeyed to Dunhuang, then crossed the deserts of demons and hot winds. 'There is not a bird to be seen in the air above, nor an animal on the ground below,' he writes of his arduous trek, finding his way by following the dry bones of the dead. After seventeen days he came to Shanshan, 'a country rugged and hilly, with thin and barren soil.' People here wore felt and rough clothing, but he writes further, 'The king professed the Law (of the Buddha), and there might be in the country more than four thousand monks, who were all students of the Hinayana.'

There was neither a courtyard with cells, nor any evidence of elaborate housing for monks at Miran, as one might expect from a monastery.

A possible explanation for this unique 'absence' could be sought in the idiosyncratic organization of the Buddhist community of Shanshan. The monks of Miran married, had children and engaged in trade. They had private households which included slaves and servant monks, a lifestyle which could have diminished the need for a large monastic structure providing living space for hundreds of monks. Accommodation for travellers and for keepers, and a place for festivals and ceremonies would have met the needs of the Miran community.

We rushed back towards the fort. I still wanted to see a series of structures south of it, collectively labelled MX, and then to reinvestigate the MV enigma.

MX was a set of three ruins lying some 200 metres from the fort, jutting into the air like a schoolmaster's finger. Judging by Stein's photographs, they had suffered severely since 1914. The northernmost structure had survived best. I climbed an eroded clay platform, from which remnants of a tower-like structure of sun-dried brick reached almost three metres. There was still part of a dome. Interestingly, the transition from the square plan to the dome was made with the aid of squinches built in fired brick, in contrast to the sun-dried blocks commonly used throughout the site. The whole edifice had apparently been rebuilt several times, and with it, its function must have changed. Originally it may have been of a Buddhist nature; later a site for smelting metal was attached to it, producing arrows for the soldiers of the Tibetan fort.

The light was turning golden and I knew that soon it would be too dark to photograph. We walked back up towards MIII, where

Xiao Liu was already waiting with the truck. I still wondered what had happened to MV. Was it completely destroyed by Tachibana, who had ripped out wall paintings three years before Stein resumed his labours at Miran in 1914? I thought that unlikely, since Stein complained only about the destruction of the paintings, not the whole shrine.

I pulled out Stein's photographs and placed them on the ground, lining up pictures with the ruins. He himself solved the riddle: what had been mapped as MV was actually MVII. The mound about fifteen metres to the east of it was MVI, as correctly indicated on the map. But where was MV? My bet was that it stood in the place where MVII was supposed to be, that is, according to Stein 'about 340 yards to the north-east of MIII'. Considering the relatively good conditions of the other structures, I found that highly probable.

The sun set quickly, and a milky blue and grey hue lay like a filter over the whole site. The boys were already waiting in the truck. I took one last photograph, and took my leave of Miran, realizing that I had only scratched the surface. I knew that more, much more, lay buried under the sand.

We were sunburnt and happy. Chang ceremoniously opened the last bottle of beer, toasting ostentatious 'gambei's.

'Did you take anything?' Xiao Liu asked protectively.

'Yeah, lots . . . everything,' I squeaked. He looked alarmed. I pointed to my camera, and he smiled relieved.

'If you're happy, I'm happy,' he nodded solemnly.

'I'm happy!'

Night had come with its usual speed.

'Is it possible to stay for another day?' I asked timidly, already knowing what the answer would be. The three young men looked at each other and unanimously shook their heads.

'My aunt invited us for food,' said Xiao Liu.

'Your aunt?' I asked astonished.

'Hm, she's been living here for twenty years.'

'Also from Sichuan?' I asked. He nodded. The village of Miran is known in bureaucratic terms as Sanshiliutuan, station number

36. I recalled that in the sixth century Miran bore the name of Tun, signifying a camp or village associated with military occupation, and Qitun, meaning 'Number Seven Military Station'.

Xiao Liu's relatives lived in a small homestead on the outskirts of the village. His aunt, a slight, middle-aged woman with a silver-streaked no-nonsense haircut, stood at the door as though she had been waiting for us. She hurried us through a dark hall into a cosy room in the back of the house, where a feast was waiting for us spread out on a narrow table. Candles and a kerosene lamp illuminated the warm space; there was a bed covered with a quilt, a few chairs and a bookcase. Aunt passed round a basket brimming with plump golden raisins.

'Ah, Miran raisins,' I said.

'No, they're from Turfan, the best raisins in Xinjiang are from Turfan,' she instructed me.

The front door slammed, and a boy of about thirteen entered the room. He threw a satchel into the corner, peeled off a thick coat and stared at us. Xiao Liu introduced him as his young cousin, and explained to him that we had been photographing the Miran site today. His eyes lit up.

'I'm interested in archaeology, my teacher, he helped with some excavations. You know they found new things, paintings, *xin faxiande dongxi* . . .'

I pulled out the site plan, and asked him to point to the spot of the new finds. But Stein's map confused him. His teacher, he said, had photographed the paintings.

'Do you think it might be possible to see them?' I asked him.

He shrugged and dashed off. A few minutes later he came back with a box and a disappointed expression. 'Teacher has gone to Ruoqiang, he won't be back till tomorrow,' he said.

'We really can't stay, can we?' I pleaded again. Chang shook his head.

The boy opened his box of treasures and dumped it on the bed. There was a large sherd of dark brown fired clay, exhibiting an applied design similar to the vessels excavated from Yotkan, the ancient Khotan capital; a number of metal objects including some three-lobed iron arrowheads from the Tibetan fort; several broken pieces of bronze and a narrow fragment of smooth grey stone with a perforation to one side.

Xiao Liu picked out an oblong bead of ribbed green glass, held it up to my ear, then put it in my hand.

'Souvenir from Miran,' he smiled. It came from the fort, the little cousin said.

I examined it closely: its semi-translucent light green colour imitating jade was reminiscent of Han dynasty glass production, which often re-worked glass imported from the West. Roman glass brought to China, re-heated and turned into a bead, traded with Tibet, brought to Miran . . . now I was taking it back to the West, I fantasized. A two-millennia journey.

Xiao Liu was getting twitchy and said we would have to go. I thanked our hostess, packed my things and my bead, and reluctantly left Miran.

We arrived back at station number 34 in the early afternoon of the next day. The Korla bus was already waiting on the village square, filled, I noticed, exclusively with Han Chinese. The rolls of film stuffed safely in my longjohns, I leaned back and dreamed about those new paintings I had not seen. Had they been excavated? If so, had they been brought back to Urumqi? Should I try the capital once more? Exhausted and satisfied, I fell into a comfortable semi-sleep, resting my head on Chang's shoulder.

A couple of hours later we pulled over for a rest stop. It was the same place I had stopped with Ma and the weasel only four days ago. It seemed like four weeks. I told Chang that I had promised to look in on the women and headed for the small shack across the road. He followed me reluctantly.

'Come on, they make the best noodles anywhere,' I cried out to him. But he walked around the shack, looked back over his shoulder to the large, concrete Chinese restaurant, shook his head and said: 'Uighurs are dirty, I don't want to eat here.' He insisted on taking lunch at the Chinese place. For the first time I got really angry with him, left him standing, and entered the small eatery. He didn't follow me.

The women recognized me immediately and with a friendly

gesture I was ushered into their 'special' room. An iron kettle simmered over an open firepit. On a *kang* reclined a large Uighur in uniform conversing animatedly with a second man in civilian clothing. They greeted me congenially, and asked jokingly whether I too thought that mutton was dirty meat. They must have overheard Chang. I laughed and said that I loved it. They invited me to fish in the large kettle for mutton bones, while waiting for my noodles. The ladies were taking their time, and self-consciously I kept checking my watch.

The Uighur man laughed, slapped me on the shoulder and said: 'Take your time, I'm the bus driver.'

Half an hour later the two of us emerged from the shack. People were crowding round the locked bus, stepping from one foot to another, trying to stay warm in the freezing temperature. Chang was fuming. He hardly spoke a word all the way back to Korla.

The question of the paintings was still eating away at me when we pulled into the bus station.

'Why don't you call Youyou,' Chang suggested. The idea had never occurred to me. We went straight from the bus stop to the post office, where we filled out the proper form. While we waited for our turn I bought a postcard, wrote on it 'Miran! I made it!' and addressed it to the Professor in Pittsburgh.

Chang re-emerged from the telephone box, puzzled. 'They say she's gone to Korla . . . she's here in town,' he informed me.

'The paintings are here,' I reacted obsessively. Chang agreed. Still high on Miran adrenalin, it was the only explanation that made sense to us. Korla was the administrative centre of Bayingolin Mongol Administrative Region, and Miran belonged to it. The paintings must be in a museum or storehouse. We asked our way to the museum. It was closed, and the guard on duty knew nothing of the Miran material.

'Let's find Youyou,' I suggested.

We marched from hotel to hotel, tired and hungry, sustained by our single goal. A clerk at a new, palatial-looking inn took pity on us, and pulled out a phone book and started calling numbers. On the third try he found her in a hotel on the other side of town. We hiked across there, and called her from Reception.

'You made it?' Youyou asked with a smile.

'What about the paintings?' I asked her, coming straight to the point. 'Are they here?'

'No, they were left *in situ*,' she answered, bursting our bubble.

'What are they, can you tell me?' I asked impatiently.

'I'm not supposed to show you anything until the material is published,' she said, but pulled out a piece of paper. On it she drew two lunettes from which rose two busts with wings.

'But those are just like the ones Stein excavated from MIII,' I said in astonishment.

'They are from MIII,' she stated, pronouncing the Roman numerals as 'III'.

So that was the answer. The MIII dado was divided into four equal concave segments, each painted with six lunettes filled with busts of winged youths. Of what must have been twenty-four figures, fourteen were found by Stein, but only seven were taken away by him. The rest he deemed too damaged to merit removal. The Chinese team had reopened the same shrine and found those damaged remnants. So, no figures with crowns, and princesses with wings, no new paintings, as our friend had fantasized in Mangai Zhen.

In a strange way I felt disappointed and relieved at the same time. Chang had fallen asleep in the chair, while Youyou and I continued to talk archaeology.

'I will make a request that you be allowed to come and work with us next year,' she said finally. 'If you would like . . .'

'I would like that.'

'You had better take your friend . . .'

'Yes, and goodbye again,' I said finally. It was past midnight.

The road to Miran ended here. Tomorrow Chang and I would make plans to go east. He would return home and resume his work as a taxi driver, and I would travel to Guangzhou, then head on to Korea and Japan.

But our journey was not quite over yet.

TWENTY-TWO

Leaving Xinjiang

'HEY, LAO WAI, WHAT YOU DOING with the China man?' shouted a gang of Uighur boys. It was after midnight; their shrill whistles echoed through the empty street. We had just left Youyou's hotel and we were exhausted.

'Don't worry . . . at home, everything will be better,' Chang said quietly, hunching his shoulders, burying his chin deeper into his scarf.

He'd been saying this a lot recently.

'Better?' I questioned. '*Hao, tai hao* . . . things are not bad, they are wonderful,' I sang facetiously, jumping over an irrigation ditch to make my point. I fell into the gutter, twisting my ankle. I screamed. There was laughter from the other side of the road. Had it not been for the agony and that awful flash of panic associated with images of broken bones, I would have thought it funny too.

Chang gathered me up gently out of the dust and asked me if I could put any weight on the foot. I couldn't. Supported by him, propped on his shoulder, muttering curses, I hopped to the door of the Sichuan restaurant. The sleepy but happy face of Chang's friend appeared at the open door. With a welcoming smile and motherly clucks of concern he asked us in. 'What about Miran?' he said, while throwing a few greens into the wok. But we were too tired and too hungry to talk and my ankle was swelling fast, turning a nasty blue.

'You stay here, while I find us a place to sleep,' Chang said finally.

241

He booked us into a hotel across the road from the restaurant; a hotel for the Chinese. The girl behind the counter hesitated. Her boss would be back tomorrow, she said, and she didn't know if it was all right for me to stay here.

'Just get her a bed!' Chang shouted. At this, surprisingly, she complied. He could be very effective in moments of crisis.

With the girl's aid Chang carried me upstairs, helped me to the toilet, got hot water to wash. Delicately, he wrapped a cold rag around my injured foot, and then left. He looked worn out; there were purple smudges under his eyes.

Despite the pain I fell asleep. Next morning the swelling had increased. I concluded, in an almost detached manner, that I would have to get an X-ray. Inwardly I was panicking. I had several months of travel ahead of me, I was in the middle of the fucking desert, and I couldn't walk.

At midday, Chang piggy-backed me downstairs. The girl from the front desk, who by now had warmed to us, was waiting outside the door with her bicycle. I balanced on the seat, my useless foot sticking awkwardly out to one side, while Chang and the girl pushed me down the road. After all this time I had still not got used to those intense mouth-gaping stares.

The hospital, a cube of concrete decorated with two red crosses, lay on the main road, not far from the hotel. Chang pushed me up a ramp into a tiled foyer where I dismounted and sat on a long wooden bench. The place was deserted.

We waited and waited. Finally, Chang went searching for some personnel. In an examining room there was a woman dressed in white, eating her lunch. She continued her meal, slowly packing away her canister, before stirring herself to inquire what the matter was. Apparently this was the doctor. Glancing at my foot, she sent me to X-ray. 'Third floor,' she called out, as she poured some tea.

There was no lift. With much effort, step by step Chang pulled me up to the third floor, found a bench, and we waited again. It was the lunch hour.

'What if someone has a serious accident in Korla between twelve and three?' I whispered.

'You die,' Chang answered, straight-faced; I swear I could not tell if he was joking.

I was X-rayed by a tall young Uighur woman, with out-of-date equipment on a crude metal table after insisting on a protective apron – I even suggested in the face of her reluctance that I might be pregnant! Efficiently twisting my foot into the correct position, the technician took the exposure and sauntered off.

Half an hour later she emerged from the darkroom, and, pronouncing the foot 'not broken', she wrote out a bill.

I slid back down to ground level, using the banister. We saw the downstairs doctor again, who, without looking at the X-ray, handed me a small bottle of tiger balm and another bill.

By donkey taxi, one of the few in Korla, we went back to the hotel, where I spent the afternoon contemplating the ceiling, the plastic chair, the table with the white plastic cover and metal legs, and tried to imagine the sky beyond the almost opaque glass of the window. It was cold. 'It'll be much warmer when we get to Sichuan,' Chang said, barely hiding his homesickness.

Next morning, he went out to organize the train tickets, but returned disappointed and empty-handed. It seemed as though everyone wanted to get out of Xinjiang. Even on the black market, the first train tickets out would not be available for three days.

To add insult to injury, the manager, who'd come back, was furious with his girls for letting a foreigner stay at the hotel. 'Strictly against the rules,' he shouted. I had to move out. We packed our bags and transferred to the Kunlun, a tourist hotel, with a barber, a restaurant and a disco.

Second of December. Departure day. I ceremoniously discarded my ruined boots, and forced my bandaged foot into a trainer. Chang had managed to hustle two tickets for an already over-booked train, and we crowded along with hundreds of other prospective passengers into the waiting hall of the station. 'Cattle transport,' I wrote in my diary.

Squeezed next to us was a middle-aged man from Chengdu holding a kitten – a tabby, perhaps seven or eight weeks old (a present for his daughter, he told us). He was friendly, and eager to start a conversation. Mr Dong had been visiting his sister in Korla. He laughed and said the cats in Xinjiang are nicer than in China, and asked me to take care of it during the trip. It was illegal to transport pets, but he thought that no one would question a foreigner. Provocatively, I asked if he thought Xinjiang was part of China. 'Of course not,' he said. I hid the kitten under my coat, and together we moved through the gates. The kitten's name was Da-ling; she kept perfectly still, tightly snuggled into my armpit. No one stopped us.

We found ourselves in a wagon in the company of 50 oil-workers, identically dressed in red trousers, red jackets and red baseball caps, with the Tarim Oil logo embroidered in English everywhere. They smelt curiously of mutton, and I later learned that shortly before their departure from the desert camp, as a bonus each man was presented with a pair of Uighur boots along with the red clothing. Uighur boots are rubbed with mutton grease.

We travelled hard sleeper. A row of doorless compartments faced the aisle, each containing six bunks. At one end of the carriage, two down from my compartment, there was a small wash-basin, a mirror, and the attendant's cabin which had a door. From the luggage racks above the windows, face towels, socks and flannels hung out to dry. During the day, the two middle bunks were folded up and the passengers sat on the lower one facing each other. The top bunk, which did not fold away, was considered the most luxurious. One of the workers gave up his, so that I could spend the journey dozing on my back, or lying on my belly watching the landscape race by. Speakers piped music non-stop into the train. I noticed that many tunes were adaptations of western compositions, such as the Beatles' 'Yesterday' arranged for orchestra, which I sang along with; but no one here had ever heard of the Beatles. The lights went off at eleven o'clock, right after the train attendant had swept out the car for the last time. Early in the morning they came on again, along with the music.

The workers had been on a two-year American contract in the Tarim basin, they said, which had just been terminated by the

Chinese government. They were going home for a few months before being shipped out to another, as yet unknown destination.

'The Americans with us had it hard, they were making lots of money, and didn't know what to do with it. Sometimes they would go over to Pakistan. But even there, nothing was up to their standards. They complained a lot,' the eldest of the group in my compartment was saying. Everyone laughed.

'We found a village in the desert, completely untouched by outsiders,' said the tall one, '. . . no one had been there for hundreds of years . . . These people didn't even know they were part of China.'

'Lucky people,' I said.

We were nearing Lanzhou. I was trying to focus beyond my reflection on the shapes passing in the night; Da-ling lay purring in the crook of my arm. Chang and the oil worker we called 'the tall one' were playing chess on the lower bunk.

There was a sudden commotion; someone was running down the aisle, pushing aside people and luggage. There were shouts, and another man made his way through the heckling crowd. I stuck my head out over the top of my bunk, to get a view of what was happening. Then there were shots. Three or four shots, I don't remember. They were quiet, oddly quiet, not like the loud bangs I knew from the movie screen. Without mercy, the two men were gunned down in the narrow gangway of the moving train. One fell against the washbasin. The force of the blast pushed him into the door to the next carriage. His head made a deep impression in the glass without shattering it, before he slid to the ground. I think he was dead. Another man collapsed directly below me, hit in the shoulder. He was brutally forced into a kneeling position by a plain-clothes policeman (those trench coats again), his hands were tied behind his back and the same rope was then connected to his ankles, his wrists and his neck. Any movement and he would choke himself. The men had been accused of stealing, but when the police emptied their pockets they found only a few hundred renminbi. That was no more than Chang was carrying, I thought. The wounded man was dragged to the attendant's compartment which had a lock. A third man, I heard, was taken into custody, unharmed, in the next carriage.

Someone commented that robbery had got out of hand in recent years.

At Lanzhou the body was taken off the train, a woman mopped the floor, and by eleven it seemed as though nothing had happened.

'*Zhe shi Zhongguo* . . . this is China,' Chang said, shrugging his shoulders, and continued with his board game, until the lights were turned off for the night.

I tried hard, but could not remember their faces.

Next day we arrived in Xian. Mr Dong and 'the tall one' also got off. We were numb and dirty, and depressed. No one spoke about the killing, but the incident hung like a black cloud over us. Chang had not reacted when the man was shot; nor had the others. Only the tall one had reached up and stroked my arm when I was shaking uncontrollably after the shooting, and told me not to draw attention to myself. He gave me his red baseball cap, trying to console me as if I were a child.

We had decided to go directly on to Chengdu and Mr Dong and the oil worker went off to organize the tickets with the black-marketeers conspicuously circling the station. They said it was easier that way.

Chang and I sat, leaning against the carved stone railing around the large station plaza, guarding the luggage. A tiny, elderly woman with small feet and a blue padded jacket approached us. She pulled Chang aside, opened her coat and showed him a magazine, while pointing at me. He shooed her away aggressively.

'What did she want?' I asked him.

'She was selling pornography,' he said.

'That little old lady?' I laughed. I didn't believe him.

'Anything to make money,' said Chang.

The other two came back waving some tickets, and Mr Dong, ever smiling, suggested finding a restaurant. There would be a five-hour wait.

'The best dumplings in China are to be found in Xian,' he said, and the tall one agreed.

I ought to have been happy to be in Xian, the ancient Changan, one of the great cities of the past, home of Emperor Qin Shi-huang's terracotta army, and the eastern terminus of the Silk Road. But instead, the hustle and bustle of cars, bicycles, shops, lights, smells and noises confused me. Urban chaos. Input overload. The last thing I wanted to do at that moment was to go sightseeing. It was like studying Roman antiquities and finally visiting Rome only to find you can't bear to look at the Colosseum. So you have a *gelato* instead.

I wasn't the only one reacting like this; both Chang and the oil worker wandered about wide-eyed, barely able to cope. I limped after them with Da-ling buried deep in my jacket. Only Mr Dong strutted ahead briskly, leading us across streets and into alleys, and found a tiny eatery specializing in *Jiaozi*, delicious steamed dumplings.

I had started to miss the quiet simplicity of the desert.

After a twenty-hour train ride, we arrived in Chengdu, took leave of Mr Dong and the tall one, and caught a train to Chongqing. We were assigned 'soft-seats', comfortable compartments with curtains and white protective covers over the cushioned seats.

The landscape had changed drastically; instead of sand colours and unrestricted vistas, luscious green hills swathed in mist and terraced into rice paddies unfolded like Song dynasty paintings outside the window. Small shacks and buildings nestled between agricultural land, people in blue Mao suits were working the fields. This was the real China.

'I'd like to show you Dazu before we go to Chongqing,' Chang said suddenly. We hadn't been talking much to each other, but neither of us had noticed until now.

'Dazu?' I asked.

'My favourite town,' he explained, then lapsed back into silence.

We alighted at Youtingpu and caught a bus waiting with its motor running in front of the station. A teenage boy was violently sick for the better part of the 30-kilometre ride to Dazu; there were cheers and laughter every time he heaved out of the bus window.

We stopped by a stack of tree trunks and a bridge. The air was delicious, cool and moist. Chang led me up a hill to a small inn with a courtyard, which during the summer months was probably overgrown with flowers.

I couldn't believe the sudden luxury of my room: the floor was carpeted instead of the usual concrete, two beds with satin covers, side-tables, lamps, a house-phone, a television covered with a piece of lace curtain. The bathroom had a tub the size of a small swimming pool, which looked home-made. Probably the shipment of tubs never materialized when the hotel was under construction, and the problem was circumvented by simply building one. The result: a tiled concrete tank. I ran the water, it would take some time to fill.

Walking over to Chang's room, I knocked, and another boy answered with a questioning look. Chang appeared immediately behind him. Although the hotel was nearly empty, he had been put with two other guests.

Pulling him out of the door, I whispered: 'I have the biggest tub in the world.'

He laughed and pointed with his thumb over his shoulder. 'So do we.'

'But I've got it all to myself,' I grinned. 'Why don't you come over?'

Apart from the industrial showers at the Academy in Urumqi and the rare pleasure of communal bathhouses of medium comfort in a few hotels, I'd been washing myself out of a thermos in an enamel bowl. There were parts of my body that hadn't seen water in months.

Putting on the thick terrycloth robe which was hanging on the door, I made a cup of instant coffee, played with the television set, turned to the trusty afternoon Beijing opera and, for the first time found it beautiful.

I had grown fond of hot baths in Japan. Slowly I sank into the steaming water. Death, trains, dust, the cold, seemed to roll off me at that moment. I was suspended, as in a Jacuzzi, a washcloth over my eyes, humming to the impossible scales of the opera, beginning to feel human again.

There was a timid knock at the door.

'Come on in, it's *wonderful*,' I groaned, without looking up.

Some noises in the other room told me Chang was stripping.

He slipped into the hot water, shivering from the heat.

'Relax,' I told him, rubbing his back with some soap and cloth.

'Too hot, too hot,' he complained and slipped beneath the water. It took me a moment to realize he had fainted. I managed to drag him out of the tub, into the next room and on to the bed. His pulse was racing, his breath came rapidly. Dark crescents were etched under his eyes, contrasting with his chalk-white face. I wrapped him in a few towels and blankets .

'A Chinese girl would never have done that,' he mumbled, coming round.

'What? . . . washing your back or saving you from drowning in the bath water?'

He laughed and some colour returned to his face.

'Give me a cigarette,' he demanded, holding out his hand.

'Have some tea.'

He glanced anxiously at the door, knowing that any moment someone might enter. I wished that, for once, I could be in a hotel room with my own key and a do-not-disturb sign.

The journey had taken its toll. Chang's body was pathetically thin, ribs and hipbones sharply defined against the smooth skin. His blood pressure had gone haywire. He was coughing. I hoped, for his sake, that now, back in his home province, things would be better. I returned to finish my bath.

'I want to eat real Sichuan food tonight,' I screamed to the other room.

'*Huo gou* . . . but it's very hot,' he screamed back.

'I like hot food,' I replied, soaping my toes.

Dazu had somehow preserved much of its pre-revolutionary charm. Tiled roofs with carved eaves bent gracefully towards the narrow main road; half-open gates encouraged peeks into meandering gardens. To the left and right market carts and stalls were wrapped up for the night. Time had stood still; it looked like the China of the picture books.

Chang was home again. He kept sticking his head into small eateries, smelling, reading menus, moving on dissatisfied. In a side street he noticed yet another sign, exchanged a few words with the proprietor and waved for me to follow.

There were three square tables, each with a metal cauldron built into the top. '*Huo gou*,' Chang called it, hot pot. Each cauldron was filled with a thick red-brown liquid and a swamp of chilli peppers.

We settled at a table and ordered beer. The proprietor lit a gas fire beneath the table, placed a bamboo grid across the receptacle, then brought a tray with vegetables, fish, meat and rice noodles. Chang called out for more. The proprietor nodded, and moments later came back with half a dozen wriggling baby eels.

'They have to be alive,' Chang explained, looking at them, pleased.

The proprietor cut their heads off with one swift smooth slice, and threw them into the bubbling liquid. Still alive, they moved through the mass, and finally disappeared from view. After a while Chang fished for one with his chopstick, popped the entire eel into his mouth and sucked the meat from the skeleton. I followed his example. Delicious.

Huo gou was hot, real hot, spicier than anything I had ever tasted. And the longer the liquid boiled, the more we ate, the hotter it got. Chang had pearls of perspiration on his face, and sighed: '*Da la*,' the big hot.

A small crowd had gathered outside the restaurant, watching our culinary workout, until the proprietor pulled a curtain closed.

They say that almost 50,000 sculptures dating from the ninth to the thirteenth centuries are carved into the hills around Dazu.

It was raining, that fine, thin rain the Japanese call *ame* – glass noodle rain. The moisture mixed with cold morning air felt unusually pleasant after months of dry, parched desert.

Chang hired a taxi, and we drove to his favourite place. He said he had been coming here for many years, to think, or not to think, or to take a rest.

'Magical,' he called it and dumbfounded by its beauty, I silently agreed.

From a collection of pagoda-shaped buildings, a former monastery, we descended into a U-shaped gorge, cut into the cliffs of Baoding Hill. It was overgrown with moss and plants, almost tropical in their fecundity; mist was rising from crevices and water dripped from boulders, shining black from the wet.

A set of stairs and bridges afforded access to the cliffs. A fairyland. Sculptures had been hewn into the precipitous rocks, and set into natural grottoes, some tiny, others life-sized, and yet others gigantic, reaching up to fourteen metres. Chang was strangely impervious to their literal meaning, and maybe it didn't matter.

The sculptures depicted scenes from the Buddhist scriptures; often an explanatory inscription was added, so one had the feeling of walking through a multi-dimensional picture book. Huge and awe-inspiring, Mara the embodiment of evil, monkey-faced with blue hair, squatted in a grotto clutching the wheel of life. Carved to depict the transmigration of the six ways, the sculptors preached the principles of causal retribution, metempsychosis and non-annihilation of the soul. There was a reclining statue of the Buddha entering Nirvana, over 30 metres long, other stories from the life of Sakyamuni, and a group of the three saints of the Avatamsaka school, with Vairocana Buddha, the mystical founder of Tantric Buddhism, in the centre.

Baoding Hill was once the centre of the Chengdu Yoga sect of Tantric Buddhism, and Dafowan, as the gorge was called, the pet project of its sixth patriarch, the monk Zhao Zhifeng.

Zhao, who was sent to the monastery as a child, was found from an early age to be a bright and eager pupil. At the age of sixteen he was sent travelling and went west to Hanzhou and to Mimu. After three years of wandering, he returned with a vision. Over the next 70 years of his life he collected funds, instructed artists and supervised the creation of more than 10,000 sculptures hewn from the living rock round his monastery. He completed his project in 1249, and died a happy man.

The Cultural Revolution never touched Dazu. Rumours have it that the Red Guards were on a destruction run towards the village and its treasures, when they were stopped by order from Zhou Enlai.

I stood on the 'Buddha Bless Me' Bridge looking down towards the scene of the Nirvana. A group of young people took turns photographing each other in front of it. I caught myself thinking how much they resembled Japanese tourists. Behind me, a few schoolgirls stopped, and watched me, giggling.

'*Lao wai, lao wai,*' I overheard them whispering to each other.

TWENTY-THREE

Chongqing

WE ARRIVED LATE IN CHONGQING. Chang flagged down a taxi which drove us across the river into the hills. Chongqing is surrounded by hills. At the end of a dirt track the driver turned off the motor and told us to get out. He complained about the bad road conditions and asked for extra money. Danger rates. Chang argued that he too was a driver, and he was perfectly aware of the correct price: 50 renminbi was too much. The man asked him how long he had been away from home, implying things had changed. Reluctantly, Chang paid up.

We continued on foot, creeping single file along a muddy path, snaking its way through rice paddies obscured by fog rising from the water, until we reached a hamlet sitting at the edge of a cliff. A row of identical buildings, arranged like steps, sloped towards the precipice. Squeezed between the cliff's edge and the houses was a vegetable patch, a shack and the communal toilets. On a bench in front of the shack was a stack of large winter cabbage.

'This is where my sister lives,' said Chang and pointed to the building next from the last, a tiny house with a flat roof and iron bars on the windows. To the left of the door was a large concrete trough. Several pairs of knitted socks hung to dry above it.

'Your sister?' I asked, slightly bewildered. I had assumed we were going to his place and had looked forward to some privacy, dreaming of 24 hours' uninterrupted sleep.

'It's better that way,' Chang said and knocked.

A short grandmother, her strands of flimsy white hair tied into a bun, opened the door, gave out a cry and greeted Chang in dialect, while ushering us into the front room. She was his brother-in-law's mother, Chang explained. I noticed she had no teeth.

There were some rudimentary furnishings: day bed, couch, a table and some chairs. The floor was concrete. A large calendar with a picture of a Chinese woman in traditional court dress, her face flirtatiously hidden behind a fan, hung above a television. A boy of perhaps nine, Chang's younger cousin, sat at the table doing homework. He jumped up, delighted to see Chang, and blushed when he was urged to greet me in English. He brought out a shy 'hello', then hid again behind his books. Chang slumped on to the couch and lit a cigarette. The house smelt of stir-fry and steamed buns.

Moments later, Chang's sister came home, a stack of books under one arm, a shopping bag slung over the other. She was handsome in a healthy way, her cheeks dimpled when she smiled, and I thought I saw some family resemblance in the distinctive jaw. She greeted me heartily, as though she had been expecting me all along.

'I'm terribly sorry I don't speak English,' she laughed mischievously. 'When I was at university, we still had to learn Russian.'

Although Soviet–Chinese friendship had chilled by 1960, it was still politically correct to study Russian throughout the sixties; English had become popular only with the re-opening of China after the Cultural Revolution. I guessed her age at mid-forties; she probably started university around 1961 or '62.

Older Sister was a teacher of literature at the middle school up the road. All of the inhabitants of this hamlet, or unit, were employed by the school, living, as is common in China, in close vicinity to their workplace. She chatted away gaily, while seeing to some dinner. Her husband, also a teacher, was out minding their shop ('impossible to survive on a teacher's salary these days') and she had a son at university. Both of them would be back tomorrow. There would be a feast, celebrating Chang's safe return. She had the calm, confident voice of a good teacher and corrected my Chinese with patient meticulousness.

Chang told me that she had brought him up and later, when he had been expelled from school as the son of counterrevolutionaries, had taught him at home. From her he got his love for literature and poetry. 'And Maupassant?' I laughed. There was a special bond between them. Almost twice his age, she was his mother rather than his sister, and I was pleased he had brought me to meet her.

After a bite to eat, Older Sister led me to her bedroom. I hadn't realized how tired I was, and after looking round the peculiarly western room, with its white self-assembly furniture and double bed, silver-framed pictures of the family and carpeted floor, I fell asleep. Only in the morning, seeing her spill of black hair next to me, did I realize I'd shared the bed with her.

Everyone had gone out. I washed in the usual way, in an enamel bowl in the kitchen, and put on lace underwear and a dab of perfume to spoil myself. Grandmother kept peeking in, observing my ritual, shaking her head and mumbling to herself. We could hardly communicate. Sichuan dialect seemed like an altogether different language. Then she served some tea and a steamed bun in a cup, watching me closely while I made some grunts of approval.

At midday Chang returned. He had exchanged his Levis and leather jacket for an ill-fitting dark blue pinstriped suit. For the first time he looked Chinese. He was sulking.

In the afternoon, we trekked down the cliff-side along a serpentine path on crude wooden steps. I was still limping. The landscape was green and luscious, and had it not been for the chilling fine rain, it would have been easy to forget it was winter. Strange, to see leaves in winter.

'Usually it's not so cold,' said Chang, drawing his coat tighter around him.

We reached a tarred road lined with municipal-style apartment buildings, half-hidden by the vegetation. Scores of female factory workers passed us, returning from their morning shift. They were all knitting what looked like long underwear, knitting as they walked. From a bus stop near the factory we took the number 22 back across the bridge into the centre of the city.

Chongqing was huge, a city of six million nestled between

wooded hills around the confluence of the Jialing and Yangtse rivers. Modern high-rises, hotels, factories and boulevards competed with markets, ramshackle wooden buildings and street vendors. Cars congested the narrow lanes, furrowing through a sea of pedestrians; there were hardly any bicycles to be seen. Food had a high profile. Outdoor cafés went side by side with greengrocers and fruit sellers, fishmongers, noodle-makers, tofu specialists, winding up narrow cobbled streets not unlike the Rue Mouffetard in Paris's Latin Quarter. Indeed, the entire city was oddly reminiscent of Pittsburgh or Paris.

Chang was playing tour guide, anxious to please, wanting me to like his home town. But things had changed – and maybe he had, too. His initial elation at returning home gave way to stark reality and a creeping depression. His pay had been cut, he said, explaining his bad mood. 'I need that much just for cigarettes,' he complained. He too was affected by the post-Tiananmen crisis which was engulfing the country.

Foreigners had left the city. Armed guards paraded in front of the university, outside the main hotels, in the streets. Unauthorized public meetings of more than a handful of people were forbidden. Special army units had been created to disperse all signs of resistance and to quell possible demonstrations. Rumour had it, they had a shoot-to-kill order.

We walked through a park overlooking the city, watching the old men with their birdcages, discussing irrelevances. In front of the closed museum, below tall and slightly ragged palm trees, an old woman was practising Taiji, the slow, elegant movements based on martial arts positions. I mimicked her graceful dance; she turned and offered to teach me.

'I don't think I will be here long enough,' I said.

That evening, the family celebrated. Chang's brother-in-law, a quiet, pleasant man of slight build, and his son had returned. 'He's my uncle,' Xiao Tan laughed, affectionately putting an arm around Chang's shoulder. He was only two years younger; they were best friends. Xiao Tan, in white shirt and jeans, hair fashionably cut in an English public-school way to fall over one eye, was studying Communications and Media. He spoke English well, with barely a trace of an accent.

Chang was the centre of attention, laughing, eating, telling traveller's tales.

'We think he is very clever,' said Xiao Tan, eyeing Chang proudly.

I sat in a corner on my best behaviour, daintily showing off my skill with chopsticks.

'Don't be so bourgeois,' Chang suddenly shouted at me.

I looked at him, and thought that he might embarrass me, were he to come back to Europe with me. I didn't like feeling judgmental, but the sentiment was there anyhow.

'I am pregnant!' The thought seemed to have come out of nowhere, lodged itself in my brain, and wouldn't go away. The more I strained against it, the more my suspicion grew. I hadn't had my period for months, something I had attributed to the stress of travel. I had been feeling weak, nauseous, and now, after eating this hot food, I lay panting in a cold sweat in Lili's bedroom.

Things had gone from bad to worse. Chang and I had spent a few days with his sister, sleeping in an empty cottage overlooking a rice paddy. We had to be secretive, sneaking there after dark, coming back before sunrise. Someone must have seen us after all. The neighbourhood committee complained to Older Sister's school principal that she was harbouring a foreigner. I decided to move to a hotel, and reluctantly, she had agreed. Grandmother cried when I shouldered my bag and left.

Chang had found us a hotel in the Chongqing equivalent of a red light district, a place where unmarried couples could stay for a night. We had deposited our bags under the watchful eyes and suggestive smiles of a sleazy-looking woman with the air of a Madam. Then we took the minibus across town to eat dinner with Lili, a good friend of Chang's, her six-year-old daughter, and a few of Chang's colleagues from work. Lili was tall, dressed in tight trousers and a leather jacket, and commented on my clothing.

'She likes it loose,' Chang explained my worn wardrobe. 'Thinks it's more comfortable.'

Lili had made *hou guo*, the 'hot pot' I had already sampled in

Dazu. We had sat on the floor of her living-room watching *Rambo* in the original English. That's when it happened. I turned white and barely made it to the kitchen sink, before the contents of my stomach emptied themselves. Lili helped me on to her bed and returned to her guests. I just knew I was pregnant.

Chang came in, concerned.

'What's the matter, Jiali?' he asked, and I just blurted it out.

'I think I'm pregnant.'

'Pregnant? *Bu shi* . . . no, you can't be!' he said dumbfounded.

'*Huaiyunde* . . . pregnant,' I repeated.

'*Zhenda?* Really, do you really think so?' he cried. His face, which had been thunderstruck with the first shock of the news, now registered an elated smile.

'Really? Really?' he cried over and over. An unexpected reaction.

'I think I should get tested,' I said, deeply worried. Chang pushed a pillow behind my head and wrapped the blanket tighter around me. Then he ran into the next room, turned off the video and announced the news to his friends. Lili opened a new bottle and they all crowded into the bedroom, toasting and congratulating Chang.

'Think how beautiful she will be, my eyes and your nose,' Chang sang happily.

'She?' I asked, stunned by the response.

'Of course, it will be a girl!' he stated matter-of-factly.

All I could think about was my boyfriend, whom I was to meet in less than two weeks in Guangzhou: 'Stefano, I love you, but there is something I have to tell you . . .' and my parents: 'Mom, Dad, a souvenir from China . . .' Chang and I had been lovers, had become friends, and neither of us had any interest in a long-term relationship. I stated as much.

'Don't worry, I can bring her up, or maybe she could live half the year in China, the other half in Europe, or maybe you could live in China . . .' he was talking rapidly, imagining.

Could I live in China? I wondered. Somehow I didn't think so. The happier Chang became about the possibility of having fathered a child, the unhappier I got about the prospect of being a mother. The difficulties seemed immense.

We left our friend's apartment late, and returned to the hotel at about two o'clock in the morning. Chang was fetching the key when the night *furen* approached us and pulled him into a corner, whispering to him.

'The PSB have searched our room. They'll probably be back.' he said, scared.

'Why?' I asked.

He gave an almost Gallic shrug, hiding his fear. 'This is China,' he repeated the over-familiar explanation.

The *furen* was on our side and opened the next room for Chang to sleep in.

'It's best this way,' he said, fetching his toothbrush.

He was right. At four, two plain-clothes policemen opened my door without knocking and spilled into my room. They poked at my luggage and looked around the bathroom.

'Alone?' they asked.

'What does it look like?' I snarled, feeling impotent.

After inspecting my passport, making it look like routine, they left.

Things were *not* better in Chang's home town.

We ate some breakfast in the food market, *douhua*, fresh beancurd served in hot water, before climbing a hill to the hospital. A western hospital, donated by the Italians, Chang pointed out.

We joined a queue in a stark hallway smelling of hospital, and took a number. It struck me that I might be the only foreigner in a city of six million Chinese. Everyone stared.

Finally it was our turn. We were asked into the examination room; a female doctor, stout and red-faced, sat behind a desk and, without looking up, asked what the matter was. A few heads hung in the gaping door, intently following the consultation.

'We think we are pregnant,' Chang announced proudly, grinning, playing to the audience as though expecting a round of applause. A ripple went through the crowd. I wished a hole would open in the floor and swallow me. The doctor did not react. She jotted a few lines on to a flimsy piece of paper, stamped it with red, and directed us to the gynaecological division in a side building. There I peed into a bottle, and was asked to come back two days later for the results.

'What happens if you really are pregnant?' Chang asked, serious for the first time.

'I don't know,' I said truthfully.

'Are you . . . *sa*?' he drew his hand across his throat, meaning, would I have an abortion.

'No!'

He looked relieved. 'I can take care of her,' he said quietly, 'China isn't such a bad place to grow up.'

I didn't answer.

We drifted around town, killing time. We purchased some peanuts soaked in salt water and sat on the edge of the concrete circle surrounding the liberation monument. A skinny, decrepit-looking old man in poor clothing and a straw hat approached us with lively chatter, incomprehensible to me. We ignored him. He insisted, pulling on my arm.

'He wants to sell you his daughter,' Chang translated into Mandarin.

'What?'

'He wants to sell his daughter as a maid. He wants you to take her out of China – don't listen, he's just a stupid peasant . . .'

With a few sharp words he shooed the old man away.

'Would you like to leave China?' I asked him.

'No,' he shook his head, and added after a moment of silence, 'but I would like to travel on the outside, for a year, maybe two.'

We took a minibus to the art academy, 'one of the best in the country,' Chang boasted, to view an exhibition of faculty and student work.

Displayed in a modern glass gallery hung scrolls and paintings in strict Chinese style, works of calligraphy, expressive and executed to a high standard, and a separate exhibition of drawings. Large, realistic pencil drawings of figures. Safe. Boring. I had seen this type of art before.

In the summer of 1984, after a year's stay in Japan, I had travelled through the former Soviet Union. In what was then still Leningrad, I had posed as an art student, and nonchalantly walked past the guards into the famous St Petersburg art academy, one of the first buildings in Europe to have been designed for this purpose. Technically accomplished drawings and sketches were hung outside classrooms, realistic, pretty, and dull. There was no abstraction, no rebellion, no experimentation, as one might expect from young art students.

A short woman in a grey skirt and cardigan had approached me. She was a professor of textile design, and was delighted to show me around. After some time I asked her about the state of contemporary art; was there any legacy of great artists like Malevich for example?

'Not here,' she had said. Soviet students might experiment in private, but that sort of activity is not supported by the school, she told me while showing off a series of colourful quilts.

I left her shortly after. She shook my hand, and almost in passing said, 'But we all remember that Malevich was a student here.'

Chang liked the drawings.

Next to the entrance to the exhibition, there were on one side large scrolls of vegetation and birds in Ming dynasty style with just a hint of western perspective, and on the other some drawings. Between these hung a large poster framed by four bold pieces of wood, painted black. The rough grey surface of the cheap paper had been systematically delineated in columns with orange crayon. Characters, different in size, and executed in various media – some in pencil, some in ball-point pen, others in brush – were strewn haphazardly over the formal structure of the background.

I pointed the poster out to Chang. He laughed and said it was only the introduction to the exhibition of drawings.

'May all those who have eyes be granted sight,' he read, slowly piecing together the floating characters.

'It's ugly,' he added.

'It's beautiful,' I said, 'do you think I can buy it?'

Chang walked up to a guard and exchanged a few words with him, while pointing at me. The guard left and returned after a few minutes with a young Chinese woman with glasses, her long black hair in a pony tail. She was the artist's wife. I pointed out the piece.

'It's not for sale,' she said and hesitated for a moment.

She invited us to visit her and her husband at their home in the academy compound in a few days.

It was time to get the test results. I was nervous and couldn't swallow my breakfast. I was craving coffee. Lili had arranged a car and together with her daughter we piled into the vehicle and drove to the hospital.

The little girl insisted on accompanying us to the clinic, grabbing both my and Chang's hand. A picture of conjugal happiness. The situation was beginning to appear perfectly ludicrous to me.

The nurse at registration took her time. Finally, she handed me an unintelligible piece of paper.

'Well?' I asked anxiously, handing it to Chang.

'Maybe yes, maybe no,' he read.

'What does that mean?' I cried. The nurse explained that the result was unclear, and that I should come back in a few days to repeat the test. I left, feeling more pregnant than ever. In the car I handed the paper to the expectant Lili. She laughed as she read out loud: 'Maybe yes, maybe no!'

'You can't trust western hospitals, let's consult the Chinese doctor,' she said resolutely as she pulled into gear.

Chang rolled his eyes, but didn't say anything.

Near the harbour in an old part of town we parked in front of a wooden building with curved Chinese eaves. We climbed a flight of stairs and entered through a carved door. Our eyes took a moment to adjust to the semi-dark hall; our noses were assaulted immediately by an odour reminiscent of liquorice, senna and moss – a smell with the consistency of the colour yellow. Behind a glass counter, spanning the entire length of the room, apothecary jars filled with herbs, snake skins, sticks, and other indefinable organic matter, lined the wall. More herbs hung from the ceiling. There was even what looked like a dried baby crocodile.

An old man, with long white hair and a Confucius beard, sat behind a table. A woman, old herself, stood by his side. We walked up to the table and my friends bowed. Lili handed the note to the woman, who passed it on to the old man. He acknowledged us with a blink of the eyes.

Chang pushed me forward, while Lili, eyes respectfully cast downward, explained the problem. The old man inspected the medical report, then looked at me, hard. He took my wrist between his thin gnarled fingers and felt for the pulse. He held my wrist for a long time, and I remember that his fingers, first cool, became warmer and warmer. Finally, he shook his head.

'Constipation,' he pronounced.

I gaped in disbelief. Both Lili and Chang seemed to accept the verdict. The old woman went behind the counter, filled a brown paper bag with a variety of herbs and told me to brew a tea from it.

Chang was devastated and stormed out of the building. I followed him. He was leaning against the railing of the boardwalk overlooking the harbour, staring into the brackish water. I laid my hand on his arm.

'Are you happy?' he asked.

'Yes.'

We walked back to the car.

Two days later, I started to menstruate.

Chang and I were saying goodbye, without mentioning my impending departure. We were both pulling back, bit by bit, back into our own lives. My thoughts were already racing ahead to the rest of my journey: Guangzhou, a short trip to Thailand, Taiwan, Korea – where some of the Otani collection was housed – and Japan. I still had two months of travel ahead of me. I was busy with arrangements, phone calls and cashing travellers cheques. Chang worried about money and thought he might leave Chongqing to find a job in one of the 'special economic zones' that were mushrooming all over the country. He needed a contact to finagle a residence permit in one of the zones.

The day before my departure we visited the artist and his wife. We had to sign in with the heavily armed guards at the gate to the academy compound. Chang was uncomfortable.

As soon as I entered the artist's small apartment I felt at home.

The tiny, two-room space had been filled with paintings, sculptures, wall-hangings and colourful home-made furniture. From the ceiling hung a Calder-like mobile, constructed from bamboo dipped in red paint, like blood. The couple's five-year-old daughter was practising scales on a piano. Chang was still uncomfortable, and tried hard not to show it.

We spent the afternoon talking art.

At dusk, just before it was time to go, the artist pulled out the poster I had admired in the gallery, fetched a series of carved stamps and red ink, and imprinted the paper with his name and symbols.

'You do understand, don't you?' he said, while shaking my hand.

'I think so,' I said.

The bus seemed to take for ever to get to the airport, winding along a narrow road through the green Sichuan countryside. It was raining lightly and swathes of fog obscured the hills. Chang was quiet.

'Let's travel again sometime,' he said suddenly.

The plane was grounded due to fog and we were forced to spend the night at the airport inn.

Next morning conditions had worsened. I complained loudly at the information desk. Quietly, a uniformed woman pulled me from the crowd. A plane had materialized, a small twin-engine aircraft, provided for the privileged few. Together with a dozen other lucky passengers, consisting mainly of wives and daughters of the well-to-do and a few party cadres, I boarded the plane.

From the window I saw Chang standing in the rain, forlorn, watching us take off. He looked ill.

TWENTY-FOUR

Epilogue

What I dreamt in the past about the future is nothing like
the present . . .

CUI JIAN, *Bu Shi Wo Bu Ming Bai*

SIX MONTHS LATER, in July 1990, I was back in Xinjiang. Back
with two buses (air-conditioned), three minibuses, a limousine,
an ambulance, a kitchen car, a security car, three television teams,
and dozens of Chinese and international scholars in re-search of
the ancient trade routes, as a member of a UNESCO project:
'Integral Study of the Silk Roads: Roads of Dialogue'.

I had joined the expedition at the very last moment, following
a letter from the academy in Urumqi saying that for the time
being, due to the volatile political situation, no foreign scholars
could obtain permission to work in Xinjiang. Going with a group
was my only chance to keep up my contacts, and to observe
first-hand the impact of the uprising which had shaken the south
of the province four months earlier, reports of which had been
enigmatic and varied.

We were the first official foreign delegation allowed in after the
uprising, and the Chinese did their best to appear in a good light.

I arrived in Dunhuang in a small twin-engine plane (each engine
a different make, I noticed, after we had landed). There I linked up
with the expedition members who had travelled from Beijing to
Xian and through the Hexi corridor, the access route to the desert.

Security was tight. The spies were obvious, and not very pro-
fessional. It took them two days to realize that I was 'Jiali', the

foreign woman who had travelled through Xinjiang's closed zones in the autumn and winter of 1989, and of whom most police stations around the Tarim basin had a description. This fact caused a small crisis among the Chinese leaders accompanying the group. I heard that meetings were being held about my 'case', 'struggle meetings', a friend called them, laughing facetiously, and I expected to be expelled at any moment. I tried not to let this bother me, but it was difficult.

We travelled through the desert surrounded by our very own glass bubble, in some ways probably truer in nature to the trade caravans of antiquity, which had often numbered hundreds. Our attentive traffic cop, surreally donning crisp white gloves, would wave us safely across the few lone intersections, so that we did not collide with camels or donkeys. Inhabitants of small villages or towns which had the misfortune to be programmed into our tight schedule were made to wait interminably in the sun, waving cultural objects and wearing bright 'ethnic' clothing. They reminded me of parades I had seen before. I kept praying that none of them would recognize me.

The effects of the April uprising hung heavily over the province.

In Turfan I found that Justin, the young Harvard scholar who had been so concerned about Chang's welfare, had been asked to leave prematurely when trouble started.

In Korla I saw a troop of soldiers harass some teenagers who had fled a midnight dance floor during a sudden rain shower and were huddling under a roof until it was over. Congregations of more than five people had been outlawed, and here in Xinjiang the new decree was enforced with vigour. The soldiers rapidly dispersed the teenagers, as if they had good cause. I rushed after them on foot, but lost sight of them.

'They are from Lanzhou,' said the front-desk girl who, together with Chang, had taken care of me when I sprained my ankle. We had recognized each other at the dance. She shrugged and smiled when I tried to get more information.

Kuqa was worse. We were housed in a government/military guest house guarded by soldiers and we were told not to wander about town alone, because someone might be kidnapped. I escaped anyway and found Arsalan at his shop. He had been denied permission to study in Pakistan. A deep, pessimistic groove had lodged itself vertically between his eyes, and he was cynical about the political situation, but didn't elaborate. Aertosen, too, was refusing to speak about the state of things. She met me reluctantly at a favourite eatery, but preferred to talk instead about her wedding. People in the market had become cold. It was no longer safe to be seen talking to foreigners.

I noticed the road from Korla to Kashgar had been paved since I was on it last.

In Kashgar we were refused permission to hire bicycles. There were rumours that six Han had been knifed in a disco, and the Chinese in our group were nervous. Trade at the Oasis Café was slow, there were hardly any tourists. While we were sitting over a beer, gazing through the Gothic windows on to the hot street, government officials came in and demanded to inspect the café's books. Tahir's problems hadn't eased much, either, I could see.

In front of the Idga, I ran into John the map-maker. He had been expelled from Khotan for mapping the city, and feared being extradited to Pakistan. He did not have a clear picture of what went on in Akto a few months back, but felt that things must have been pretty bad.

There had been plenty of rumours. The most persistent was that locals had been barred from building a new mosque in Akto, south of Kashgar, and had demonstrated violently against the ban, a demonstration which was brought down by military force. Hundreds of Uighurs and Chinese had reportedly been killed. Others said that the Chinese had provoked the uprising to provide an excuse for quelling the growing unrest by an overt show of power, following a series of miscalculated policy decisions coupled with a general economic low.

I wandered through the bazaar around the Idga; someone told me the bazaar was about to be levelled, to be replaced by a concrete parking lot. An old man at a bookstall on the corner of Jiefang Road talked about the uprising. Following the occupation of Xinjiang by Maoist troops, the East Turkestan Party, a remnant of the short-lived East Turkestan Republic, had gone underground. It had survived all these years, and had grown strong again over the last decade.

'Every Uighur in the province pays taxes to the party,' he explained.

'Everyone?' I asked astonished. I knew about East Turkestan, but I had never heard of the East Turkestan Party.

'Almost every Uighur,' he nodded. 'You wouldn't be a Uighur otherwise.'

For the last 40 years of its clandestine existence, I learned, the aim of the party had been the eventual secession from Chinese rule, with the slogan, 'small trouble every three years, big trouble every ten'. The old man laughed.

During the last decade the leaders of the illegal party in the north were easing up on more militant policies. Voices favouring a democratic solution, calls to work within the system, began to be heard; there was even talk about the possibilities of a federation. Many of the leaders were profiting from the sudden economic boom which Xinjiang was experiencing under Deng's move towards 'market socialism'.

Gradually a split developed in the party, along a north–south divide, which manifested itself finally in the creation of a Fundamentalist Muslim wing (FMP), still using the name of the East Turkestan Party.

Their aim was not only to secede from China proper, but also to leave the north of the province behind, to create a sort of new Kashgaria. Their influence reached from Aksu, over Kashgar to Yarkant and Khotan. Liberally supplied with funds from Pakistan and Iran, who later also supplied weapons, a number of militant mullahs established, without the knowledge of the government, private schools based on the principles of Islam in all the major southern towns, and began to groom an ever-growing number of youngsters for a forthcoming *jihad*, a holy war. (These schools were closed in an organized raid in 1989, which had caused some of the tensions I was feeling then.) The mullahs also started to train a militia.

In order to create a mobile army they began to buy up horses in and around Kashgar throughout the winter of 1989–90, causing the price of horses to soar. This is where the story of the 1990 uprising began.

One of the militia groups based near Blaqsu, a hamlet belonging to the Akto district south of Kashgar, had focused on a young Uighur who raised horses. 'He was quite good at it, too,' the old man mused. The young man refused to sell his stock. The militia applied pressure and when he did not budge, confiscated the horses, including his prize stallion named Rakhta. For the revolution, they said.

The young man, upset by the loss of his animals and disagreeing with the revolutionary cause, reported the incident to the local police station. The police did nothing. A week later, finding there had been no action taken on his complaint, he went higher up, to a police station in Toqsak, a larger town in the same region. At this time he also reported on the FMP and the militia. Though it does not appear that the authorities took the report too seriously, they did send a car with four Han officers as well as a Uighur to Akto to investigate the claim.

The militia, young, hotheaded and primed for action, captured the policemen, killed the Han Chinese ('they killed them the Muslim way,' said the man, nodding a reflective sort of nod, which I supposed meant that their throats were cut) and sent the Uighur back to report.

Urumqi at this point sent in a platoon. The officers were lured into a mosque under the guise of negotiations, surrounded by armed men and held hostage. The officer in charge was beaten up. This is when Urumqi became alarmed and notified Beijing. The government responded with all-out military action, by both ground and air. Both Uighur and Han Chinese were killed, the militia fled into the mountains, pursued by helicopters.

'They levelled a mountain top,' the man said.

Following this aborted uprising, caused by a bunch of young hotheads, the general climate in the province chilled even more. Hundreds of party officials were relieved of their posts, there were public executions in Urumqi.

The governor, Tumur Dawamet, blamed the 'problem' on 'international bourgeois liberalization', an evil to be resisted and eliminated.

It is still impossible to get verifiable news in Xinjiang.

In Urumqi a letter from Chang was waiting for me. I had not heard from him in several months. He had given up his job as a taxi driver and was planning to do business in Shenzen, the new special economic zone just across the border from Hong Kong. No forwarding address.

The members of the expedition were requested not to refer to Xinjiang as 'Eastern Turkestan' as many had the habit of doing, but to use the term 'Western China'.

Two days before my final departure, a senior archaeologist was chosen to bring me the following message from the Chinese leaders: 'The misunderstanding of last year has been forgiven.'

'Face,' said a friend of mine, 'it was a matter of face. You've been very lucky. Best stay out of politics from now on,' he warned me.

At the end of the journey I flew to Beijing. I stayed in a hotel where three attendants worked in the toilet. One opened the outer door, another opened the toilet door and removed the 'sanitized' strip of paper, and a third turned on the tap, hovering over me while I washed my hands, then handed me a towel when I was finished.

I had Beijing duck in an air-conditioned restaurant overlooking the city, serenaded by a harp plucked by a competent musician dressed in tails. I felt completely out of place.

That evening, at the Seven Star, a club on Airport Road, I met the musician Cui Jian, a short, shy man in his late twenties with a cigarette pack rolled up in the sleeve of his T-shirt. I asked him what music he liked listening to these days. He gave a wry laugh, glanced left and right and said: 'Public Enemy'.

A recent letter from Chang told me that he'd been interrogated for hustling ten tons of processed steel rods. 'When they arrested me it was the height of summer,' he wrote. 'Chinese prisons are damn cold in winter.'

Index

Nick Danziger

Danziger's Travels

Beyond Forbidden Frontiers

'A marvellous account of a truly epic journey . . . Puts him in the forefront of modern travel writers.'   *Mail on Sunday*

Nick Danziger's graphic account of his hair-raising adventures during an eighteen-month journey 'beyond forbidden frontiers' in Asia makes a vivid and unforgettable impact. Travelling in disguise as an itinerant Muslim, his journey on foot and using traditional means of local transport cost him £1,000 in all – exactly one-third of the Winston Churchill travel fellowship he received in London.

After walking and hitch-hiking through southern Turkey and the ayatollahs' Iran, he entred Afghanistan illegally in the wake of a convoy of Chinese weapons and spent two months dodging Russian helicopter gunships with rebel guerrillas. He was the first foreigner to cross from Pakistan into the closed western province of China since the revolution of 1949.

Living and travelling with local people and pitting his wits against officialdom, Danziger broke barriers and crossed boundaries of all kinds. Written with engaging humour and a great zest for life, *Danziger's Travels* is an exceptional travel book in every way, handsomely illustrated with the author's own outstanding photographs and drawings.

'Danziger is the stuff of which legends are made . . . His remarkable story contains some of the most exciting travel writing I have ever read.'   William Dalrymple, *Literary Review*

'Even the most travel-crazy person I know looks unadventurous alongside Nick Danziger.'   *Midweek*

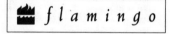

William Dalrymple

City of Djinns

A Year in Delhi

Winner of the 1994 *Sunday Times* Young Writer of the Year Award.

Alive with the mayhem of the present and sparkling with the author's ubiquitous, irrepressible wit, *City of Djinns* is the fascinating portrait of a city as has never been attempted before. Meeting an extraordinary array of characters, from the city's elusive eunuchs to the embattled descendants of the great Moguls, from the rich Punjabis to the Sufis and mystics, and investigating the resonances of these people and their modern ways with the India of the past, this is a unique and dazzling feat of research and adventure by one of the finest travel writers of his generation.

'A sympathetic and engaging portrait of this age-old city . . . It is fine, entertaining, well-written stuff, thoroughly researched but with none of the stern academic tone that so many historical profiles adopt. What sustains it, apart from his erudite knowledge of Moslem architecture, medicine, music, military architecture, and arcane religious principles, is Dalrymple's sense of historical adventure. Just open your eyes, he says. If you know how to look, even the empty tombs and abandoned ruins of the past are alive . . .' *Financial Times*

'Unlike much of modern travel writing *City of Djinns* is informative, learned and funny . . . a lively and sometimes profound book.' *Economist*

'Scholarly and marvellously entertaining . . . A considerable feat.'
Dervla Murphy, *Spectator*

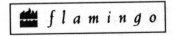

Benedict Allen

The Proving Grounds

A Quest for Manhood

The only 'whiteman' to have undergone the gruelling male initiation ceremony of a remote Papua New Guinea tribe – as described in *Into the Crocodile Nest* – Benedict Allen opens the powerful, eloquent story of *The Proving Grounds* by returning to his tribal village, only to learn from his clan brothers and sisters that the trials of induction are far from over. He is sent traversing the Central Range of New Guinea, through the forest mists, to discover the living magic of the uncontacted Yaifo people, forced to cross the treacherous Torres Strait by flimsy canoe to Australia and scorched by the red sands of the Gibson Desert. Whitefella Benedict undertakes this breathtaking journey in an extraordinary bid to achieve a unique level of acceptance – earning beyond dispute his right to be treated as an adult in a tribal community.

'An extraordinary solo journey through Thailand, Papua New Guinea and the deserts of Western Australia. Offers rich insights into aboriginal life.'   *Daily Telegraph*

'A stern and unquestionably brave endeavour . . . One of the most outstanding, certainly the most original, travel books to come my way.'   John Hillaby

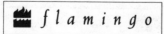

Heinrich Harrer

Seven Years in Tibet

Heinrich Harrer, already a famous mountaineer and Olympic ski champion, was caught by the outbreak of the Second World War while climbing in the Himalayas. Being an Austrian, he was interned in India. By an almost superhuman effort, and on his third attempt he succeeded in escaping into Tibet.

After a series of remarkable experiences in a country never before crossed by a Westerner, he reached the forbidden city of Lhasa. He stayed there for seven years, learned the language and acquired a greater understanding of Tibet and Tibetans than a Westerner had ever before achieved. He became the friend and tutor of the young Dalai Lama and finally accompanied him into India when he was put to flight by the Red Chinese invasion.

'Some books, like some mountains, are lonely and unrivalled peaks, and this is one of these.'   *Economist*

'Few adventurers in this century have had the combined luck and hardihood to return with such news as this. Fewer still have rendered it so powerfully unadorned.'   *Times Literary Supplement*

'Like the voyage of the Kon-Tiki, it deserves to take its place among the few great travel stories of our own times.'   *The Times*

flamingo

Where the Indus is Young

Walking to Baltistan

Dervla Murphy

'Altogether the most appallingly fascinating travel book I have ever read'
JAN MORRIS, *The Times*

Dervla Murphy and her six-year-old daughter Rachel walked into the Karakoram mountains in the heart of the western Himalayas and along the perilous Indus Gorge. Accompanied only by a gallant polo pony, they endured conditions that tested the limits of their ingenuity, fortitude and courage.

Yet even when beset by crumbling tracks over bottomless chasms, an assault by a lascivious Kashmiri, the unnerving melancholy of the Balts – and Rachel's continual probing questions – this formidable traveller retained her enthusiasm for her surroundings and her sense of humour. Hair-raising, gloriously subjective and with the quirky vitality of fiction, the resulting book is a classic of travel writing.

'The lasting impression left by this book is one of sheer joy'
COLIN THUBRON, *Sunday Telegraph*

'It is her real reverence for natural beauty that gives her writing its special quality . . . Dervla Murphy is a writer one should be profoundly grateful for'
Daily Telegraph

'Miss Murphy is a connoisseur of lost Arcardias'
Times Literary Supplement

ISBN: 0 00 654801 6

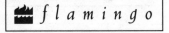

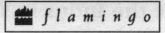 **flamingo**

Flamingo is a quality imprint publishing both fiction and non-fiction. Below are some recent titles.

Fiction

☐ No Other Life *Brian Moore* £5.99
☐ The Kitchen God's Wife *Amy Tan* £4.99
☐ A Thousand Acres *Jane Smiley* £5.99
☐ A Yellow Raft in Blue Water *Michael Dorris* £5.99
☐ Tess *Emma Tennant* £5.99
☐ Pepper *Tristan Hawkins* £5.99
☐ Dreaming in Cuban *Cristina Garcia* £5.99
☐ Happenstance *Carol Shields* £5.99
☐ Blood Sugar *Suzannah Dunn* £5.99
☐ Postcards *E. Annie Proulx* £5.99

Non-fiction

☐ The Gates of Paradise *Alberto Manguel* £9.99
☐ Sentimental Journeys *Joan Didion* £5.99
☐ Epstein *Stephen Gardiner* £8.99
☐ Love, Love and Love *Sandra Bernhard* £5.99
☐ City of Djinns *William Dalrymple* £5.99
☐ Dame Edna Everage *John Lahr* £5.99
☐ Tolstoy's Diaries *R. F. Christian* £7.99
☐ Wild Swans *Jung Chang* £7.99

You can buy Flamingo paperbacks at your local bookshop or newsagent. Or you can order them from HarperCollins Mail Order, Dept. 8, HarperCollins*Publishers*, Westerhill Road, Bishopbriggs, Glasgow G64 2QT. Please enclose a cheque or postal order, to the order of the cover price plus add £1.00 for the first and 25p for additional books ordered within the UK.

NAME (Block letters)_____

ADDRESS_____

_____

_____